AMERICA IN TWO CENTURIES:
An Inventory

AMERICA IN TWO CENTURIES:
An Inventory

Advisory Editor

DANIEL J. BOORSTIN

*See last pages of this volume
for a complete list of titles*

Sports in American Life

BY

FREDERICK W. COZENS

AND

FLORENCE SCOVIL STUMPF

ARNO PRESS
A New York Times Company
1976

796
C 88a

Editorial Supervision: ANDREA HICKS

————••⦿••————

Reprint Edition 1976 by Arno Press Inc.

Reprinted from a copy in
  The University of Pennsylvania Library

AMERICA IN TWO CENTURIES: An Inventory
ISBN for complete set: 0-405-07666-5
See last pages of this volume for titles.

Manufactured in the United States of America

————••⦿••————

Library of Congress Cataloging in Publication Data

Cozens, Frederick Warren, 1890-1954.
    Sports in American life.

    (America in two centuries, an inventory)
    Reprint of the ed. published by University of
Chicago Press, Chicago.
    1. Sports--United States. I. Stumpf, Florence
Scovil, joint author. II. Title. III. Series.
GV583.C68 1976   796'.0973   75-22810
ISBN 0-405-07681-9

Sports in American Life

Sports in American Life

BY

FREDERICK W. COZENS

AND

FLORENCE SCOVIL STUMPF

THE UNIVERSITY OF CHICAGO PRESS

THE UNIVERSITY OF CHICAGO PRESS, CHICAGO 37
Cambridge University Press, London, N.W. 1, England

This book is affectionately dedicated
to four fine sons and splendid sportsmen

FREDERICK KERRON COZENS

JAMES BEHARRELL COZENS

WILLIAM ALAN STUMPF

MICHAEL SCOVIL STUMPF

Preface

THIS BOOK HAS BEEN WRITTEN FOR ALL PERSONS INTERESTED IN games, sports, and recreational activities and for those who are eager to understand the basic sociological significance of this aspect of culture. Students and teachers, parents and professional workers in the field, as well as the general reader, are becoming increasingly aware that all human activities are interrelated and that none is so trivial that it may not influence others which may seem more important. The tools they use and the food they eat may determine the chances for survival of a people, but the games they play and the stories they read may establish the character of a nation. All individuals who are interested in the enterprise which is American education, and who are groping their way toward an understanding between social phenomena and the educative process, must eventually recognize that it is as important to understand the recreational phase of culture as it is to understand the economic, familial, religious, or political phases.

Sports and physical recreation form an integral part of cultures everywhere, and the authors believe that an awareness of the common heritage which all men share in this area of human experience can contribute to increased understanding and sympathy, our most potent weapon against the forces of intolerance, bigotry, and prejudice.

The materials for this study have been drawn from many sources, as can be seen from an examination of the "Notes and Bibliography," but the interpretation and implications set forth are the responsibility of the authors.

We are deeply indebted to many friends both within and without the profession for encouragement in our undertaking and to hundreds of writers for perhaps unwittingly presenting materials which in one way or another have helped us in developing the point of view presented here.

The authors wish to thank the publishers and writers who have generously permitted quotations to be taken from their works.

FREDERICK W. COZENS
FLORENCE SCOVIL STUMPF

UNIVERSITY OF CALIFORNIA
BERKELEY
March 1953

Table of Contents

ix

1. *Introduction*

A BOOK ON SPORTS IN AMERICAN CULTURE WOULD SEEM TO NEED no justification beyond the fact that it chronicles and submits to some analysis a fascinating, colorful, and sometimes inspiring section of the total picture of American life. Few observers of life in America have failed to comment on the large place which sport fills in the public consciousness throughout all classes of society. This fact alone would make sports something worth investigating and understanding with regard to their relationship to the culture as a whole.

Sports and physical recreation activities belong with the *arts* of humanity. Such activities have formed a basic part of all cultures, including all racial groups and all historical ages, because they are as fundamental a form of human expression as music, poetry, and painting. Every age has had its artists and its amateurs, its adherents and its enemies. While wars, systems of government, plagues and famines, have come and gone in the long record of mankind, these fundamental things have always been present in greater or lesser degree.

The obvious explanation as to why it is difficult to find an acknowledgement of sports as an important item in cultural history is because sports did not function in many of the fields *conventionally* credited with making important contributions to history. In fact an examination of the works of early historians would lead the reader to believe that individuals were born and they died, they earned a living, fought in wars, and elected other individuals to political office, *but they never played!*[1]

Just a year before the twentieth century began an English writer commented that modern historians have erred in not giving games their due place and that no greater mistake could be made than to consider the subject of recreation as being below the dignity of the Muse of History.[2] Some forty years later Dixon Wecter, whose untimely death deprived America of one of her most promising young social historians, wrote as follows:

> Some day sport will find its wide-visioned philosopher. He will show us how cricket, with its white clothes and leisure boredom, and sudden crises met with cool mastery to the ripple of applause among the teacups and cucumber sandwiches, is an epitome of the British Empire. Or the bull-fight with its scarlet cape and gold braid, its fierce pride and cruelty, and the quixotic futility of its perils, is the essence of Spain. Or that football with its rugged individualism, and baseball with its equality of opportunity, are valid American symbols, while Soviet Russia favors mass games in preference to the Olympic sports which aim at world's records and other tacit assertions of one man's superiority over another. Most of these things have been felt or hinted before, but their synthesis has never been made.[3]

The authors modestly reject any claim to the role of "wide-visioned philosopher" but with a feeling of mixed pride and humility present to the general reader as well as to the student and teacher a small segment of this total story which will some day be written.

Sports and games provide a touchstone for understanding how people live, work, and think and may also serve as a barometer of a nation's progress in civilization. If there be any validity in the premise that athletic efficiency may be considered a by-product of a country's general cultural and economic status, then the high level of social and economic life in the Scandinavian nations, the industrial and engineering achievements of Central Europe, the strength of scientific and technical initiative of the United States and of the British Empire have been truly reflected by the athletic superiority of these countries over the rest of the world.[4]

SPORTS AS AN AID TO INTERNATIONAL UNDERSTANDING

As distinctive a feature of the twentieth century as some of the scientific and technological discoveries has been the amazing development and popularity achieved by sports, competitive athletics, and games. Within a few decades, sports and games have spread over the whole world, leaping barriers of race, religion, and social class. The language of sport is truly universal, and in the sportsman's code there is neither East nor West, neither white nor black, neither exploiter nor exploited.[5]

In spite of the world-wide economic, political, and social disorders and difficulties existing at mid-century, a great deal of attention and interest are being given to the promotion of physical education and sports all over the world. The acute economic difficulties in many parts of the world and the emphasis on the need for hard work and greater production seem to make it even more important that encouragement be given to all workers to gain fitness and refreshment in their leisure hours through physical recreation.

While the form and organization of physical education and sports varies widely from country to country and is profoundly influenced by national traditions and characteristics, by climate and by natural and artificial facilities, there seems to be evidenced everywhere a desire to add to the welfare and happiness of people by working toward better provision and encouragement of physical education and sports. This international growth is concerned primarily with three phases, sometimes closely interrelated and sometimes seemingly headed in different directions:

1. Physical education as a subject taught in the schools.

2. Sports and physical recreation as provided and encouraged for the out-of-school population.

3. More competitive opportunities for the top-level performers drawn from Groups 1 and 2.

In this last category the developments in Asia and the Near East are especially significant. As an illustration there is the organization of the Mediterranean Games, held at Istanbul, Turkey, and including competitors from Italy, Spain, Lebanon, Syria, Egypt, and Turkey; and the Asian Games Federation, involving competitors from the Philippines, Burma, Siam, Ceylon, Indonesia, Nepal, Afghanistan, Pakistan, and India.

Throughout recorded history sports and athletic contests have been most closely related to one or the other of two great areas of human culture—religion and nationalism. With the advent of Christianity the religious significance of such activities began its gradual disappearance from the scene in Western civilization. The lack of religious connotations seemed to intensify the nationalistic and militaristic emphasis. Certainly no observer could fail to note that the promotion of programs of sports and physical recreation played an important role in the developing nationalism of many European countries.

The emergence of nationalism in the countries of the Far East and Near East in the historical period of the twentieth century is an acknowledged fact. A resurgence of interest in physical education and an increased emphasis on sports form an integral part of the programs of reform, reconstruction, and development in the various countries of this part of the world. Egypt is building one of the most up-to-date arenas in the world near the center of the city of Cairo, with a seating capacity for a hundred thousand spectators; and the Institute of Education at Giza has become an important training center for teachers of physical education, not only within Egypt, but serving the neighboring countries of Iraq, Syria, Lebanon, Transjordan, Yemen, and Tripolitania. The National Planning Commission of the Government of India included major recommendations for the improvement of physical education in its five-year plan of national development. The National Sports Club of India has ambitious plans for the construction of modern sports facilities in the principal cities of India, the first item on the agenda to be Jawhar Stadium in Delhi, named in honor of Pandit Jawharlal Nehru. A representative from Siam made a survey of sport and physical education in Great Britain for the purpose of using such information to raise the standards in his own country. In Ceylon the city of Colombo started plans for a modern stadium when approximately half the crowds had to be turned away from matches held between Ceylon and Indian football teams.[6]

The nations of the world at mid-century are in the precarious position of finding ways and means of living together with some degree of amity or facing possible destruction. In this situation America has been thrust into a leading role. If a structure of international understanding and good will is to be built which will be strong enough to sustain a peaceful world toward which the people of the earth are striving, it must rest on a wider foundation than economic interests *alone*. There must be a patient and constant search for the shared enthusiasms and rituals which form man's noneconomic life. One such common denominator is to be found in the existence of athletic sports, dancing, and games, which are an integral part of every culture known to history or ethnology. Understanding, like charity, begins at home, and thoughtful Americans realize that an important part of the hope for success in assuming the sobering position of leadership in the world will depend upon the degree of understanding which Americans have of their *own* culture, its operation, and its interrelationships.

STUDY A MAN'S PLEASURES, AND THE HALF OF HIM IS KNOWN

In the task of seeking and examining the factors which have gone into the process of making games and sports, particularly those which are ordinarily thought of as forms of physical recreation, the important part of life which they are in America, a sense of the inseparableness of each element of the culture with all other elements deepens and grows. There is a developing realization of the validity of the premise that a balance between work and play, between the things that must be done to sustain life and the things people want to do to make life worth living, is of primary importance in any successfully

functioning culture. It follows that a knowledge and an understanding of all the things within the culture which either help
or hinder the fulfilment of this balance are of vital interest.

Sports are one index to the national genius and character of
the American people. The story of their expansion, change,
and adaptation parallels the chronicle of expansion, change,
and adaptation in the culture as a whole. As the dramatic
story of industrialization and urbanization unfolded in the
years of the twentieth century, so did the tale of the nation's
sports life. The increasing popularity of sports and the growing
importance of physical recreation in the lives of more and
more Americans have profoundly affected city and regional
planning; the architectural design of homes, schools, churches,
and industrial installations; and the building of highways.

Progressively since the beginning of the twentieth century
adult men and women, adolescents and children, have been
presented with more and still more leisure time. Leisure has
become, for many Americans, the largest block of time in their
lives. And Americans have developed a myriad of amazing
and amusing ways of spending their leisure. But in competition with movies, night clubs, reading, and a hundred other
modern diversions the popularity and the appeal of sports and
games have persisted and grown.

The manufacture and sale of sporting goods equipment of
all types has for many years formed a substantial subsection of
our national economy. This does not mean merely the balls,
bats, rackets, guns, fishing tackle, clubs, etc., but a thousand
and one accouterments—the equipment needed for swimming
pools, for stadiums, grandstands, tennis courts, and the many-
sided picture of personnel and property in connection with
spectator sports. Add to this all the investment and expenditures involved in the tourist trade throughout the nation, so
much of which is motivated by the desire for outdoor recreation.

Consistent with a tradition of free enterprise and individual economic initiative, commercially sponsored and promoted sports and enterprises for the provision of physical recreation activities for the public have grown and flourished. Operating standards have been improved as competition increased and as customers became increasingly discriminating in their desires. Such ventures are to a degree under public control, since they are dependent on customers to survive.

The impact on the American school system of sports and later of a modern concept of the worthy use of leisure time has resulted in an acknowledged educational obligation—an obligation to supply direction, to provide instruction, and to foster opportunity for the fullest possible growth and development of each individual's recreational potential. The increase in quantity and in quality of such school instruction has added to the ranks of sports enthusiasts, participants and spectators alike.

Sports and physical recreation have provided a fruitful field in the culture for the expression of the American propensity for humanitarianism. Certainly the playground movement was actuated by humanitarian concern for the underprivileged urban youngster. The hundreds of youth-serving and welfare agencies have utilized physical recreation activities to counteract the more deleterious effects of an increasingly complex, industrialized culture on the lives of children and youth: the lack of space for wholesome outdoor play, the too-easy availability of sedentary entertainment, the constant increase in labor-saving and time-saving devices which curtail the outlets for physical energy.

The extensive provision of municipal recreation facilities and leadership for sports and the activities of the federal government in helping the average citizen to realize his ambition to share in the outdoor pleasures of the nation are a part of a revolutionary development in American culture. This development concerns the acknowledgment that in a complex society equality of opportunity cannot be taken for granted, that sometimes it must be contrived. It carries the implication that adequate nutrition, adequate housing, and adequate recreational opportunities may belong among the inalienable rights of man, and that without them the pursuit of happiness may become a race on a treadmill.[7]

An earlier America saw the development of two great types of character, one exemplified by the New England Puritan and the other by the Southern Cavalier. In the Puritan tradition the idea of God was the dominant molding force, and in the southern tradition the idea of the gentleman. The historian, Stuart Sherman, advanced the theory that since the Civil War there has developed an American Type, one that is best exemplified by what he calls "athletic asceticism." The optimistic view that "the whole upward movement of our later American culture indicates a type of athletic asceticism as the necessary and inevitable corollary of our civilization"[8] remains an ideal to be sought. And yet would anyone who is familiar with the conduct of American soldiers in two world wars, and since, argue that they were soft, effeminate, or lacking in nerve power?

It is a certainty that, since 1900, Americans have been busy ridding themselves of the Puritan heritage of associating pleasure with sin. There are only a few localities remaining in which it is not possible or entirely acceptable for adult men and women to go forth with golf clubs, tennis rackets, fishing reels, skis, or what-have-you and have no other reason than the pursuit of pleasure.

An examination of intercultural relationships such as this book undertakes should aid in an understanding of two of the most widely deplored and consistently criticized aspects of the nation's sports life. These aspects represent a growing tendency to overorganize sports and leisure-time activities and to overemphasize and overpublicize athletes and athletic events. Yet in the organized world of today—with mighty governments, corporations, associations, political parties, pressure groups, and institutions, each with its own publicity machine—it is a little unrealistic to expect sports and athletics to escape the overwhelming trend of the times. Also, and largely due to a highly developed system of communication, American culture has developed what might be termed a "star" psychology. Names of individuals in government, in the criminal world, in society, and in business are highly publicized, quite without regard to the fact that their individual accomplishments are more often than not the work of many people, or of complete organizations. Hollywood has done much to push the national psychology in this direction. It is inevitable that the same thing is found in the realm of sports and athletics. It is the individual coach, the individual player, who is overpublicized, sometimes with hero-worship and sometimes with villification.

Political and economic happenings and activities have absorbed much of the time, interest, and energy of twentieth-century Americans. But, important as are such issues as trusts, monopolies, and strikes, politics, business, and war, men and women still sought to enjoy themselves in such leisure time as they had and were absorbed in the cares and pleasures of family life. Thus, how the people lived, the amusements they sought and the sports in which they indulged, the clothes they wore and the songs they sang, all are as much a part of history as the great events that made the newspaper headlines.[9]

It has been said, "Study a man's pleasures, and the half of him is known." It is hoped that this volume will form a part of that search for what was valid in the American past and what is sound in the American present and encouraging in the American future.[10] In a world where such words as "democracy," "freedom," "liberty," and "sportsmanship," and the ideals they represent, are being challenged, ridiculed, and repudiated, it becomes increasingly difficult to take them for granted. To what better task can a citizen give himself than an understanding of the national character, fashioned as it has been from such a strange mixture of inheritance, environment, and historical experience.

2. *A Frame of Reference*
for the Study

IT WOULD BE AN ENDLESS TASK TO TRACE ALL THE INTERRELATION-
ships which exist between sports and vigorous physical recreational pursuits and the various elements of the culture of the
United States, even if the period of time were restricted to the
first fifty years of the twentieth century. A list of the factors
which affect the sports and recreational life of a given people
would eventually include virtually all major manifestations of
the culture, with only a *degree* of influence as the differenti-
ating characteristic. No knowledge of how people dressed, ate,
thought, worshiped, governed themselves, educated their children, built their homes and cities—nothing would be irrelevant
to a complete understanding of the how, when, what, and why
of their sports and recreational life.

Sports and play activities of a vigorous physical nature have
been an integral part of every culture in so far as is known,
but the peculiar and particular development of such activities
in a progressively more industrialized and urbanized society,
and under a democratic form of government, has a history all
its own. Much as may be learned from studying the sports and
recreational patterns of other cultures, from the most primitive
to the most highly developed, an explanation and an understanding of how this pattern evolved in the United States may
be gained only through a study of those features of the culture
and the sports life of Americans which are in some ways quite
unique.

In considering a framework within which a study of sports
and American culture in the twentieth century might con-

ceivably be explored with some hope of completeness, it seems desirable arbitrarily to select for emphasis those areas of the culture which seem to have the greatest degree of interrelationship with the nation's sports life. This framework must also be dictated to some degree by the data which are available. Since it is impossible to be actually projected in time, to cover the period 1900 through 1950, reliance on the written and spoken record of the period is inevitable.

In a primitive culture the physical environment, geographical factors, may be a powerful influence in the sports life of the people. Whether the country is flat or mountainous, subject to extremes of heat and cold, the annual incidence of rainfall—all are important in understanding the choice of activities as well as the frequency or infrequency with which certain activities occur. This is, and has been, increasingly less true in modern America. The automobile and other forms of transportation have practically eliminated distance as a factor vitally influencing sports life. Ice-skating is more often carried on inside a building and on an artificially created rink than it is out of doors. The absence of natural bodies of water, lakes, streams, and beaches, is compensated for by the steady growth of swimming pools. Basketball, America's own, is carried on the year round, regardless of snow, rain, or heat. It may be concluded, therefore, that this factor of physical environment and geography is not one of *prime* importance in a study which pertains to twentieth-century United States.

The level of energy which exists among a given people is something which cannot be ignored in the search for an understanding of their sports life. Sports flourish where there is, among sufficient numbers of the population, abundant energy to engage in vigorous recreational activities. Many examples could be cited of populations subject to endemic disease of the debilitating type which most seriously affect both their ability and their desire to engage in such activities.

No more than small groups of our total population have

been the victims of such disease in the twentieth century. The nutritional status of the average American undoubtedly compares very favorably with that of any other group in the world and is far superior to that of many groups. It may be assumed, therefore, that the factor of level of energy is not of prime importance to an over-all study of sports in twentieth-century American culture.

If it is acknowledged that there exists a progressively high degree of control over the physical environment and the geographical factors, and if it may be assumed that there is a sufficiently high degree of nutritional status (level of energy) among a major portion of the total population, what, then, are the great influencing elements in American culture that have shaped the sports life of the nation?

HOW AMERICANS HAVE LEARNED TO LIVE WITH INDUSTRIALIZATION AND URBANIZATION

The family represents one point of departure for understanding any culture, since it forms the basic and fundamental unit of all human societies. In America every large city presents a contrasting picture of homes and families, ranging the scale in extremes of wealth and poverty, of literacy and illiteracy, of social prestige and complete obscurity, of high ideals and antisocial practices. Out of these homes and families come the children who fill the schoolrooms and innundate the playgrounds, the future patrons of the ball parks and stadiums, the prospective readers of the sports page, and the future purchasers of the nation's billion-dollar output of sporting goods and equipment. Since every participant and every spectator in the total panorama of the nation's sports life is the product of a family, the potential power of the family to mold, to channel, and to supply recreational experiences becomes a matter of vital importance.

To understand the drive that lies behind the picture of a nation which leads the world in variety of games and sports played, watched, listened to, and paid for, one must go back to the Declaration of Independence. The third of those unalienable rights in that famous triumvirate of "life, liberty, and the pursuit of happiness" has been something that Americans have taken seriously! Nothing less could explain the movement which began in the earliest years of the century toward civic improvement of recreation facilities and the provision of playgrounds. Cities struggling with almost overpowering problems of housing, sanitation, police and fire protection, cities where living conditions for low-income groups were deplorable, still found leaders, energy, and funds for making the "pursuit of happiness" a little nearer reality.

Reputable businessmen and disreputable adventurers competed in efforts to provide, by commercial means, avenues through which citizens could find some joy and self-expression. New forms of relaxation and amusement flourished as an urban population struggled to adjust itself to new food habits, new living habits, and the intensified nervous strain involved in complete dependence on a money-making and money-spending basis. Here was a different sort of mass population, increasingly self-assertive as well as prosperous. An urban population who bought their clothes instead of making them, rented their houses instead of building them, and paid for their food instead of growing it would quite logically expect and be willing to pay for their recreation.

The provision of recreation, as a phase of business management, had been initiated more than a hundred years before with the early beginnings of the industrial revolution and the efforts of Robert Owen in his model community of New Lanark in Scotland. The United States "inherited" the industrial revolution from England, but what happened in the United States was quite different from what happened in England, and for a number of quite understandable reasons. Here was a vociferous and youthful democracy, a free-enterprise system, an extremely heterogeneous population, almost unlimited room for expansion, and a wealth of natural resources.

Industrial recreation in America has developed without benefit of direct government legislation; in fact, much of the early growth was a result of spontaneous, self-organized activities, initiated by employees. Whether the twentieth-century efforts of industry are motivated by a concern for the welfare of workers or by an interest in promoting greater efficiency, the belief is widely held that such programs "pay dividends."

THE EFFECTS OF THE CHANGING ROLE OF SCHOOL AND CHURCH

Some of the most powerfully influencing factors affecting the sports, play activities, and over-all recreational life of people are to be found in the realm of the social institutions within a given culture. There is probably no more powerful social institution in American culture than the school. The almost overwhelming task of attempting to provide free and universal education for all citizens was first undertaken in this country.

From all the multitude of subjects, ideas, and customs which form the whole of a culture, society selects those which it feels are most essential—in fact, indispensable—in the education and training of its youth. This selective process goes on all the time and represents an attempt to provide more help to youth in understanding and adjusting to the society in which they are to live. Thus we see in the last fifty years many changes in the curriculum of the school. A study of Latin and Greek, considered in the year 1900 to be indispensable in the curriculum of the college, is no longer so considered. Conversely we have schools of business administration and of social welfare and curriculums in physical education which did not exist in 1900.

Another institution in our society which has many interrelationships with the physical recreational life of the people is the church. Most of the major church groups in our culture, regardless of denomination, have undergone a tremendous change in attitude in this regard within the last fifty years.

In 1900 the most common attitude on the part of most churches with regard to vigorous sports and games was one of complete disapproval. At the turn of the century the church did not show too high a degree of sensitivity to the changes which were taking place in the culture: the increase in leisure time and the growth of all forms of recreation and the increased standard of living, which was making it possible for more and more people to participate in such activities. But gradually the awareness came that the church *as an institution* was in competition with many other forces in the culture for the time, thought, and the energy of individuals.

THE IMPACT OF DEVELOPMENTS IN COMMUNICATION
AND TRANSPORTATION

America is a literate nation, and it is important to understand how public opinion and reaction and public tastes have been shaped and influenced by the published word. Observers of American life have frequently commented on the preoccupation of the people with sports and games, both as participants and as spectators. In attempting to understand the "why" of this universally acknowledged trait in the culture, it is essential to remember the part played by the newspaper, the periodical literature, radio and television.

Despite tremendous advances in speed and in the coverage of the railroads since 1900, despite the advent of the airplane and the luxury of the present-day ocean liner, the form of transportation which is of paramount importance in the first half of the twentieth century is the automobile. As Strunsky puts it, the average man in an automobile "has the world at his wheels. To the limits of his tires and his gasoline he is monarch of all he surveys."[1]

The automobile, though it may be the cause of four hundred deaths on any given Labor Day week end, has brought zest into the sports and out-of-door life of countless millions. The businessman to his golf course, the children to the beaches and parks, the whole family to the state and federal land preserves for a camping and fishing trip—these are but a small portion of its recreational uses.

THE INCREASING CONCERN OF GOVERNMENT FOR THE WELFARE OF THE PEOPLE

As the process of industrialization and urbanization is speeded up in a society, the government of that society tends to become more powerful and more highly centralized. It must of necessity assist in finding solutions for problems which affect the welfare of the nation as a whole. Since the early years of the twentieth century, government on all levels, from the local town council to the federal bureau, has shown an increasing concern for the physical recreation of citizens.

With regard to children there is the whole story of the playground movement which began as a private philanthropic venture in most cities, promoted, sponsored, and financed by individual groups of citizens, under the leadership of a woman's club, a local YMCA, a settlement house, or one of the many welfare groups which exist in any large city. But within a relatively short time citizens were advocating the provision of playgrounds and leadership for such playgrounds as a municipal responsibility. They felt that such ventures should be financed from public funds and not depend exclusively on private philanthropy. The result is that today this is a fully acknowledged public, governmental function. And, further, the movement has expanded from merely supplying playgrounds for children to the provision of extensive recreational facilities of all kinds serving all age groups.

The federal government has acquired and is preserving some fifteen million acres of land which have present or potential recreational value and ten times that area of forests. Through the National Park Service it has set as an objective the job of securing the maximum recreational use of these lands. During the period 1932–37 the federal government is said to have spent a billion and a half dollars in constructing and improving permanent recreational facilities.

In that division of government concerned with law enforcement we find a definite interrelationship with physical recreation. Most penal institutions have accepted the fact that programs of sports and games, planned for the inmates, are extremely helpful in promoting morale and aiding in the process of rehabilitation. Since the first children's courts were established in the United States and the words "juvenile delinquent" replaced the phrase "young criminal" in our language, police officers, judges, and social workers have praised the efforts of society in striving to provide more and better recreational facilities for this age group as a preventive measure in combating potential delinquency.

THE PROBLEMS OF WAR

There are many ways in which war affects the sports life of the nation. Great masses of men in the various branches of the armed services are thrown together with periods of enforced leisure but under certain restrictive controls. To many of these men it means their first opportunity to learn sports skills and their first chance to participate. And war's ending sends back to civilian life millions of young men who have come to know sports and to cherish the opportunity to continue participation as one of the things for which they fought—both for themselves and for their children.

War puts women into men's jobs and thereby increases their freedom and independence in matters of dress, manners, and recreational pursuits. War brings problems to solve in providing leisure time outlets for war-impacted communities.

War steps up the rate at which adolescents in our society are pushed toward maturity and invariably brings an increase in juvenile delinquency. This in turn stimulates community and governmental action in promoting vigorous physical recreation activities and participation opportunities for this group.

Only during a war emergency does a nation make a careful survey of its manpower. During World War I such a survey was made, and the revelations of the draft statistics shocked the nation. The compulsory state physical education laws which resulted failed to accomplish the promised miracle of making the nation's youth physically fit, but they did finally result in an almost universal sports program in the schools.

Since World War II all our armed services have made a careful study of programs of sports and vigorous recreational activities for their personnel, with the resulting growth of provision for participation in sports and an almost total dismissal of the formal programs of gymnastics so dogmatically imposed in the early years of the century. This approach is based upon a realization of the *dual* role of sports in contributing to the morale of men as well as to their physical fitness.

THE NARROWING GAP BETWEEN RICH AND POOR

If it were necessary to set down the most unique feature of the development of sports in American culture, it would be the gradual transformation of the idea of sports for a privileged few, "gallant sportsmen to whom a dollar was just something for tradesmen to fret about," to sports for all those who had the desire or the ability to indulge.

People in a mood to play are people who feel comparatively safe regarding the elemental needs of life. In this fact lies a part of the explanation of the prevalence of play in primitive society.[2] In an industrialized, urbanized society sports are sometimes a luxury, not to be indulged in before the individual has attained a degree of tranquillity, a measure of relief from the harassment of the stress and strain of penury, which converts all of life into a frightening problem. In conditions of abject poverty one cannot hope to breed sportsmen. An indispensable ingredient is a basic feeling of leisure, derived from some measure of economic security.[3]

Nothing is more characteristic of twentieth-century America than the narrowing gap between rich and poor. Balanced against admitted ineffectiveness of governmental machinery and many instances of unrestrained economic exploitation, we have a rising standard of living for greater numbers, an increase in the availability of public education, the standardization of dress and fashion obliterating long-standing marks of class, and democratization of all forms of recreation through motion pictures, radio, television, the park systems, and municipal recreation programs.

The growth of newspaper circulation and periodical publications has brought knowledge as to other ways of life and has stimulated the desire to share in what American culture characterizes as the "good things of life." The automobile alone might be called the great leveler, eliminating as it does the age-old distinction between "he who rides and he who walks."

THE INFLUENCE OF IDEAS, IDEALS, TRADITIONS, AND DEMOCRATIC CONCEPTS

In spite of the importance of sociological factors in molding the lives of individuals within a given culture, these factors are not the sole determinants in influencing individual or group behavior. Each generation of children is fitted into the social pattern by a process of indoctrination which includes knowledge of rituals and opinions, laws and taboos, legends and folk tales. In other words, every society has what the anthropologist calls a system of "conventional understandings" which are transmitted more or less intact from generation to generation.[4] These understandings constitute a set of standards against which the individual judges himself and is judged. Many of these "conventional understandings" influence and are influenced by the sports life of the nation.

There is no higher compliment which, in the common parlance, can be paid to any American boy or girl, man or woman, than to designate him as a "good sport." As a cultural ideal it has almost entirely supplanted the titles of "lady" and "gentleman." This ideal of sportsmanship is continually reinforced in the culture by citations in the press, on the radio, and in television. It is an ideal which imposes a type of self-control which in many instances is more effective in preserving and promoting satisfactory human relationships than the invocation of the written law.

No analysis of national characteristics would be complete without a word about Americans and their passion for voluntary associative activity. From the time of De Tocqueville's observation that the meeting of three Americans meant the election of a president, vice-president, and secretary, to Will Rogers' comment that two Americans could not meet on the street without one banging a gavel and calling the other to order, it has been obvious that this impetus to associative activity is a sovereign principle of our democratic life.

To be known as a nation of "joiners" has its amusing side, but there can be little doubt that such organizations have afforded the people their best schooling in self-government. Through the process of membership and participation citizens have learned from youth to seek each other's counsel, choose leaders, harmonize differences, and obey the majority will. The habits of thought and action so engendered have enabled Americans to take effective action in the conduct of most of the major concerns of life—spiritual, economic, political, and recreational.

Perhaps because of a pioneer background the tradition of physical strength, the ability to "play the game," has a greater appeal to the American imagination than intellectual or artistic accomplishment. Herein lies a part of the explanation of the "drive" which goes into our sports life. The team is never beaten until the last man is out in the ninth inning, the game is never over until the gun has sounded—these axioms have an appeal to all and are accentuated by the public press, particularly on the sports page.

Mention must be made of one of the most pressing among the many national problems awaiting amelioration and solution in the United States and its interrelationship with the sports life of the nation. This is the dilemma of racial segregation, discrimination, and the general status of certain minority groups within the culture. Much attention has been focused on the important efforts that are being made toward a solution of employment, education, and housing difficulties. There is still another line of attack, where the battle for human freedom, equality, and dignity has made admirable progress—the sports arena. Perhaps the spirit of sportsmanship, the genuine admiration engendered for a champion, regardless of color or creed, may help some Americans to shed their prejudices and bring the nation a step nearer to the ideal of "liberty and justice for all."

At mid-century attention is focused on grave international problems of all sorts, and in this area too sports have played a part. A complicated and widespread network of international athletic competition, amateur and professional, has existed over the last hundred years of American history. Each athlete, from the humblest individual competitor to the members of the powerful contingent of Olympic representatives, has had a share in forming the total pattern of reaction to America which exists in the world today.

Sport, like every other invention of man, can be used for good or evil purposes. If international contests between individuals or teams are treated as involving national prestige or as proving racial or national superiority, then they may serve only as an additional source of international misunderstanding. And, yet, in a world that has no common religious or political philosophy to share, perhaps the field of sport and the universality of the ideal of sportsmanship may provide a meeting ground where co-operation and understanding, a respect for the rules, and a sense of fair play will prevail.

Spectator sports have provided a "whipping boy" in the American athletic picture since the century began. Yet the fact of the intensity and width of the enthusiasm of the general public for such contests is beyond question. The spectator role seems an inescapable concomitant of America's complex twentieth-century development.[5]

3. *The Family Survives—but the Pattern Is Changed*

THE FAMILY IS AN IDEA AND AN IDEAL; IT IS ALSO A SOCIAL IN-stitution—in fact, it is the basic and fundamental unit of society. But, most important of all, the family is the particular group of individual human beings of which it is composed, father, mother, and children. In the first fifty years of the twentieth century the American family has undergone many changes in mores, composition, location, and degree of stability and in the role which it plays in the lives of its members. These changes have perhaps been inevitable in the light of other cultural changes which have so transformed the pattern of daily living, working, and playing of most Americans.

It is in the home that the child's earliest play ideas, patterns of participation, and ideals of sportsmanship are learned, and the child's mother is ordinarily his first model and teacher. Thus a part of the foundation of the sports life of a nation is built by the mothers of the nation. Our Puritan tradition is most often blamed for the incapacity of some adults to play with pleasure. A prominent psychiatrist has stated that from his own observation a much more powerful deterrent to the frank enjoyment of recreation among adults was a sense of guilt, an echo of parental prohibitions.[1] The fact that more adult Americans know how to work than know how to play may be due in part to the circumstance in which most punishments of their childhood were for lawlessly following the impulse to play, and nearly all rewards were for aptitude and industry in work.[2]

Many of the functions formerly performed by the family

23

have been taken over by agencies outside the family, in whole or in part, and this has intensified the importance of those that remain. Modern families must be held together not by the performance of specific acts but by the more subtle and stronger bonds of affection, social and psychic dependence of each on the other. The new criteria of success are in terms of mutual and complete respect, trust, confidence, and co-operation in all matters. The cultural lag in thinking about the family is seen when emphasis continues to be placed upon the organization and material activities of family life and when these are credited with the emotional development, the growth of personality, and the attitudes which are considered significant.[3]

An increase in leisure time and a rising standard of living have been reflected in increased problems and possibilities in the recreational life of families. In this chapter an attempt will be made to examine the interrelationships, both existing and emerging, between sports and physical recreation, as well as some of the history of this aspect of life with the total picture of the family in American culture.

THE STATUS OF CHILDREN

This great, careless, self-satisfied country of ours is being aroused to consciousness of the fact that it is no longer a paradise of the poor as well as the promised land of the oppressed. Our timeworn democratic policy of "letting alone" has been sadly over-worked in every direction, but it is no longer even respectable when applied to children. The playground idea is a mighty protest against the flagrant inequalities of opportunity for those who are too young to appreciate their theoretical equality and freedom. Let us not repeat the errors of yesterday by expecting results without means to secure them, efficiency without training, and success without carefulness.[4]

The new century was ten years old when these words were written, and a tremendous groundwork had already been laid. The inspired writings of Jane Addams, Jacob Riis, Henry Curtis, Luther Gulick, and a host of others had dramatized the deplorable conditions of life as they existed for the children and families of the tenement and slum areas in American cities.

There was abundant evidence that conditions were not due to any abnormality or innate viciousness of individuals but, in many instances, to sheer helplessness. Industrialization and urbanization, particularly in the early years of the century, were responsible for the herding-together of immense populations into inadequate quarters, under conditions shockingly unsanitary and completely lacking in that degree of privacy which is essential in forming moral habits and attitudes.

The great majority of the thirteen million immigrants who entered the United States between 1900 and 1914 settled in the large cities.[5] Many of these families were ignorant of civic institutions, of laws of sanitation and hygiene, and even of the protections which were offered by laws and philanthropic institutions. Frequently the children in such families, in their contact with the schools and the playground, formed the most substantial link with the new culture. But this fact in itself was a threat to the stability of the family, since such children frequently came to resent the Old World ways of parents. Thus another factor was added to the delinquency potential. These children and youth were breaking away from the controls exerted by their alien culture but had not become effectively adjusted to the discipline imposed by American customs. The constant hope and faith are expressed in the literature of the period that the playground, with its socializing influence and training in sportsmanship, will help to accomplish this difficult task. The work of the social settlement provided much constructive help to the foreign-born by realizing the necessity of proceeding slowly in breaking down cultural barriers and imposing new beliefs and standards.

It was well understood that the provision of playgrounds would not solve the entire situation, but as Theodore Roosevelt wrote to Jacob Riis:

It is an excellent thing to have rapid transit, but it is a good deal more important, if you look at matters with a proper perspective, to have ample playgrounds in the poorer quarters of the city, and to take the children off the streets so as to prevent them growing up toughs.[6]

The early years of the century have been characterized by historians as an era of quest for social justice. Nowhere is this quest better portrayed than in the work of women in America who were beginning to enjoy their first tentative steps toward widespread participation in public affairs and particularly their work in alleviating the misery and unhappiness of urban mothers and children who were so inadequately equipped to help themselves.

The story of the extraordinary spread of new ideas of child care during the first third of the twentieth century will be told in Chapter 9.

Multitudes of American women were being made acutely conscious of the need of something better than the traditional background that had for so long dominated parent-child relationships.[7] Prominent among the new concepts of child care were those concerned with play—play as an indispensable part of physiological growth and development, play as a vital educational means, and play as an irreplaceable sociological factor in total development.

The added knowledge and leisure time of the middle- and upper-class women gave them opportunity for social observation and for the cultivation of social sympathies. In some cases sentiment was aroused by the awareness of human misery, and in other cases the self-preservative instinct forced women to work among their neighbors; "for in cities one's neighbors may murder in innumerable ways besides with the pistol or dirk."[8] For whatever combination of motives, there is a tremendous record of achievement in all branches of child welfare which the women of America, working individually and in groups, have accomplished in the twentieth century.

THE CHANGING STATUS OF WOMEN

To approach an understanding of the emerging pattern of the modern American family, it is essential to trace the changing status of women in the culture during the last fifty years. The most obvious symbol of the contrast between women of today and those of fifty years ago is the outward freedom achieved by women—their physical freedom of movement, their freedom from hampering and constricting clothing, their freedom to engage in sports and to go independently where they will, alone or with men. The most obvious proof of the revolutionary effect of sport on the life of the modern woman is to be found in the manner of dress. More profound implications exist, however, than are indicated by such outward and visible signs as clothing when women are considered in their vital role as mothers. If one examines the realities of daily life which lie behind the military and political events recorded by historians, it is evident that everywhere throughout the history of mankind there has been exercised by women a focal cultural influence. In the past such influence was confined almost exclusively within the family and home. The twentieth-century emancipation of women has widened the circle of influence but has not changed the fact that the home is still the focal point.

America is the home of the Declaration of Independence and the cradle of democracy, but prior to the twentieth century the democracy which functioned was one of adult males, not one of men, women, and children. The nineteenth century seemed convinced that women were physically and mentally inferior to men, and, while great tribute was often paid to their spiritual insight, the social status of women was somewhere between that of a child and a man.

The cultural shift which brought woman to a near-equality with man in every aspect of her social career is cumulative, the result of a gradual but constant mass movement of events and of the personal practices of a multitude of persons both men and women. Women were never merely spectators or inactive partners, but in present-day America they contribute to the culture with the same sense of self-determination that man possesses. Girls are currently being brought up to think of themselves as *persons* first and as *women* second.[9]

Women and sports.—With the single exception of the improved legal status, no social achievement has had more far-reaching effects than the entrance of women into the realm of sports, which brought with it emancipation from the type and quantity of clothing in which they had been imprisoned for years.[10] Many of the changes in our cultural ideal of womanhood with regard to gentility, acceptable standards of modesty, and physical vigor show a directly traceable influence to sports participation and sports costuming.[11] There is a significant cultural implication in the fact that American women golfers refused to follow the precedent of Great Britain and call their tournament the "Ladies' Championship." They insisted that the distinction was one of sex and not gentility and have always called their big tournament a "Woman's Championship."

Throughout the years preceding the twentieth century there was always the subtle influence of fashion, inhibiting even the very young girl from enjoying the free physical life of her brothers. This curtailment was the sort of thing John Stuart Mill had referred to in his famous treatise on the *Subjection of Women* when he said that, so long as women were brought up as a variety of hothouse plants, shielded from the wholesome vicissitudes of air and temperature, and untrained in occupations and exercises which give stimulus to the circulatory and muscular system, it would not be surprising to find they showed morbid characteristics.

Dress reform in America had been rather vigorously promoted in the 1840's and again in the 1870's, mostly on the basis of morals and hygiene. But it remained for the coming of a simple mechanical invention to bring an end to the tyranny of the corset, the bustle, and the trailing skirt.[12] It was not the arguments of reformers but the factory and the bicycle, the first World War and the automobile, the tennis racket and the turkey trot.[13] Once the freedom and comfort of the new sport clothes had been experienced, neither newspaper ridicule, masculine disapproval, adverse legislation, or ecclesiastical prohibition stopped the twentieth-century woman from adopting the new fashions.[14]

The innovation of the low-wheeled bicycle was but the beginning of a trend which was rapidly reinforced by women going into all sorts of outdoor activities, and, as the dress changed, so did the ideas of modesty. The outward and visible change was the least important, since it was merely a symbol of a deeper revolution in standards, ideals, health, and physique. The new woman would be in many ways stronger, more healthy, and more ambitious. The transformation of women from a sensory to a motor basis meant replacing coercion with volition, the cultivation of an enthusiasm for social ends which gradually replaced the moral restrictions that bound them to the past.[15]

Sports clothes, which eventually came to include the modern bathing suit together with shorts and slacks, symbolized the new status of women. "It was the final proof of their successful assertion of the right to enjoy whatever recreation they chose, costumed according to the demands of the sport rather than the tabus of an outworn prudery, and to enjoy it in free and natural association with men."[16]

The athletic era also brought an end to the chaperone. The older women couldn't be persuaded to ride bicycles, and the younger ones couldn't be kept off! There must be many a present-day grandmother who remembers the unparalleled sense of freedom that was hers the first time she and a party of friends set off on their "safeties" unaccompanied.[17] The growing camaraderie of young men and women is an important part of current social change, and nowhere is it evidenced more than in the field of sports. This has potentiality for positive social gain, since, when young people participate together in such sports as tennis, golf, skating, and swimming, they have an excellent opportunity to appraise the stamina, energy, persistence, sportsmanship, and the reaction to success and adversity as displayed by their partner. Such knowledge may play an important part in the selection of a future mate and was not possible to secure in a generation when any activity on the part of woman more strenuous than croquet or a sedate canter on the back of a gentle horse was considered to be "unmaidenly."[18]

The old Greek proverb which says that the man who gives his child to a slave to be educated will soon have two slaves is as true of mothers as it is of teachers. Until women had achieved a reasonable degree of equality and freedom for *themselves*, they could not fully participate in the task of passing along this precious heritage to their sons and daughters.

EXPANDING ROLE OF THE FAMILY IN RECREATIONAL SERVICE AND LEADERSHIP

The modern family provides an atmosphere more friendly and more emotionally satisfying and makes provision for greater freedom and development of the individual personality.[19] Few things bring the generations together better than play, with the laughter and good spirits that real play should engender. Parents and children become temporarily the same age when they face each other across a table-tennis net, toss a game of horseshoes, share a game of golf, or play "catch." Few things will serve to heighten family unity like vacations which all members enjoy together, camping out, hiking, and fishing. When each member has a vital role in such projects, in terms of play rather than work, the family unity is close to that achieved in the old-time rural family, but without its drudgery and rigid discipline.

The prevalence of summer camps has diminished to a degree the role of the family vacation. One benefit from this circumstance that is too frequently unappreciated is this: a vacation for parents, freed from the responsibility and care of their children, may be a particularly unifying experience for husband and wife. Given an opportunity, modern women want to play more adventurously, more lightheartedly, more companionably with their husbands than was considered possible by a previous generation.[20]

Parents who learn to play *spontaneously* with their children are building more solidly for parental happiness and satisfaction. If all occasions for play are initiated by the child and the response is merely an acceding to the child's request, then such play is on the parent's part just another of those sacrificial acts performed with inner strain. A parent should feel free to initiate play, noise, to "rough house" when *he* feels in the mood. Children are much too perceptive not to sense the difference. As one author puts it, "the best fathers and mothers probably do some physical things—walk, skate, climb, swim, whittle, build models, shine the silver—with their children."[21]

In a modern family it is possible for the wife and mother to become a key figure in the recreational life of her family, as manager of leisure. This does not imply a dictation of what the various members of the family should or must do. It does mean studying the leisure needs and interests of the family members and helping each to do more adequately what he really wants to do. So many vital impulses toward worth-while and enjoyable recreation activities are never satisfied simply because of inertia or mechanical difficulties. The equipment is out of place or in need of repair, the information is not readily available or is inadequate, and the time schedules are not properly arranged. An alert and interested woman in the home can accomplish wonders in conquering the inertia of family members who are inclined to fritter time away in a less desirable manner simply through efficient planning and the contagion of her willingness and enthusiasm.

Family reaction to the acquisition of sports skills can be a very influential factor in the life of each member of the group. A generation or two past boys went to the old swimming hole, usually without parental interest or support, and were content with the ability to stay afloat and propel themselves through the water. Today both boys and girls are encouraged to learn how to swim and are not long content with crudities. There is real striving for efficiency and form. This is also true in golf and tennis, and many girls have through this means been persuaded to forsake the idleness of the front porch to join their brothers in the practice of sports.[22]

To make good bread it takes flour, milk, salt, sugar, lard, and yeast. It simply is not good if the yeast is left out. So it is with the ingredients which go into making a happy and successful home. Food, clothing, and shelter remain as basic essentials, but, unless the "yeast" of recreation is included, the result may be heavy and spiritually indigestible.[23] The tremendously increased complexity of modern life has brought about a tendency toward overorganization of leisure, and the home is often confronted with the problem of competing for the child's interest with agencies outside the home. To obtain a satisfactory balance between the home, the school, and various community agencies and attractions requires the greatest degree of cooperation and understanding. The extracurricular activities of the child with his own age group are a positive need, just as is the proper home environment which so largely conditions his attitudes toward life. An exclusive absorption of the child's energy by either home or school will result in a malformed product.[24]

The home as a center for recreation.—There is some evidence that where homes are more adequate and living standards high, the organization of the individual's leisure life more often centers in the home. The growing practice of building play and game rooms in homes indicates that as housing becomes more adequate, additional space will probably be used more and more for leisure-time activities.[25] Just as there have been in the past members of religious cults who voluntarily lived in poverty to serve the Lord, perhaps there may develop a cult of families which agrees to live without conventional aesthetic luxuries for the sake of raising and enjoying children. In a home that contains a minimum of breakable, stainable, and otherwise damageable equipment, the child may never have the experience of discovering that the cover on the sofa is of greater importance to his mother than his ability to crawl over it.

It might almost be imagined that the designers of metropolitan housing projects hate the family, they seem sometimes so ignorant of its requirements or so unable imaginatively to interpret them. Families need space so that neither physically nor spiritually will they have to live from hand to mouth.[26] A house that lacks facilities for play, has no floors that can be danced upon, no room for children's games, and no external playground for throwing a ball is as incomplete as a furnace without a flue.[27]

In future planning, the neighborhood, not the individual house, must be considered the basic unit. To encourage the growth of neighborhoods, there must be a group of families large enough to support the neighborhood institutions and facilities such as the school, the church, the shopping center. And the spiritual life of the people must be sustained by recreational areas, parks, and playgrounds made accessible and patterned for their use.[28]

In modern American culture the isolation of the home cannot be preserved, and its self-sufficiency is a myth. The easy availability of means of transportation; the constant impingement of the multiple channels of mass communication, radio, television, newspapers, periodicals; the multiple activities of the school, the church, and the youth agencies—all these establish connections and filaments throughout the community. "To achieve the results of individualism it [the home] cannot escape the duties of co-operation. Today no one can build an adequate house who does not also take pains to create an adequate community."[29]

4. *Commercial Recreation and Spectator Sports to the Rescue*

THE PROVISION OF RECREATION ON A COMMERCIAL BASIS IS AS legitimate and as inevitable in modern America as is the supplying of food or any other commodity required in daily living. The quantity and the variety of recreational outlets and opportunities made available on a commercial basis are enormous and provide for a very considerable share of the leisure time of millions of Americans.[1] The widespread interest and enthusiasm of the public for sports and games has made this type of recreation a very lucrative one for commercial promotion. Today the role of commercially sponsored physical recreation is less important than earlier in the century, owing to an increase in municipal facilities, to a much more progressive school system which includes wide opportunities for learning sports skills, and to the manifold efforts of various private agencies and the church in providing both facilities and leadership. All these factors tend to keep commercial interests from dominating the field.[2] Thus, while community recreation is not free—its cost is borne by users and nonusers alike—in commercial recreation the cost is solely to the consumer.

Many more voices have been raised to criticize and condemn than to praise commercial sports and recreation, and yet such enterprises have undoubtedly increased the opportunity of many city dwellers to swim, to skate, to bowl, and to play golf. As to the charge so frequently made that professional sports have created a generation of spectators, the real cause of "spectatoritis" is the modern big city, and the remedy, if one is needed, lies not in curtailing or abolishing professional sports but in enlightened city planning which will provide greater opportunity for participation.[3]

Interest in sports has assumed such proportions in American culture that amateur contests are completely inadequate to supply the demand. The average follower of sport prefers a game of football played by well-trained amateurs to one played by professionals even better trained. But, if the choice lies between a professional game and none at all, there is no question but what he will patronize the professional game. The present trend seems to indicate that the professional and amateur sports will fight it out side by side *with an audience large enough to support both.*[4]

There are four principal areas in which commercially sponsored sports and physical recreation have functioned in the recreational life of America in the years of the twentieth century. First, with regard to participant sports, there have been, among other things, promotion of and provision for bowling, golf, skiing, and swimming. Second, there has been a phenomenal growth of vacation spots, hotels, summer resorts, etc., with their provisions for boating, horseback-riding, fishing, hunting, swimming, tennis, golf, and other sports activities often being a prime drawing card. Third, there has been an extensive provision of first-class summer camps for children with their wide variety of sports opportunities. And, fourth, the whole tremendous field of professional spectator sports. An examination of the many interrelationships of commercial sports and physical recreation with the emerging pattern of American culture in the last fifty years necessitates some attention to each of these four major areas.

EARLY COMMERCIAL RECREATION

Before undertaking that task it may be interesting to take a backward glance at three of the most popular forms of commercial recreation which were being provided for urban America at the opening of the twentieth century. These were the amusement park, the trolley-park, and the exposition. Each of these enterprises included some provision for both active and passive participation by customers in various forms of sport and physical recreation.

The pages of the periodical press of these early years are full of comment on that strange American creation, the amusement park. Statesmen, philosophers, foreign visitors, and poets discussed this phenomenon and attempted to analyze its relationship to American life and culture. Richard Le Gallienne wrote in the *Cosmopolitan* in 1905 of the "Human Need of Coney Island," calling it the tom-tom of America. His reaction was that every nation has its need of orgiastic escape from respectability from the world of what-we-have-to-do into the world of what-we-would-like-to-do.[5] Another famous writer described the scene as follows:

Here, on the beach, wading, swimming, leaping, diving and shouting, was a myriad of human beings of all ages, forgetting the city's heat, forgetting everything but the joy of the riotous water, the battle with the lifting, toppling surf, the wild stimulus of the flying foam.[6]

From 1904 to 1907 there was a veritable hysteria of park promotion, followed by a panic. Those that survived the stress and strain embodied the elements that made for better performance and profit. It had been proved that "novelties" *alone* could not hold the crowd, and, while the "novelties" continued, there was growing evidence of the things which give title to the name of park—trees, grass, lakes, playgrounds, and athletic fields.[7]

Manhattan had its Coney Island, but nearly every city in the land had a trolley-park on its outskirts. Street and surburban railway companies had entered the amusement field on an extensive scale. These outlying breathing spots became popular centers of recreation for clusters of small communities newly linked by electric current. Such parks, combining natural and artificial diversions, became a mecca on Sundays and holidays not only for the working classes but also for the "middle millions."[8] It was not unusual to have fifty thousand people gather in the more extensive trolley-parks owned by companies in Philadelphia, Detroit, Minneapolis, and Baltimore, listening to band concerts, watching or taking part in ball games, boating on the lake or river, or simply strolling along the shady walks.

James Sullivan, then president of the Amateur Athletic Union, recorded a glowing description of the role of athletic sports in the Pan-American Exposition held at Buffalo in 1901.[9] In a stadium especially constructed for the exposition, the sports program opened with a game of baseball between the Carlisle Indians and Cornell University. The program ran from May to October and covered, in addition to baseball, championship contests in basketball and many contests in intercollegiate and interschool track and field events.

At the famous Louisiana Purchase Exposition held in St. Louis during 1904, the exposition authorities offered to the American Physical Education Association six gold medals to be awarded for the six most valuable articles submitted on the subject of physical training.[10]

BOWLING

The rise of bowling to the top ranks of participant sports in modern America epitomizes in its own small way the triumph of the common man. It seems strange that bowling, the most harmless game conceivable in itself, should have been an object of repressive legislation and edict for more than four hundred years. An English statute in the year 1477 forbade the practice of bowling by "the meaner sort of people," specifically "servants, labourers, mechanics and other vulgar persons."[11] The existence of a Connecticut law prohibiting the game of "9 pin bowling" was the reason for the organization of the modern ten-pin game when the American Bowling Congress came into existence in 1895.

The story of the unsavory atmosphere of gambling and

drinking which surrounded the game in early England as well as in America is well documented. The work of the American Bowling Congress did much in the early years of its existence toward cleaning up the sport, but it was when women began to play the game that it really became respectable. As one writer phrased it, "Mom took it [the bowling alley] out from behind the pool room and put it in the church basement."[12]

By mid-century there were a million and a half bowlers in the American Bowling Congress, an organization dedicated to "uniform rules" and the "spirit of good fellowship." Also within this organizational jurisdiction were 300,000 sanctioned teams and 56,000 sanctioned alley beds, each required to be level within four-thousandths of an inch. Women bowlers had their own International Bowling Congress formed in 1916.

Headquarters of the American Bowling Congress are in Milwaukee, and the annual tournaments, held since 1901, now average 30,000 contestants. Customarily 100,000 spectators pay admission to see the contests, and another 100,000 are admitted free for various reasons. National championships have been staged in other cities, but the privilege of playing host depends to a large extent on the ability of a city to furnish the essential facilities. These include a building with forty alleys, sufficient dressing rooms, checkrooms, and waiting rooms for competing bowlers, and a grandstand for as many as four thousand spectators. Entry fees collected from competing bowlers go to make up the cash awards, which usually amount to more than $400,000.[13]

In addition to commercially operated bowling alleys, there are uncounted thousands scattered throughout the United States in lodge halls, private homes (including the White House), industrial plants, universities, and church basements. A truly national sport, bowling is most popular in the Middle West and highly industrialized Central States, least popular in the South. Manhattan has fifty-eight bowling places, seven of which offer twenty-four-hour service for the benefit of waiters, cab-drivers, bartenders, and show people who drop in for a game on their way home.

Although it may never be possible to catalogue with complete exactness the reasons why any one sport enjoys such tremendous popularity at a given time and place in history, there are obvious reasons for the popularity of bowling in twentieth-century America. For a relatively vigorous sport a minimum amount of space is required, which makes the construction of bowling alleys well adapted to highly congested urbanized areas. Bowling continues throughout all seasons of the year, and, being an indoor sport, its profitable operation is not dependent upon the weather. All ages and both sexes may play with equal pleasure, and it constitutes an ideal corecreational activity. There is no great outlay of expense for equipment, since many alleys furnish shoes as well as the bowling balls. Bowling is a highly competitive sport and seems to afford its devotees an excellent outlet for aggressive impulses, both operators and players agreeing that the "crash-bang" of the alley is an indispensable part of the game!

GOLF

Many students of the game of golf believe that the establishment of the game at the eastern and southern resorts of the ultrarich marks the real start of its widespread popularity. By 1900 Poland Springs, Saratoga, Manchester in Vermont, Shennecossett near New London, and Lake Placid had added golf courses to their other attractions. Florida had seventeen courses ready for the winter vacationists in January, 1901.[14]

Throughout the history of the game in America, golf has been the recipient of a great deal of concerted commercial promotion. Much of this promotion was in addition to the actual construction of courses, although this building program was often intimately connected with real estate schemes, lucrative club promotion, and the hotel and resort business.

The name of A. G. Spalding Company is closely related to

the commercial side of the development of golf. The story began with the trip of a young salesman to England in 1892 and
his subsequent return with $400 worth of golf clubs and balls.
The young man was Julian W. Curtiss, later president and
chairman of the board. The firm of Spalding's good-naturedly
dismissed the investment as "Curtiss' folly," but within a very
few years they were engaged in a competitive battle for the
growing market in golf equipment. By 1936 supplying golf
equipment represented more than 40 per cent of the company's
entire business.

Spalding's brought Harry Vardon, Britain's number-one professional golfer, to the United States in 1900 for an exhibition
tour, and incidental to this their product, the Vardon Flyer
ball, was highly advertised and exploited. There is little doubt
that this tour greatly stimulated American interest in the game.
The Vardon Flyer, a gutta-percha ball, was eventually knocked
out of the market by the introduction of the new type of
wound-rubber ball with balata gum for an outside covering.
Spalding's met this development by buying a rubber company
with right to a balata process and set up its own rubber refin-
ery.[15] By 1922, as a curb on further increasing the range of the
long-sailing ball, the United States Golf Association acted to
standardize the weight, dimensions, and liveliness of balls to be
used in official play. The competition and efforts still go on
among manufacturers of clubs and other equipment to make
it possible for the average man to play a better game. Spalding's is cited here in the role of pioneer in the industry, but
the list of firms which have made significant contributions to
the promotion and improvement of the game is long and
distinguished.[16]

Since 1921 a co-operative arrangement has existed between
the United States Department of Agriculture and the USGA
concerned with turf research. Extensive experiments have been
conducted at government test plots at Arlington, Virginia,
and at Beltsville, Maryland, which have resulted in finer turf

for golf courses and better and more economical management by greenskeepers. The USGA has expended hundreds of thousands of dollars in the work.[17]

Prior to World War I there were in the United States approximately eighteen hundred golf courses. This number had increased to approximately six thousand by 1930. Of these, forty-five hundred were private-club enterprises, some two hundred and fifty were municipal, and the balance were conducted for a handsome profit by hotels, real estate promoters, and others with a knack for making money.[18] The availability of such courses took care of that portion of the golf-playing enthusiasts unable to pay the high membership fees required by most clubs and to whom municipal facilities were not available.

The growth of commerically financed golf courses kept *proportionate* pace with that of municipal and club courses. By 1932 there were reported to be 611 nine-hole, pay-as-you-play links with at least 213,850 regular players.[19] One such course in Chicago showed a net profit of $50,000 in 1929 "despite the world's keenest competition in public golf facilities."[20]

Professional golfers have existed from the game's early beginnings, but it was not until 1937 that professional golf graduated into big business. Much of the credit for this successful transition goes to Fred Corcoran, who became what amounted to tournament director for the Professional Golfers Association. His genius for convincing chambers of commerce and other publicity agencies for ambitious cities and resorts of what a golf tournament could do for them produced remarkable results. In 1936 touring professionals played about twenty-two tournaments a year; ten years later the schedule was forty-five weeks of the year. Where tournament purses had totaled $100,-000 in 1936, by 1947 the prize money exceeded $600,000. The same ten-year period also brought an increase of 300 per cent in the size of the galleries.[21]

SKIING

Winter sports, and particularly skiing, are today a major American sport, and they also represent a tremendous business enterprise. Much of the credit for this development goes to the Civilian Conservation Corps boys and their work during the depression, which work laid the foundation for the future. After the III Olympic Winter Games at Lake Placid in 1932, where one event brought three thousand people up from New York City and over fifteen thousand watched the jumping, winter sports looked like a paying proposition even to the skeptical eyes of businessmen. By 1937 Madison Square Garden was giving nightly audiences of twelve thousand a view of Hannes Schneider and his kids from North Conway in that "daredevil sport, Skiing."

Skiing areas developed across the United States represent practically every variety of means of financing. Where a more concentrated population or tourist tradition exists, commercial interests are developing ski areas. In the northern Rockies where no great urban population centers are found, and because it is possible to ski on the mountains behind practically every town, most of the development has been of the club variety. In Pennsylvania developments center around various large hotels. A sample development is Mohawk Mountain in the Berkshires, where a hundred-thousand-dollar commercial investment provides nine tows serving nine trails and four slopes. The center is open four days a week and features a Kiddie Ski Pen with a registered nurse in charge. It is reported that the New England farmers who furnish sleeping quarters and meals to many thousands of skiers consider them as just one more crop, hardier than winter wheat and more profitable than maple sugar.

Most spectacular development is that of Sun Valley, started in 1936. This represented a four-million-dollar program to build the world's finest winter resort, located at the head of a

Union Pacific railroad spur at Ketchum, Idaho. Here will be found eight chair lifts with a total length of four and one-half miles, and there is a single 3,224-foot downhill drop.

As in the case of golf, the sport of skiing has benefited by various commercial promotional devices. Macy's Department Store in New York City erected a fifty-seven-foot slope of boraxed carpet which attracted thousands of visitors, and at Saks–Fifth Avenue professional instructors gave lessons to young ladies about to take their first ski week end. These sales techniques were duplicated in various large stores across the country. "Learn To Ski Week's" have been featured by the top-bracket ski centers such as Alta, Aspen, and Sun Valley, where board and lodging, lifts and lessons, are offered at budget prices. Many stores dealing in the sale of ski equipment have added rental departments where skis, poles, boots, and other essential equipment may be rented by enthusiasts who cannot afford to invest in personal equipment. Through these means, and also through the unlimited co-operation of railroads and busses in scheduling special means of low-cost transportation, the possibility of participation in the fascinating world of winter sports has been made possible for hundreds of thousands of Americans.[22]

SUMMER RESORTS AND VACATION PLAYGROUNDS

In assessing the role of commercial recreation in the sports life of the nation, it is well to remember the thousands of summer resorts and vacation spots that are offered as alluring playgrounds to the city dwellers. In the year 1911, before the automobile came into widespread use and put the whole nation on wheels, *Good Housekeeping* ran a section on "Where To Go."[23] The magazine recommended Estes Park in the Rockies, where athletic classes were conducted and which offered mountain climbing and hiking. Readers were reminded that the Isles of the Sea were only three miles from Boston and offered swimming, boating, fishing, and sailing. Just thirty-eight miles from Los Angeles was Camp Rincon (accessible by steam cars on the Sante Fe or electric cars to Azusa and then by four-horse stages to the camp in three and a half hours), where one lived in tents and had access to swimming pools, tennis courts, saddle horses, and pack animals. Ortley, New Jersey (which could be reached by the Pennsylvania line), offered swimming, fishing, and sailing.

By 1928 the Vacation Service Bureau was operating in New York City and publishing an annual "Vacation Guide" containing information on 943 selected resorts, summer camps, and week-end resorts in New York, New Jersey, New England, and eastern Pennsylvania.[24]

Today the business of catering to vacation-seeking Americans and of providing them with opportunities for participation in sports and a wide variety of physical recreations has assumed an important role in the economic life of the nation.

PRIVATE CAMPS FOR CHILDREN

Since there are a total of some two thousand private, commercially operated camps in the United States, they represent an integral and significant chapter in the sports life of the nation's youngsters. Many of these camps, by reason of the fact that they are operated for profit and usually charge sizable fees, are able to offer a richer and more fully rounded program than the so-called "organization" camps.

Ernest B. Balch, who started Camp Chocorua in New Hampshire in the year 1881, is considered by many authorities to be the real founder of the organized camping movement in this country. The plan of operation of this camp served as a pattern which was followed by many who subsequently started other camps. Among the recreational activities, all of which were planned by the campers, were tennis, baseball, swimming, and other aquatic activities.[25] Camp Kehonka for Girls, also in New Hampshire, was established in 1902, the first camp founded exclusively for girls.[26]

The cultural pressures behind the growth of the camping movement are not difficult to trace. The influence of the confinement, the regimentation, and the many action inhibiting features of urban living on the children of the cities were things of which many parents were acutely conscious. Added to this realization was the nostalgic memory of their own rural upbringing, which served to strengthen the determination to give their children at least a taste of the joyous and carefree contact with nature which had been a part of their own happy childhood.

The periodical press, and particularly the women's magazines, did its share of publicizing the value of a camp experience for both boys and girls. Luther Gulick explained to readers, "The 'Why' of the Summer Camps for Boys and Girls,"[27] and during the 1920's *Good Housekeeping* was devoting three to four pages each month to camp advertisements. Camping for girls developed almost as rapidly as that for boys, and hundreds of girls from the more economically privileged families traveled to northern and western wooded areas each year for a summer of healthful outdoor living.[28]

The *Ladies' Home Journal* repeatedly emphasized the wonderful opportunities for girls to develop physically, morally, and socially by living for periods in girls' camps during the summer. Alluring photographs and well-written articles extolled the joys of outdoor sports and games and told of the wonderful benefits to be gained by active participation in outdoor living and playing. Swimming and canoeing, horsebackriding and hiking, seemed to be the principal activities.[20]

The multiplication of camps—public, private, and organizational—in the first two decades of the century brought about a relationship between the various types of camps that was decidedly unfriendly and antagonistic. Each regarded the other as an unfair competitor, the basis for much of the misunderstanding being the differences in fees charged by the various types of camps. The work of the Camp Directors Association (later to become the American Camping Association, Inc.) in its agreement on a code of ethics did much to correct former misunderstandings and prevent future ones from arising. The organized camping movement is bigger than any one type of camp, and the keynote must be co-operation, not competition. There is sufficient room, and plenty of opportunity, for all types of camps to function within the American scene and to work together for the welfare of boys and girls and the good of the movement.[30]

SPECTATOR SPORTS

The amount of time and money spent by Americans in viewing sports events has been a continual source of pro-and-con argument and comment throughout the years of the twentieth century. All shades of opinion, ranging from high praise to scathing denunciation, are to be found in the periodical literature of the time. A sample of the more optimistic point of view is given in an article published in *World's Work* in 1913:

> Altogether our amusements are a vast and varied industry, employing millions of capital and the time and skill of hundreds of thousands of people. . . . We may well be hopeful of them, for with few exceptions they tend to be cleaner, more wholesome, more truly recreative, and more genuinely representative of the national appetite of a healthy-minded people for innocent and helpful diversion.[31]

One of the gloomier prophets who has consistently and most articulately decried the growth of professionalism and spectatorism is the venerable John Tunis. Whether or not one shares his pessimism, the literature of American sports would be less colorfully and carefully documented without his many contributions to the field.[32]

Madison Square Garden.—Just as Coney Island was symbolic of a certain phase of American life and American amusement in the nineties and the early years of the century, Madison Square Garden is the symbol of certain spectator sports in mid-twentieth century. From its opening on June 16, 1890, until 1925 the old Garden was not only the home of boxing but the scene of many other sports events. Six-day races of all types, Wild West shows, aquatic exhibitions in the huge pool, and the first automobile show were all held here. The Garden also housed MacLevy's Gymnasium, training quarters for local and itinerant fighters, and headquarters for "classes and reducing courses for business men at night, working girls in the evening, and matrons and housewives in the morning."[33]

The arena of the new Madison Square Garden, opened in November, 1925, and built at a cost of five and a half million dollars, seats 18,903 for boxing, 15,500 for hockey, and 14,500 for bicycle races. It is so equipped with modern devices that the multiple use of the building is rather amazing. Four hours after a hockey game the ice can be cleared, 4,200 seats added, and a ring set up for boxing. The Garden was not originally equipped for ice hockey, But Tex Rickard agreed to let Canadian promoters put in an ice-making plant (at their expense) and in return let them have certain dates at the Garden at the top guaranty price. The sport proved so popular that there soon developed a substantial clientele in New York, Boston, Chicago, and Detroit.[34]

Many sports were added to the Garden's repertoire in the 1930's, and among these were basketball, tennis, and ice-skating. It was in the winter of 1936–37 that ice-skating for the first time became officially a spectacle, and 64,000 customers flocked to see Miss Maribel Vinson perform. The following season a Silver Skates Gymkhana was sponsored by a New York newspaper. The Perry-Vines tennis match in the Garden in 1936 attracted 17,630. Madison Square Garden also played host to national champions in America's fastest-growing spectator sport—basketball.[35] Between 1938 and 1947 more than 575,000 persons paid over $1,500,000 just to see the annual national invitational basketball championships at Madison Square Garden.[36] Thus the Garden prospered, and Madison Square shares were affectionately termed "Cauliflower Common" on the New York Stock Exchange.

Boxing.—The modern championship prize fight has aroused an interest and achieved a prestige which could not have been foreseen fifty years ago.[37]

Until the Dempsey-Carpentier fight in 1921 only one match had attracted over $400,000 at the gate—the Dempsey-Willard fight. Between 1920 and 1948 twenty-one fights went over that figure and eight of them over a million dollars. The only two-million-dollar gate on record was the Dempsey-Tunney fight in 1927 at Soldier Field in Chicago, where Tunney received the highest pay a professional athlete had ever received, $990,000 for thirty minutes!

Boxing as a business was a relatively uncomplicated affair before the twentieth century began, being conducted on a side-bet, winner-take-all system for rewarding the fighters. Today the financial reports involve expenses for advertising, promotion, taxes, ushers, special police, carpenters, mechanics, guarantees or compensation to the participants (including semifinal and preliminary bouts), rentals, lighting, construction, and many other items. But also there are, in addition to the gate receipts, radio, television, and movie rights as well as testimonials and other advertising contracts.

Mike Jacobs' famous Twentieth Century Boxing Club, which had a virtual monopoly on title bouts, is reported to have run, in the first thirteen years of its existence, 478 fights with 73 world's titles involved and to have grossed $25,546,-099.[38] The complicated story of the breakup of the Jacobs monopoly in 1949 and the formation of the International Boxing Club, with its interlocking financial interests, is a saga of "big business"; and the suggestion was made at the time that it might merit the investigation of the Antitrust Division of the Department of Justice.[39]

By 1951 a federal grand jury in New York was investigating the alleged monopoly and such obvious facts as these: IBC owns the Chicago Stadium, the Detroit Olympia, and a big share of the St. Louis Arena; only IBC can promote fights in St. Nicholas Arena, Yankee Stadium, or the Polo Grounds in New York.

Boxing as big business no longer depends solely on the actual attendance at bouts. IBC's television contracts include $20,000 per show from the Gillette Safety Razor Company for its Friday night fights from Madison Square Garden and St. Nicholas Arena in New York and $10,000 per show from the Pabst Brewing Company for the Wednesday night fights from New York, Chicago, Detroit, and St. Louis.[40]

In spite of the fact that boxing is the most "commercial" of all professional sports and that an undeniably unpleasant odor has surrounded many so-called "title" bouts, sufficient numbers of fans remain interested and loyal to make it a profitable business. The sport has been labeled a modern American substitute for the chariot race, the gladiator's duel, and the bull fight. Its fascination for the average citizen has been explained in the following manner:

Their lives are usually devoid of opportunities and motives to exhibit courage, endurance, ability to take punishment and other qualities which go to make up a successful prizefighter. It is precisely because they suffer from the lack of anything heroic or thrilling in their own experience that they work themselves into a frenzy over the dubious and necessarily brutal efforts of two professional bruisers to knock each other out.[41]

Baseball.—Professional baseball has retained its premier position as the favorite spectator sport of Americans throughout the years of the twentieth century. The year-round coverage of the game provided by the sports pages of the nation will be discussed in Chapter 8 and an indication of the extent of coverage by radio in Chapter 10.

As a business enterprise, organized baseball is one of the largest and richest monopolies in the United States, with real estate holdings worth many millions of dollars. Its status is practically that of a public utility, with protective legislation extending to the Supreme Court. Contracts of famous players compare with the value set upon talents of Metropolitan Opera stars and the country's finest musicians.[42] Although occasionally overshadowed by a million-dollar boxing gate, on a day-by-day basis it is probably more profitable than any spectator sport with the possible exception of horse-racing.

There is, of course, a reverse side to this bright picture of financial success. In common with other business enterprises, organized baseball has had its serious reverses and difficult times. During the early depression years some big-league clubs had a difficult time finding banks which would extend loans to cover operating expenses. The situation in the minor leagues was much worse, with many Class B and C leagues suspended and the Class AA and A leagues barely able to operate.[43] There were also sharp declines as a result of both world wars, but in each instance organized baseball has recovered and gone forward to even greater popularity and financial success.

Attendance figures as taken from various sources show many differences, but the *magnitude* of all figures is an indication of the economic growth and health of organized baseball. The ebb and flow of public support of minor leagues is considered by many experts to be the most valid measure of the status of baseball. The curve of growth and decline over the last fifty years shows the close interrelationship of the fortunes of baseball with those of the American people and of the culture as a whole. In 1949 the paid attendance at minor-league games reached 41,872,762, and at major-league games 20,324,987.[44] An additional and substantial annual income results from the many business concessions operating in a ball park. It has been estimated that baseball fans consume in an average year, in a large ball park, "nearly 700,000 bottles of pop, about 600,000 hot dogs, over 500,000 slabs of ice cream, about 400,000 bags of peanuts."[45]

It would be extremely difficult to determine the capital investment in baseball, since it depends on resale values, replacements, and property investments. But an idea of the tremendous economic value of baseball as an industry may be obtained by contemplating the extent of the manufacture of baseball goods, uniforms, balls, bats, and supplies; all the concessions at baseball games; and costs of operation, traveling and hotel expenses, salaries, and the turnover of wages of all employees engaged in all phases of the game.

So many attempts have been made to analyze the factors which have given baseball the hold it has on Americans, to explain how it has woven itself so deeply into our way of living, that only the briefest comment will be attempted here. Certainly some deep-seated mores and beliefs of the people are both reflected and reinforced by the national game. Baseball has the competitive team play which football has, but it is also *highly* individualistic. The individual player has a record of day-by-day failure or accomplishment which may function in the minds of the "fan" almost independently of the team of which he is a member. All physical types have at one time or another made successful players, small men and large, old men and young, tall men and short. It seems as though neither shape, size, nor intellectual capacity limits the baseball player.[46] But perhaps it is most of all the essentially democratic nature of the game. Inside the baseball park every man is as good as, if not better than, the one next to him.

5. Labor and Industry Attack the Problem of Recreation

THE PICTURE OF SPORTS LIFE IN TWENTIETH-CENTURY AMERICA would be incomplete which did not include an examination of the part played by organized industrial recreation. America's working population is some sixty million plus. Of this number, approximately twelve million work for themselves; the balance are employees. Today more than twenty million people directly employed by industry are active in industrial sports, and the provision and management of sports and recreation facilities for the public in more than a thousand communities are in total or in part financed by industry.[1] Industrial teams alone buy more athletic goods (with the exception of football supplies) than the combined purchases of all schools and colleges.

In 1900 the industrial recreation programs of today would have been considered fantastic. Employers felt little or no responsibility for the welfare of employees. Far from considering the provision of *recreation* as a responsibility of employers, laws regarding elementary protection of health and safety still had to be fought for and enacted. No form of workmen's compensation for injury was provided by law in 1900. However, as industry grew in size and labor grew in strength, welfare programs of all sorts came into existence. The first survey of importance, conducted by the United States Bureau of Labor Statistics in 1913 on "Employer's Welfare Work," involved case studies of fifty-one companies, and 53 per cent were found to have some recreation in connection with their welfare work.[2]

EMPLOYEE WELFARE AND "TIME-MOTION" STUDIES

Quite early in the century the more forward-looking students of the problems of labor and industry were making a plea for more consideration of the worker as a human being. Norman Hapgood, in addressing the 1910 graduating class of the Sheffield Scientific School of Yale University, emphasized the fact that there was a growing belief that a need existed for a "welfare manager," not responsible for the money-making side of business, but who would study the needs and wishes of employees.[3] And he stated further that opportunities for diversion, whether in intellectual directions or in such amusements as dancing and games, should be provided.

It was about this same time that Frederick Winslow Taylor, the pioneer in scientific management, was publicizing the results of his initial "time-and-motion" studies and attempting to convince management that the solution to the problem of securing a full day's work would not be found until the standard of what constituted a full day's work could be established by scientific experimentation. Taylor deplored the fact that the *spirit* evidenced by workmen in their sports life did not carry over to their work life. He declared that the English and Americans were the greatest sportsmen in the world and that, when playing cricket or baseball, they strained every muscle and nerve to secure victory. But when these same men returned to work, instead of using every effort to turn out the largest possible amount of work, they deliberately planned to do as little as possible.[4]

The expression of such a point of view very naturally made Taylor and his theories very unpopular with the men who worked and was bitterly resented. Taylor was accused of wanting to create a human machine who would depart from the door of the factory with a very minimum of surplus energy for recreation, family life, civic duties, or trade-union activities.

The mistake of early scientific management and its utilization of the motion-and-time studies was in viewing industrial relationships as mechanical and material rather than as psychological and human. The modern concept of industrial engineering has supplemented the economic ideal of efficient working with the social ideal of happy, harmonious living. This means not only wages sufficient to maintain decent standards of living but a working day which will permit sufficient leisure for health and recreation.[5] The basis for programs of industrial recreation is therefore both humanitarian and selfish, both idealistic and practical. Industry has learned that it can hire human energy for mechanically operated machines but that it cannot hire enthusiasm for the job or the good will of employees. Successful programs of recreation have frequently helped to foster such reactions by the contribution they have made to man's ability to live more happily and harmoniously with his fellows in effective group life.

THE AMERICAN SCENE CHANGES

In the last fifty years there has been a gradual but persistent change in the American labor scene from industrial paternalism to industrial democracy. Nowhere is this better exemplified than in the history of industrial recreation. American trained and educated workers inevitably carried over into their working life their individualism and ambition. The environment of the factory created a society in which "their experiences with the gang, fraternal orders, baseball teams, and Rotary Clubs"[6] were applied to the task of meeting needs imposed by modern industry. This explains the failure of some of the early recreation programs, which succeeded primarily in creating antagonism, suspicion, and outright rejection by many employees. The paternalistic and patronizing approach was evidence to workers that such programs were (or might be) a substitute for higher wages, better safety measures, and improved working conditions.

In the late nineteen-thirties the National Labor Relations

Board found it necessary in a number of cases to order employers to cease and desist from recreation programs, where they had been found guilty of violating the National Labor Relations Act by coercing or intimidating employees through such a program.[7] The board indicated that it was not seeking to discourage such programs, but fair play and good sportsmanship demanded that employers completely divorce their recreational programs from any attempt to interfere with self-organization or collective bargaining.[8]

GRADUAL DEVELOPMENTS IN THE FIRST FOUR DECADES OF THE CENTURY

Industrial recreation as a phase of business management has a long and not too-well-known history in America. The traditional yearly picnic for employees and their families was a time-honored institution long before any regular programs came into existence. Many small companies had programs of recreation and welfare which flourished without publicity and within their own small orbit. As an example, the Ludlow Athletic and Recreation Association organized in 1896 had status as a corporation under the Public Statutes of Massachusetts.[9] The National Cash Register Company, which today has one of the finest recreational centers in the country, actually started in 1904 when the founder of the company made a part of his wooded estate available to factory employees.

Miss Ida Tarbell, one of the most famous and most astute of observers of American business life, wrote a series of articles for the *American* in 1915 entitled "The Golden Rule in Business." One of these articles is devoted to a factual and philosophical examination of the status of recreation in industry.[10] She concluded that, in spite of the obviousness of the values of the social spirit, industry had been both slow and stupid in utilizing it. Miss Tarbell found "thousands of offices, shops and factories in this country where there is no more cohesion than in a keg of nails."

The role played by the factory athletic program in the Americanization of the extremely heterogeneous group of industrial employees of the day is a recurring theme in the early history of such efforts. In describing the rivalry between the forty or more baseball teams in the Connellsville District of Pennsylvania, Miss Tarbell said that it was doubtful "if more than two or three men on a team spoke the same language," but this did not seem to interfere with either the enthusiasm or the efficiency of the players. Five thousand spectators, miners, their wives and children, and officers of the company from the president on down witnessed the final play-off.

While baseball in 1915 was easily the favorite factory game, many industries had a variety of sports offerings to match a college or an athletic club. One factory in Rochester had baseball, lawn tennis, bowling on the green, volleyball, croquet, soccer, and quoits.

A reminder of the fact that the battle for shorter working days had not been won came from the director of an urban YWCA through whose hands some three hundred thousand girls employed in industry had passed. "Our swimming pools and our gymnasiums were of no use to the entirely exhausted person. Even our cafeterias could not do much for the girl who is only able to pay seven cents for a meal."[11] The opinion was expressed by this writer that the majority of the working population suffered from partial disability due to fatigue. The economic waste resulting from overwork was probably greater than that produced by the great preventable diseases.

The workingman's view of the interrelation of recreation to modern industry was expressed by Frank Hodge, then secretary of the Miner's Federation in England, speaking not only for workers in England but throughout the world. What workers want is not merely a means of living but life itself. Under conditions of standardized machine industry they must find their real expression as human beings outside working hours—in the use of leisure for family life, education, recreation, a hobby. Hodge considered this the vital question at the back of the whole labor program.[12]

LABOR UNIONS AND INDUSTRIAL RECREATION

Two outstanding examples of what can be accomplished by labor unions in organizing recreation for their membership are illustrated in the programs of the United Automobile Workers (CIO) and the International Ladies Garment Workers (AF of L).

The UAW set up a Recreation Department in 1937, based on a policy of organized recreation for all age groups and both sexes, to be operated on a strict policy of no racial or religious discrimination[13] and to be related to the total union program. The UAW constitution provides that one-half cent of the per capita dues shall be set aside for a special fund for recreation programs, to be apportioned to each region. This is a minimum amount. In addition, locals may set aside any amount they choose for recreation. In some locals this is as much as four cents a month per member.[14]

Activities offered under the UAW recreation program include almost everything in the way of leisure-time pursuits. Among these are team games and individual sports, social recreation, dancing instruction, handicrafts, and cultural and educational activities, such as choral groups, dramatics, movies, children's hobby clubs, orchestras, and health and charm classes. The men and women from the shops and production lines who lead recreation programs on the local and regional level get their formal training at summer-school recreation institutes conducted each year in UAW regions and usually held in public park camp sites leased for the purpose.[15] The UAW's Recreation Department is directed by Olga Madar, the only woman department head in the UAW International setup.[16]

When hearings were being held in Washington, D.C., during June, 1949, on H.R. 2026, the Community Recreation Services Act, a letter from Walter P. Reuther, head of the UAW, was

read into the record. Mr. Reuther said that he spoke for one
million auto workers and nearly four million persons in UAW
families, a significant numerical percentage of the nation's total
population. He explained that the program of the UAW is
linked to and dependent upon the recreation program of communities and that, therefore, "the success of our program, its
benefits to participants is affected directly by the potency of
community programs, facilities and leadership."[17] Mr. William
Green, then President of the AF of L, also gave his support to
the passage of the act. He pointed out that the union was particularly conscious of the lack of wholesome recreational opportunities in most industrial communities. He also emphasized
that, as the fight for shorter hours and a shorter work week
goes on, the problem of adequate facilities becomes increasingly important.

The members of the International Ladies Garment Workers
Union produce most of our four-billion-dollar annual volume
of women's wear. Seventy-five per cent of its membership is
female. This union owns and maintains a thousand-acre playground in the scenic Pocono Mountains of Pennsylvania, within easy distance of the garment center, New York City. Union
president, Dave Dubinsky, insists that the pioneers who
founded the union in 1900 and carried the banner of social
protest in 1910 laid important groundwork.[18] But Dubinsky's
work in the nineteen-twenties in applying education and recreation as tools has accomplished many things. He simply refused to recognize any reason why golf, tennis, fishing, and
hunting should be reserved for any particular group of people.
What has been accomplished is evident at Pocono and in the
fact that in 1950 seventy locals, joint boards, and councils were
active in sports. Union accomplishments in the dramatic field
are better known to the general public. The ILGWU produced a smash hit *Pins and Needles* that ran for more than a
thousand Broadway performances, made two national tours,
and staged a "command performance" in the White House.

INDUSTRIAL TEAMS BECOME INTERNATIONAL

One development which has taken place in the field of industrial recreation within the past decade has both national and international implications. The National Industrial Basketball League was formed in 1946 and has become one of the finest amateur basketball organizations in the country.[19] By mid-century there were eleven teams in the league, and there is every indication that it may be expanded. An examination of the sponsoring agencies reveals quite a cross-section of American life and industry.[20]

During the past several years teams in the NIBL have been publicizing not only the names of the companies they represent but the United States itself in many corners of the globe. In the 1950–51 season the Blue and Golds played in the Far East, seventeen games in fourteen days, a tour that took the team through Hong Kong, China, and the Philippines. Seven players of the Blue and Golds, combined with a contingent of college players from Indiana State, won the Pan-American title by defeating Argentina, 64–52. The Argentina team had previously defeated another touring NIBL team (the Denver Chevrolet's) in the finals of the World's AAU Tournament in Buenos Aires. The 1952 Olympic squad had many industrial players, and the coach of an industrial team was selected to head the Olympic group.[21]

This international participation has not been confined to basketball alone. In 1951 the team selected by the Amateur Hockey Association to represent America at the world championship amateur hockey matches in Paris were all employees of the Lewiston's Bates Manufacturing Company of Maine. The team sailed on January 19, 1951, for a three-month exhibition tour of France, Holland, Finland, West Germany, and Sweden. Following the matches in Paris in March, five exhibition games were held in London.[22]

MODERN TRENDS

There are indications of progress toward a solution to the rivalry, distrust, and duplication of services and facilities which have hampered the full development of industrial recreation in the last fifty years. The modern trend is toward a co-operative arrangement between community and industry in facilities, leadership, and planning to better serve *all* the people. There has been some experimentation with setting up incorporated nonprofit organizations for welfare purposes. Such community foundations are tax exempt, and companies contributing funds or deeding property obtain tax deductions.[23]

One example of the new trend is seen in the city of Denver, Colorado, where fifty-six firms, employing over thirty thousand persons, have been brought together by the municipal recreation department to form "The Denver Industrial Recreation Federation."

Years of experimentation and experience have shown that workers want three things in a recreation program: first, to be able to choose the activity that suits them; second, to have a hand in the management of that activity either directly or through their representatives; and, third, to feel that the program is primarily their concern and not the concern of management.

A viewpoint of management regards programs of industrial recreation as a potential factor in accomplishing the following: building a feeling of individual importance in workers; bringing employees closer together in living as well as working; providing activities which others may enjoy in a *community*, because of their availability and the time element involved; preparing employees for eventual retirement and a vastly increased leisure; contributing to pleasanter working relations and greater co-operation by cutting across departmental lines; and, as an integrating factor in making workers feel more like members of a "community."[24]

Although industrial recreation programs are most often praised and promoted for their psychological and sociological worth, there are certain basic physiological reasons for justifying their continuance. In modern industrial work fatigue is chiefly that of the central nervous system, although the worker often localizes his fatigue in the muscles. Among the causes of industrial fatigue are: machine-imposed rhythms, highspeed production, monotonous processes, noise, vibration, visual fatigue, unfavorable atmospheric conditions, infrequent rest pauses, lack of exercise, inadequate or faulty nutrition, and emotional strain such as might result from fear of unemployment. The factory worker may undertake recreational activities such as swimming, bicycling, or tennis which are more strenuous than his occupation but without the fatigue characteristic of his work.[25]

One study of the relationship of recreational participation to industrial efficiency showed a high degree of relationship between recreational participation and industrial efficiency, but the results cannot be interpreted as meaning that special activities which had a positive or negative relationship to industrial efficiency are the cause of that degree of relationship.[26] There are numerous problems of this sort that offer fruitful fields of investigation for individuals in recreation work and in physical education.

Athletics, outdoor sports, and vigorous physical activities have formed the core of the majority of industrial recreation programs. Even today, when such programs have been expanded to include practically every known variety of leisure-time activity and hobby, sports still maintain their place as first choice. Athletic facilities have consistently headed the list of company-supplied facilities in the past and continue to do so thus far in the twentieth century. A recent survey reveals the following:

1. The number of different activities now used in programs exceeds one hundred.

2. Bowling continues to be the most popular but is closely followed by softball, basketball, and golf. Other sports are not far behind and include baseball, table tennis, lawn tennis, fishing, shooting, and archery.

3. Between six and seven thousand companies, labor unions, and employee associations are known to be active in promoting sports as a phase of their recreation programs. Some unofficial estimates indicate that there are as many as twenty thousand organizations promoting some type of industrial recreation.[27]

6. The Role of the School in the Sports Life of America

THERE ARE THREE SIGNIFICANT REASONS WHY ANY STUDY OF sports in American culture must necessarily give considerable space to the role of the school. First, it must be considered a training ground for the sports tastes and habits of future adults. Second, it is the actual locale for much of the sports and play life of a sizable group of the population, the students themselves. Third, the sports activities of the school often form an integral part of the recreational life of the rest of the community.[1]

A VIEW AT THE TURN OF THE CENTURY

The place of sports in the school curriculum at the beginning of the century is illustrated by the report of the famous Physical Training Conference of 1889.[2] In the entire discussion of thirty-three participants, mention was made of athletic sports only twice, once by Hartwell of Johns Hopkins and once by Hitchcock of Amherst. Sports were valued only as pastimes, and systematic gymnastics were considered to be the forms of exercise yielding the best results in the physical training of school children and college students. This represents a reasonably accurate point of view regarding the place of sports in the school curriculum just prior to the turn of the century, since it came from men who were considered *the* authorities.

It is a far cry from this point of view to one in which the program of sports is of paramount importance in the instructional program as well as in the so-called extracurricular aspects of competition—recognized by the school and presided over by schoolmen. It will be the purpose of this chapter to indicate how these changes came about and how cultural change and pressure were able to overcome the twin traditions of Puritanism and work.

Our early settlers needed no prodding to work because of their previous indoctrination in their homeland and because of the labor shortage in America. But the worship of work made it difficult for Americans to learn how to play. "The first mitigation of the daily grind took the form of hunting, fishing, barn-raisings and log-rollings—activities that had no social stigma because they contributed to the basic needs of living."[3]

The beginnings of recreation (or play) as a serious business were laid in the middle of the nineteenth century. Americans played not for fun but to win "with all the fierce energy that once felled the forests and broke the prairies."[4] However, the idea of play as an integral part of life was difficult to assimilate, and it is little wonder that at the beginning of the twentieth century there were grave misgivings about making it a part of the school curriculum.

CULTURAL PRESSURES EVENTUATING IN A SPORTS CURRICULUM IN THE SCHOOLS

Early twentieth-century educators emphasize the value of play.—One of the cultural pressures which gradually exerted an influence on the school program in general and on physical education in particular was the wide dissemination of the idea of play as an educative process. The philosophy of secondary education around the turn of the century was away from the classical course of study, made up chiefly of Latin, Greek, and mathematics, designed primarily for those who were preparing for a college education. It gave consideration to the whole child, not just to the mental part of him. Whitton, for example, pointed out the common tendency of the schools to consider their duty done when the students left the classroom, when actually the function of the school had just begun.[5]

Prior to the opening of the century the reform philosophy of Horace Mann and that of the disciples of Pestalozzi remained largely in the realm of theory.[6] However, despite a great deal of conservatism, there appeared to be an awakening on the part of some educators to the narrowness of the traditional classical curriculum with its emphasis on mental discipline and mental power and one program for all.

Along with the new philosophy of education stressing the free activity of children came a very decided increase in enrolment in the secondary school, which helped to bring the play idea to more boys and girls. Drastic changes in the ideas of child-training, publicized by such magazines as the *Ladies' Home Journal*, were responsible for a revision of the previous attitude toward play. Widespread changes in the school curriculum were a part of the adjustment of the culture to the new ideas of play. School playgrounds, lessened homework loads, Montessori methods in the kindergarten, President Theodore Roosevelt's support of the idea of play in the school curriculum, and recess game periods were all evidences of cultural interaction which made way for a new philosophy of education in America.[7]

The periodical literature of the day stressed the point that participation in sports and games tended to influence young people toward better citizenship. Teamwork and good sportsmanship were associated with competition in vigorous athletic games. It was recognized that group behavior on the playground served as a powerful democratizing force, particularly in the big cities.

Some of the leaders in physical education recognize the potential value of sports.—While it is true that gymnastics carried by far the major emphasis in any school program of physical education, a number of leaders recognized the poten-

tial values of sports and games despite well-founded objections
to their manner of conduct. Sargent, one of the most dis-
cerning men of all time in the field, extolled the favorable
effects of athletics (and by that he meant athletic competition).[8] George E. Johnson, a school superintendent and
famous for his book on *Education by Plays and Games*, made
a plea for the use of games in the school instead of gymnastics
or at least giving games an equal opportunity with gymnastics.[9]

Much more was written in the early years of the century
about college sports than about sports in the secondary school,
but some idea of the place of sports at this level can be obtained from a survey made by McCurdy in 1905 embracing
555 cities in all parts of the country.[10]

It must be assumed from his report that the instructional
program of physical education was almost exclusively one
of gymnastics. He found, however, that the large majority
of school superintendents approved of competitive athletics
in high school and desired to place the supervision of the
boys' sports in the hands of a regular teacher. While such
a condition indicates no particular change for the class program, it does show a favorable attitude toward accepting interschool sports as a part of the school's over-all responsibility.
However, it should not be inferred from McCurdy's report
that all was "sweetness and light" in so far as interschool competition was concerned. Meylan, of Columbia University,
characterized three sets of individuals holding general views
on the question of intercollegiate athletics: (1) the extremists
—nothing but good can come from athletics; (2) the dispensers
—do away with athletics; and (3) the middle-grounders—
athletics have many advantages as well as some bad features.[11]
His concluding sentence could have been taken from any
number of statements written fifty years later and merely
illustrates the fact that social problems are never solved once
and for all but remain to be re-examined in terms of changing

cultural conditions. "The abuses of athletics are in the direction of excess, inordinate desire to win at any cost, the spirit of commercialism, and the tendencies to professionalism and to gambling." Though interschool competition forms a considerable part of the picture given to the public regarding the role of the school in the sports life of America, it must be regarded as only a small part, relatively, since only a small segment of the school population took part.

The content of the physical education programs in the early part of the century showed a cultural lag—gymnastics in the instructional program and sports in the afterschool program. This lag was undoubtedly due to a number of factors. In the first place, educators were still not fully willing to accept play (and hence sports) as a part of the school program. They recognized the necessity for a certain amount of vigorous physical activity in the school as a relief from the tension of continuous mental effort and were willing to include gymnastics because it afforded such relief, did not take much time, and could not be construed as play. There was little tendency to have fun in a gymnastics class.

Second, the vast majority of individuals who were available to serve as teachers of gymnastics had been trained in one of the European systems or had picked up their knowledge of gymnastics by themselves. McCurdy's survey of 1905 showed that about two-thirds of the teachers had some normal school training, while one-third had not. Very little sports instruction was given in such normal school courses, and it is probably safe to assume that teachers of gymnastics were not well prepared to handle a sports program.

Third, the time element, the size of classes, and the facilities available were not well adapted to instruction in a program of sports. Gymnastic classes of a hundred can be accommodated easily in a gymnasium sixty by one hundred feet, but such size is impossible for even one-third that number in basketball. The out-of-door facilities were either woefully inadequate or entirely lacking. As a consequence, gymnastic exercises were almost the only type of program which could be offered.

Over the years from the beginning of the century to World War I, little evidence of a sports program can be found in the physical education class period. Almost all the discussion in the literature was concerned with various aspects of inter-school sports—aspects that were causing difficulties of one sort or another. One forward-looking fact was brought out in Lowman's study of physical training in the secondary schools of the United States and commented on by McCurdy's editorial.[12] The private high schools and academies were better equipped for physical education than the public high schools. Here was to be found a much higher percentage of both directors and participants. In all probability, much of the participation was of the intramural variety, and it could well be that a reasonable share of the "athletics for all" movement which gained prominence in the second decade of the century came from programs in the academies, a heritage from the private schools of England.

One of the great contributions to the fundamental idea of play in the education of the child was demonstrated by Hetherington in a summer program on the Berkeley campus of the University of California beginning in 1913. While it might seem to the casual observer a far cry from the play-school idea to sports in the physical education program of the secondary school, the point which needs to be stressed has to do with the necessity for the provision of skilled leadership in play activities in the early years of the child's life.[13]

The development of sports for women.—Throughout the first decade of the century there was growing evidence of the right of girls and women to participate in sports both in and out of school, and it must be kept in mind that school sports are not and should not be limited to the boys' program. Sargent's voice in the pages of the *Ladies' Home Journal* was carried to the girls and women of the nation in answer to several articles decrying the desirability of freedom for girls and women in athletics.[14]

Early in the century attention was being given to the sports program for women in some of our leading colleges. At Vassar, for example, the introduction of athletics into the program of physical education did much to stimulate the interest of girls in their physical welfare. Apparently the girls were not satisfied with a program of mild gymnastics.[15] Lavinia Hart, writing on a girl's college life in the *Cosmopolitan*, indicated that open-air athletics were very popular the year around.[16] Among the sports mentioned were skating, tobogganing, rowing, tennis, golf, lacrosse, swimming, riding, cycling, and certain events in track and field.

The rise of intramural sports.[17]—Perhaps the most persistent criticism leveled at the intercollegiate athletic program by both the public and educational administrators centers around the lack of opportunity for participation offered to the mass of the students. A partial response to this criticism is to be found in the rise of intramural sports. College boys who wanted to play on a team and were not good enough to make the varsity joined together and challenged another group which had done the same thing. Class teams were organized, and fraternity and living groups formed teams, originally without the help of varsity athletic or physical education administrators.

As the movement grew, it became apparent that an overall organization was needed to stabilize and centralize control. Michigan and Ohio State in 1913 took the lead and created a staff position in physical education, "Director of Intramural Sports." Aided by the success of mass competition on the playgrounds and in the War Training Camps, other institutions began to realize the value from such organization. Following World War I, the growth of men's intramural sports began to assume great proportions in the colleges, soon filtering into the women's program and into the high schools.[18]

National associations made a place for the discussion of intramurals at their yearly meetings,[19] and it was not long before the interest in afterschool play began to have an effect upon the class program where instruction in sport fundamentals could be given. Widespread attention to the new state requirements offered the opportunity of giving instruction to many thousands of boys and girls who had not hitherto been reached. Team play began to be recognized as a legitimate part of the instructional program, and provisions were made for a broadening of the scope of activities offered to the student in "required" physical education. As a consequence, the ideal physical education program for girls as well as boys now offers instruction as well as some competitive experience in a considerable number of sports activities designed to meet their needs.

SPORTS IN THE CULTURE PRODUCE CHANGES IN THE SCHOOL PROGRAM

Beginning soon after the organization of the Playground and Recreation Association of America and with the establishment of playgrounds in many cities all over the country, the idea of out-of-door play in programs of physical education was stressed by play leaders.[20] Professional personnel through the leading journal of physical education (*American Physical Education Review*) came face to face each month with "propaganda" regarding many phases of the playground movement—the opening of new play facilities, the amount spent by various cities on playgrounds, data on playground legislation, the value of playgrounds in a community, the activities conducted on the playgrounds, municipal administration of play facilities, and the like.

The same children who were subjected to gymnastics in the school found delight in a play program on the playgrounds and often under the same leadership which was present in the school. It is not strange, therefore, that both the children and the leadership recognized a play or sports program as being infinitely more fun than one composed largely and sometimes exclusively of gymnastics exercises. Playground programs, particularly in the summer months, were reinforced by organized competitions in which large numbers took part. The Athletic Badge Tests, promoted by the Playground and Recreation Association of America beginning in 1913, were used as motivating devices to promote the physical efficiency of the boys and girls of the nation and were undoubtedly helpful in interesting hundreds of thousands of boys and girls in their physical skill status.

Prior to World War I there was a strong demand all over the country to use school facilities for play purposes in the evenings, on week ends, and in the summer. "The wider use of the school plant" became a slogan which caught the fancy of taxpayers and municipal officials, and, despite some objection from schoolmen, there was a gradual "opening-up" of school facilities for all types of recreation, and in gymnasiums and on playgrounds sports programs flourished.[21] Thus, early attempts to introduce sports into the class program of physical education were reinforced.

THE SCHOOLS APPLY THE PRINCIPLE OF ASSOCIATIVE ACTIVITY TO THE CONDUCT OF SPORTS

The movement for athletic competition in colleges which swept across the country in the last years of the nineteenth century spread to the public and private secondary schools of the nation, and the many problems of control arose as with the institutions of higher learning. Lack of interest on the part of school administrators and domination of partisan spectators were particularly condemned by leading physical educators.[22] The Society of Secondary School Physical Directors realized this, and part of its program was concerned with a careful study of many and varied athletic problems such as the organization by colleges of championships for high-school boys, competition outside of the school, the management of contests, the periods of training, the amount of participation, medical examination, and recruiting of high-school players by colleges.[23]

The New York Public School Athletic League.—Early in his work as director of physical training of the New York City public schools, Luther Halsey Gulick, saw the need for organizing athletic competition which would provide for the average boy rather than the one who was highly skilled.[24] He initiated a movement which resulted in the formation of the New York Public School Athletic League in 1903. One of the interesting things about this organization was that, although sanctioned by the board of education, it was not made a part of the work of the board but rather a separate organization set up through the co-operative efforts of the superintendent of schools, the presidents of the board of education and the City College of New York, the secretary of the AAU, the chairman of the Intercollegiate Athletic Association, and several prominent businessmen influential in the political and financial world.[25] Realizing the necessity for good publicity in this venture, Gulick secured the assistance of nine newspapers in metropolitan New York, and the league was dramatically launched in 1903.[26]

Because of the large number of entries and the fact that groups had to be handled rapidly, the program of the big meets consisted largely of running and relay racing with boys classified by weight rather than age. However, other activities involving team competition were approved and included baseball, basketball, football, soccer, cross-country, swimming, ice- and roller-skating, and shooting. Baseball was especially popular, and in 1907 there were 106 teams in competition, with fifteen thousand spectators for the final game.[27]

Rifle-shooting soon became a prominent activity of high-school boys, with seven thousand boys receiving instruction in 1908 and annual contests held between different high schools. Marksmanship badges were awarded and President Theodore Roosevelt, during his term of office, always wrote a letter of commendation to the boy showing the greatest proficiency during the year. Prizes were awarded by E. I. du Pont de Nemours Powder Company to the school team having the highest score. General Wingate, president of the PSAL, believed that none of the activities conducted by the league was "likely to have as important an influence upon the country at large as the system of instruction in military rifle shooting."[28]

The operation of the league program was supported by membership fees and contributions from citizens, among whom were to be found such prominent financeers as J. Pierpont Morgan, Andrew Carnegie, John D. Rockefeller, and Harry Payne Whitney.[29]

In 1905 the Girls' Branch of the league was established, not independent from the school system but as an integral part of the physical education department. The activity most successful in the girls' program was folk dancing, and, though there was no interschool competition, play days were arranged where thousands of girls took part.

In speaking of the Public School Athletic League, which he called the world's greatest athletic organization, Reeve stressed the work of the league in developing cleaner, better lives for thousands of boys and the fact that athletic competition had been instrumental in increasing scholarship.[30]

There can be little question that the New York Public School Athletic League served as a pattern for the formation of other city school athletic organizations.[31] Seventeen cities are reported to have formed similar leagues, and inquiries about league organization came from Chile, Argentina, India, and Turkey.[32]

The National Federation of State High School Athletic

Associations.—In the early part of the century high-school boys were just as eager for competition in sports as were college men, and, like the college situation, sports grew up in a very haphazard fashion.[33] They were ignored or tolerated until the schoolmen finally decided that, since they were fast becoming an integral part of the school's extracurricular program, something must be done about their regulation and control.[34] This led to a school organization or association for the purpose of establishing policies within a school, then to an association between two or more schools, and, finally, after a number of intermediate steps, to a state-wide organization charged with the responsibility of developing uniform regulations suitable for all. This development went on simultaneously in a considerable number of states in the years just preceding and just following 1900. Forsythe reports that by 1925 there were athletic associations in all states, though "not all state organizations are called athletic associations."[35] Prior to 1920 there was strong feeling that the control of all high-school contests should be in the hands of schoolmen and not representatives of colleges, clubs, and promotional organizations. In 1920 the secretary of the Illinois High School Athletic Association invited representatives from neighboring states to come together in Chicago for a discussion of the problems which had arisen. As a result of this meeting and another in 1921, involving four midwestern states, the 1922 conference, attended by representatives from eleven states, officially adopted the present name of the organization—The National Federation of State High School Athletic Associations. Forty-four states now hold membership in the federation, and over the years it has done much to stimulate member organizations to reach agreement on such matters as eligibility rules, elimination of national championships, regulation in regard to interstate meets and tournaments, the formulation of rules for high-school players, and national policies in regard to suitable equipment and sports adaptations.[36]

The National Collegiate Athletic Association.—Reform in college athletics, particularly football, received a considerable amount of journalistic attention in the early years of the century.[37] As has been so well stated in the published literature on the subject,[38] school and college athletics had undergone an evolution from an "institution" that was almost universally opposed by schoolmen in the latter part of the nineteenth century to one which was tolerated as a more or less necessary evil to a final stage at the turn of the century where a considerable amount of recognition had been given athletics as an established part of the educational program. However, school and college administrators were faced with serious problems when the decision was made to "take over" their control, since within educational institutions an almost innumerable number of variations of faculty and/or alumni, student, and trustee committees or boards had been set up.

Because intercollegiate competition in sports was inevitable from the start, it was logical that colleges of similar size, ideals, and geographical location should effect an association for intercollege control as each had done for intracollege organization. Similarly, when competition commenced to go outside of a rather narrowly defined geographical area, some organization of a national character was equally inevitable.

The number of fatalities and serious injuries during the football season of 1905 served as a spark to touch off widespread indignation regarding the conduct of sports in general and football in particular. In an attempt to save football, a game he loved, President Theodore Roosevelt called a conference of college representatives at the White House and urged immediate action. In December, 1905, a national football conference of college and university presidents and faculty members was called by Chancellor McCracken of New York University. Among the thirty institutions represented, a number favored immediate abolition of football, but constructive suggestions in regard to the elimination of mass play and unnecessary roughness saved the game and provided for vast improvement.[39]

The McCracken conference resulted in the organization of the Intercollegiate Athletic Association of the United States, later (1910) to become the National Collegiate Athletic Association, the first body actually to be established for the purpose of regulating and supervising college athletics throughout the United States. It is primarily an educational body and at first served only in an advisory and consultative capacity, but since World War II its policies have changed. Now membership in the NCAA can be retained only if institutions adhere to the principles which have been established.[40]

Thus, in keeping with the regulations which have been set up from time to time for the control of other aspects of our culture, it was found necessary to bring to task those colleges violating the spirit of a program which, because of its connection with institutions of higher learning, had appeared to be unassailable. It is worthy of more than passing note to point out that the lay public has taken an active and at times a vociferous part in the condemnation of aspects of college sports which appeared to be out of control. If education belongs to the public, any phase of it may also come under public scrutiny.

The formation of intercollegiate athletic conferences in the past half-century has played no small role in the standardization and stabilization of competitive sports in the schools and colleges of the nation. This movement began with the formation of the Western Intercollegiate Conference in 1895 and since that time has embraced more than seventy-five groups[41] composed of colleges of similar size and academic standards located in a particular geographical area.[42]

Other groups apply the principle.—The principle of associative activity in the conduct and control of sports was not limited to the formation of athletic conferences. Among the national organizations which have had a vital interest in such programs are the American Association for Health, Physical Education and Recreation, the College Physical Education Association, the Society of State Directors of Health, Physical Education and Recreation, and the National Association of Physical Education for College Women.[43]

In the field of sports for women the National Section on Women's Athletics has had a tremendous influence on the development of standards in competitive athletics for girls and women. Organized originally by a group of professional women in physical education for the purpose of establishing a set of basketball rules for girls and women, it developed into a very strong section of the American Association for Health, Physical Education and Recreation. Nor can we neglect small professional groups which gave intensive study to the development of basic principles in the conduct of physical education and athletics. Among these was the Athletic Research Society, which, despite its brief existence of twelve years (1907–18), contributed materially to the acceptance of competitive sports as an integral part of the school and college program.[44]

The National Amateur Athletic Federation.—Another organization deserves specific mention, not for what it actually did, but for what it tried to do. The National Amateur Athletic Federation, organized in 1922, attempted to bring together all national groups and agencies in any way promoting athletics and physical training in the United States. There was a general awareness that the promotion of athletics for all boys and girls, young men and young women, would be a stepping stone to the physical fitness of a nation found comparatively unfit in the medical examinations for armed service personnel in World War I. The development of high ideals in amateur sport and the raising of American citizenship to a higher plane were stressed as fundamental in the federation's platform.[45]

Because of the vision of representatives of the founding

organizations, it became clear that girls and women were as vitally interested in nation-wide athletic participation as boys and men. As a result, there was formed, almost immediately, a Women's Division of the NAAF which grew and prospered but was finally merged with the American Association for Health, Physical Education and Recreation and became in 1940 the National Section on Women's Athletics of that body.[46]

Several of the independent forces which were brought together to make up the NAAF (Men's Division) were too strong to submerge their special interests, and the organization was not successful for more than a few years. However, the attempt to set up a body devoted to the "unity of sport," wherever found in America, indicates a desire on the part of many groups to work toward the ideal of national health and soundness through a program of universal participation in athletics, sports, and games.[47]

The junior colleges organize.—With the growth of the junior college in the early part of the century, it was quite natural that here too athletics should become an integral part of the educational program. Some fears were expressed almost immediately regarding the manner in which athletics should develop. Men of experience insisted that athletics should be controlled and made a part of the educational program.[48] Community pressures for successful athletic teams undoubtedly gave rise to an emphasis which resulted in the organization of junior-college athletic conferences throughout the country. As early as 1930 a questionnaire sent to 320 junior colleges of the nation indicated that twenty such conferences, embracing a total membership of 120 schools, had been formed.[49] In California the junior-college athlete made good when he transferred to the university,[50] indicating a high type of training in the junior college or superior ability as a high-school player. But it is well known that, more often than not, the junior-college athlete does not have the scholastic entrance requirements to come immediately to the state or private university of his choice.

The principle operates at mid-century.—In sports the principle of associative activity has taken various forms, from the organization of student associations in particular institutions to the co-operative efforts of a number of schools and colleges and, finally, to the banding-together of educational institutions from all parts of the nation.

These national organizations were well established by 1930, but their work had only just begun. Though many devious ways have been found to evade the regulations of associative groups, school and college sports leaders are still pinning their faith on this typically American principle. Today we see the rise of the conference commissioner in college sports and the formation of various associations of coaches. In mid-century we have top-level educational bodies, notably the American Council on Education through its Committee of College Presidents, seeking to set up further regulatory measures which will attempt to insure the stability of a phase of college life which has almost universal appeal to the American public.

The proper conduct of school and college sports must be regarded as a social problem and, like many other social problems, cannot be solved by laws alone. One possible solution would appear to be an attempt to get each institution to assume full responsibility for the conduct of its sports program as an educational project rather than as a business enterprise. Essentially, then, the problem becomes one of the downright, homely honesty of each institution.

WAR BRINGS COMPULSORY PHYSICAL EDUCATION PROGRAMS

Wars, terrible as they are, do cause an acceleration in development in many fields of human endeavor—in medicine, in industrial production, and certainly in sports. It may be that professional educators would have succeeded *eventually* in setting up compulsory physical education programs in American schools had there been no World War I. It is a matter of record, however, that a direct result of the preparation for and participation in World War I produced cultural pressures which resulted in the passage of such state legislation.

Four distinct pressures finally culminated in the passage of state legislation regarding the teaching of physical education in the public schools: (1) the movement toward preparedness which began more than two years before the United States declared war on Germany in April, 1917; (2) the fear that the Congress would pass federal legislation requiring universal military training perhaps extending into the elementary schools, or that federal legislation requiring universal physical training would be enacted; (3) the invocation of the states' rights doctrine on matters pertaining to the prerogatives of individual states; and (4) the deplorable physical condition of the youth of the nation as revealed by statistics from the Selective Service Act of 1917.

No one thing or no one set of circumstances produced the sports program in the school. Rather, such programs came from a combination of circumstances sparked by almost universal physical education requirements throughout the nation. In other words, had it not been for the requirement, the millions of boys and girls of school age six to eighteen (possibly twenty-five million) would not have had the exposure to the program which was afforded them. This statement should not be presumed to mean that, as soon as a compulsory program started to function in a state, immediately a sports program was instituted. A considerable number of other factors were involved. Schools found themselves lacking in personnel, equipment, and facilities. But almost immediately a number of states followed the example of California in introducing into the programs of physical education sports skills and tests for these skills to motivate progress in their acquisition.[51] Thus a gradual change from a gymnastics to a sports program developed in the years between World War I and the early thirties.

The need for teachers.—The enactment of legislation in many states following World War I presented a number of problems. In order to comply with requirements, school systems had to have teachers immediately and could not wait until colleges and universities instituted teacher-education programs. As a result, many men and women were recruited who were not well prepared. Men particularly were selected from the ranks of college athletes who had a Bachelor's degree, many of whom had attained officer status in World War I. These men knew their sports, and it was logical that they should use this knowledge in their programs of physical education. As a consequence, more and more attention was given to this aspect than ever before. The class program became the seasonal major sport program on a less intensive basis. During the football season, football fundamentals were taught; next came basketball, then track, and finally baseball, where softball was substituted for hardball.

Later the demand for teachers of physical education and sports coaches was met by four-year Bachelor's degree curriculums in state and private institutions supplemented by summer courses including coaching schools and clinics for both men and women, where the emphasis was almost entirely on technique and strategy in team games. While not organized in such great numbers as in the twenties, these coaching schools and clinics have continued to thrive as a means of in-service training. However, comparatively little attention was given to activities other than the traditional major sports, or to the class program, despite some emphasis on the organization of intramural sports.

THE YEARS BETWEEN WORLD WARS I AND II

There is no question about the effect which various aspects of World War I had on sports in schools and colleges during the years between World Wars I and II. The emphasis placed upon sports as a most valuable preparation for conditioning and morale of soldiers, the tremendous spectator interest developed in France as a result of the sports competition placed before the armed forces during and after World War I, the indignation of the people at home in regard to the physical unfitness of draftees—all of these became pressures in American culture to set the stage for the great boom in sports participation and interest which developed in the nineteen-twenties. This was the period in which the public created a demand for the erection of huge stadiums on the campuses of colleges and universities and to a lesser degree on high-school campuses of the nation. Sports became available to out-of-school youth and adults as well as to those in school. Owing in part to war experiences, the in-school program gradually changed from gymnastics to sports.

Pressures for the enactment of state laws regarding the teaching of health and physical education in public school systems did not end with the cessation of hostilities and the return to civilian life of armed service personnel. From 1921 through 1929 ten additional state legislatures had passed such compulsory laws, thus making twenty-seven states which had enacted public school health and physical education legislation as a result largely of World War I.

School sports in the depression.—The financial crash of 1929 did not immediately affect the school situation, but by 1932 the schools were hard hit. Budgets were cut, teachers' salaries were lowered, and teaching loads were heavier due to the increase of student enrolment as a result of unemployment.[52] Physical education, along with other so-called "frills" as, for example, art and music, experienced some difficulty.[53] Equipment and facilities were drastically curtailed, and the dollar was wrung dry. Interschool competition involving out-of-town trips was often eliminated. Smaller schools, in order to economize, adopted a new type of football—six-man football. Competition in this activity spread rapidly, and by 1941 it was played in forty-five states.[54] Intercollegiate football attendance reached its lowest level in 1932 but thereafter started to increase. The sale of sports goods declined 57 per cent from 1929 to 1933, partly due to export and partly to the financial condition of the nation as a whole.

However, out of the depression came some things favorable to the development of sports in the schools. A considerable share of WPA and PWA funds was used for the building of school sports facilities—gymnasiums, swimming pools, tennis courts, and athletic fields. By 1937 it was estimated that $75,-000,000 had been spent for such projects.[55] In Michigan alone sixty gymnasiums were under construction.[56] The WPA Recreation Projects instituted for the community affected the sports program of the school. There was a demand for the teaching of sports for which the community was providing facilities—golf, tennis, badminton, and swimming. It appears to be a reasonable assumption that the inclusion of many individual sports in the school program of physical education came as a direct result of cultural pressures during the nineteen-thirties. Intramural activities developed at all levels of education. Schoolmen had become increasingly aware of the inadvisability of interscholastic competition at the junior high school level and were substituting intramural activities to meet the demand for competition.

In the field of interscholastic and intercollegiate competition for girls and women there was a steady growth of play-days during the the depression. Following the ideal of "sports for all" rather than for the few, the professional women of the nation went all-out for the encouragement and promotion of sports and games for all, to be wisely chosen, wisely promoted, and wisely supervised. The National Section on Women's Athletics in 1937 set up important standards for the guidance of girls and women in their competitive programs which were described by a male member of the profession as a contribution destined to be of far-reaching importance in the field of health and physical education.[57]

The value of sports in the use of leisure time by both youth and adults was given serious and detailed study by many organizations, and in the middle of the depression (1935) the newly created American Youth Commission gave its undivided attention to the consideration of the needs of youth and plans for the development of programs most helpful in solving their problems.[58] In its recommendations the commission stressed the close relationship between education and recreation and emphasized the major responsibility of the school in this regard and the importance of establishing a program which would offer every school boy and girl "the opportunity to cultivate physical fitness through games, sports and outdoor activities."[59] Because there was no place on the economic market in the depression years for young people of school and college age, enrolments increased. Since society virtually said to the schools, "Keep our boys and girls happy and out of mischief," opportunity was given to educational institutions to expose more young people to a program of sports than ever before.

THE PREPAREDNESS PROGRAM

The early armed services rejection statistics caused even more concern to the nation than those of World War I. High government officials and members of the medical profession and of physical education attempted, early in our serious consideration of war, to persuade the Congress to vote national legislation which would attempt to remedy the condition of our national fitness by providing federal aid to states. The famous Schwert Bill (10606), which died in committee with the close of the Seventy-sixth Congress, and its successor (H.R. 1074), though vigorously supported by such organizations as the American Legion, the Benevolent and Protective Order of Elks, and the National Congress of

Parents and Teachers, did not come to a vote of the Congress but did do much to direct the attention of the people toward preparedness through physical fitness.[60] Another bill was introduced which called for a survey of the nation's facilities and personnel for the purposes of improving our efforts in the field of physical education and athletic participation and the preparation of a program of physical activities to meet the needs of youth.[61]

Physical fitness emphasized.—To meet the demands of the armed services for men in better physical condition, teams of experts toured the country in 1942 holding institutes and demonstrations for educators particularly in regard to wartime programs of school physical education which would emphasize vigorous and rugged activities. Sponsored by the United States Office of Education, the personnel of the institutes included representatives from the armed forces and the American Association for Health, Physical Education and Recreation.[62] To supplement the work of these institutes, the United States Office of Education, Federal Security Agency, published two handbooks on physical fitness, one for high schools and one for colleges and universities.[63] Both publications stressed the necessity for emphasis on sports where large numbers participate (intramural) and where the element of endurance as well as that of skill was prominent. Another publication, a Navy manual, adapted for the use of schools and colleges, came as the result of many requests from educators to set forth the program of sports developed at the preflight schools and training bases.[64]

Unquestionably, the almost universal emphasis placed on physical fitness did much to strengthen school and college *class* programs of physical education. Particular attention was given to those sports which had the possibility of developing endurance. Among these were included football, boxing, wrestling, basketball, ice hockey, lacrosse, water polo, soccer, speedball, handball, squash, track and field, and swimming.

Since many colleges and universities were concerned with programs for men in service, the type and extent of the activities offered depended to some degree on the approval of commanding officers. Many intercollegiate athletic teams were made up largely of armed services personnel, in some instances almost exclusively of Navy students. In intramural competition, however, the other armed services permitted sports participation. It seems fair to say, however, that the general emphasis in school and college programs was on so-called physical fitness activities rather than sports requiring a considerable area for competition. Competitive areas required for a large number of teams in such sports as football, baseball, soccer, and speedball were seldom available either at colleges or at high schools. Daily participation at a given hour had to be limited to those sports requiring a minimum of space and hence the stress on boxing, wrestling, tumbling, and mass exercises of various kinds. Swimming was, of course, a must. Obstacle courses were built on many school and college campuses, and, when inclement weather drove participants indoors, a variety of gymnasium obstacle courses was devised. The flair for obstacle courses during World War II resembled that for miniature golf courses during the depression years. As the war ended, their demise was just as rapid.

Despite the emphasis given to physical fitness in school programs of physical education during World War II, it is apparent that this emphasis produced no lasting effects. The impetus given to sports in school programs during the twenties as a result of World War I and the state legislation which followed, the attention given to sports as valuable assets in the use of leisure time during the depression years, both within and without the school, seem to indicate an American point of view which could not be changed by expedient adaptations. Here, then, is a reaffirmation of the philosophy that physical fitness is only one outcome of physical education as an educational means and that the program, to be lasting, must contain the element of fun to be found in sports.

WORLD WAR II AND ITS EFFECT ON THE SPORTS
PROGRAM IN SCHOOLS AND COLLEGES

With the advent of World War II, the talk of physical
fitness centered around the value of sports in the building
of morale as well as in the building of physical stamina necessary to its succesful prosecution. Educational leaders turned
their attention to the matter of what should be done with
sports in schools and colleges, both in the class program and
in the competitive program.

Two schools of thought emerged. One school believed sincerely that physical condition was the primary requisite for
induction into the armed services: Give the boys (all of them)
strenuous, all-out exercises and get them into conditon quickly
so that when they are called they will be ready! The propo-
nents of this school were not antagonistic to the values inherent in athletic competition but were insistent that the time
element was of the utmost importance and that to condition all
men and boys by means of athletic sports alone required
facilities and personnel far beyond available resources.[65]
The other school of thought believed that the values to be
gained in sports participation should not be discarded because
of the expediency of condition and that to subject men to
drudgery would produce disadvantageous results,[66] Although
there was some rather sharp debate in the professional literature, the extent of the feeling as a national issue would be difficult to discover. When leaders disagree as to what ought to be
done, the "little people" often wonder where to turn,[67] but,
despite the confusion, by and large school physical education
people as well as those in the armed services did the best possible job under existing conditions.

Interscholastic and intercollegiate competition.—Interscholastic and intercollegiate competition were very definitely
handicapped during the war period. The depletion of manpower in many colleges and universities resulted in the aban-
donment of competitive schedules. Other institutions, particu-

larly those which were training Navy personnel, played a limited schedule with due consideration for long trips and time given to practice.

Most state departments of education vigorously encouraged interschool competition for high-school boys even though it was necessary to limit schedules because of gas rationing and the lack of athletic supplies. In many instances the lack of trained personnel caused difficulties, but volunteers from the teaching staff were able to replace temporarily those who had gone into the various services. Brace, in reviewing this phase of the program (1944), says:

Interschool athletics are probably now being conducted on at least 80 per cent of the prewar basis. Regrouping of competing schools has reduced length of trips. . . . As regards intercollegiate athletics the present picture appears to be one in which college coaching staffs have struggled to keep some kind of team in the field. Many colleges have been forced to give up intercollegiate athletics for the duration and still others will probably have to follow suit. Nevertheless the value of athletics is probably more clearly recognized now than ever before.[68]

WAR'S END AND THE AFTERMATH

Long before the end of World War II, leaders in all aspects of our culture were giving serious consideration to what should be done in postwar America. The type of physical education program which should be carried on or instituted in schools and colleges was widely discussed and widely publicized. Physical fitness continued to receive a considerable share of attention; swimming programs were emphasized; the question was raised as to whether a games program was sufficient to obtain physical fitness; the needs of the veterans returning to college were considered to be of particular importance; the old question of too much time spent on the stars to the neglect of the masses was given attention; the broadening of the competitive athletic program for both boys and girls received special consideration. These and many other problems, including the professional preparation of teachers of health education, physical education, and recreation, were treated at length in the professional literature and discussed in conferences and institutes.

The work of the Athletic Institute since 1947 in promoting and financing five national conferences under the sponsorship of leading organizations in physical education, health education, and recreation is highly significant.[69] A nonprofit organization subsidized by more than a hundred and fifty producers of athletic equipment, the Athletic Institute endeavors to develop a community consciousness of the need for providing better facilities, programs, and leadership to the end that more wholesome living will result. Its publications have been well received and include not only a body of literature resulting from the conferences which represents the best national thinking but printed aids in learning and teaching sports skills, in addition to motion pictures and slide films in archery, badminton, baseball, basketball, bowling, boxing, fishing, football, golf, hunting, softball, tennis, track, tumbling, volleyball, and wrestling. The institute's board of directors includes fourteen national leaders in athletics, physical education, and recreation, two of whom are women.

It would appear, however, that World War II has changed the school program but little, except in the matter of emphasis on interschool and intercollegiate competition. At the college level, particularly, war's end produced problems which were to have serious repercussions in the early nineteen-fifties. The immediate eligibility of athletes returning from service in the armed forces, together with government subsidy under the G.I. Bill, caused spirited bidding for players—"shopping around" of players and the old problems of recruiting and subsidization. War breeds a certain amount of delinquency among servicemen. They were out to get whatever they could, and this applied equally to the college as to the armed services. The problems, however, were not much different from those of the early nineteen-hundreds, except that in the late forties and early fifties athletics were supposed to be under the control of the colleges.

Mid-century "athletic" scandals.—The basketball gambling scandals of 1950 and 1951, followed by the West Point cheating affair, brought indignation to sport lovers throughout the country. They started a flood of scathing denunciations against school and college sports in rather wholesale fashion, some justified, some unjustified. The rotten apples must be removed from the barrel lest the entire lot be contaminated; but, in writing about the rotten apples, the good apples must not be forgotten, nor should we overlook the nourishing food they provide. It is most unfortunate for sports that some filth has been discovered in their conduct as well as among the players, but the answer to the rottenness in athletics, as it is in government, is not "do away with athletics or government" but "clean them up." Cultural pressures have been exerted to produce unfortunate conditions, but, by the same token, pressures will be exerted in the other direction.

Two issues of the *Saturday Evening Post* of October, 1951, offer frank accounts of college football as a big-business enterprise and the pressures exerted on the big-time coach and are indicative of the tremendous and often morbid interest which thousands of fans have in the game.[70]

The pressures exerted on athletes, at least in some institutions, are brought out by John Lardner, veteran sports writer.[71] It is his contention that college sports are today performed by specialists, hand-picked from the high schools. Their function is to increase revenue, bring glory to the college via the sports page, and thereby attract more specialists to keep the cycle in operation. He further contends that the varsity becomes the athlete's life, overpowering him to such an extent as to subject him to fears, tensions, and hypocrisies.

Lardner would have us believe that all big-time college sport is rotten, and he is undoubtedly sincere in his condemnation of what he has seen and heard, but he has not conducted a nation-wide survey, and there are big-time teams which can refute everything he has said.

Clair Bee's article in the *Saturday Evening Post* is an excellent exposition of the way in which some colleges get into big-time athletics.[72] He explains why the recruiting system used in many places, coupled with overemphasis and the need of money to support a bigger program, can backfire when gambling pressures are put on the players.

In all likelihood, the events of 1950 and 1951 brought pressure to bear on the American Council on Education that led to the appointment of the famous committee of eleven college presidents. This committee, charged with the responsibility of recommending remedies for college athletics out of control, set forth, early in 1952, a ten-point program which was to be administered by the six powerful accrediting agencies throughout the country. The hope was that the "code" would be enforced by the refusal to accredit schools which violated it.

Reactions to the report were varied. There was some sentiment in favor of every item in the report, and there was considerable opposition to a number of items. Spokesmen for the NCAA, which was holding its annual meeting during the time press releases of the ACE committee's action were made, indicated that changes should be made by working through the NCAA, a body already sanctioned by college presidents in general. There were sharp differences of opinion on at least two points, namely, the ban on bowl games and out-of-season practice. However, it was the opinion of the president of the NCAA that, if colleges as a whole approved the ACE report, then, in essence, it would become the code of the NCAA.

Within two months two eastern college-accrediting agencies, the Middle Atlantic States Association and the New England States College and Secondary Schools Association, had met and announced that they could not enforce the ACE code because it was impractical and beyond their function.

The newspaper publicity which was given to the entire situation is an indication of the apparent importance of intercollegiate competition in the minds of both college administrators and the general public.

So long as educational institutions operate without centralized government control, solutions to their problems, including the problem of competitive athletics, must be sought through the medium of voluntary associative activity. This is the time-honored principle which America has used for a hundred and seventy-five years in business, in politics, and in education. It is often a slow process, because democracy is a slow process; it makes mistakes, and some corruption appears, but it offers the only acceptable means within the framework of our American culture. Solutions to social problems become acceptable only when a majority of the cultural forces involved co-operate to make such solutions effective. Thus when the public and the press, as well as our educational leaders, are agreed on a plan of action even though it be a compromise, the distressing problems of competitive athletics will be minimized.

7. The Changing Role
of the Church

WITH APOLOGIES TO ANY READER WHO MIGHT CONSIDER THE remark irreverent, the role of the church in the sports life of the nation could best be described in the colloquial phrase, "If you can't lick 'em, join 'em!" In tracing the changing attitude of the church in twentieth-century America with regard to sports and physical recreation, the church is thought of as a social institution functioning in the culture in a manner similar to the school and the home. It seems possible to examine the habitual behaviors, practices, attitudes, and experiences grouped under the term "religious"—viewed as traits of human groups—without raising questions as to the validity of underlying conceptions and beliefs. Every successful attempt of a religion to perpetuate itself involves means of propaganda, education, and discipline, and these are impossible without some degree of institutionalization. This study is concerned, therefore, with the church as an institution and with the use it has made of sports and physical recreation in the accomplishment of its purposes.

When one speaks of the "church" in America, it is well to remember that the term comprises the greatest number and variety of denominations which has ever existed in any one country at any one time. The lastest census records a total church membership of 65,000,000 divided into 256 separate denominations. The larger units of this group of 256 comprise 95 per cent of the nation's church membership, while some 200 denominations comprise but 3 per cent or a matter of 2,000,000 out of the total of 65,000,000. This extraordinary diversity of denominations seems to be a concomitant of democracy, distinctive of a free society.

THE TRANSITION IN ATTITUDE

The development of a more liberal attitude within the church began early in the century and has progressed to the present time. This has meant a development of lines of intercommunication and interrelationship with other civic organizations and agencies and a growth of community spirit, bringing a sense of common function with other social institutions in the culture.[1] No area of endeavor shows greater progress than that of the understanding of, and the provision for, a fuller recreational life for church members. Many churches have acknowledged that one of their tasks as a social institution is to help establish a standard of recreation for the community and then assist the community to find and maintain a proper balance between work and play.[2] Many churches have taken full advantage of the opportunity for constructive service by interesting themselves in the people's play and by demonstrating more tolerance, more sympathy, and more appreciation of the reasons which lead people to do the things they do in seeking amusement.

The assumption is frequently made that the church in America has consistently been a negative and deterring influence in the realm of sports and vigorous physical recreation. While the assumption is justified to some degree, it is countered by numerous instances of farsighted, liberal sentiments as expressed by many individual churchmen and through the pages of official publications of various religious bodies. The briefest sampling of such expressions will serve to illustrate.

The twentieth century was but six months old when the rector of Holy Trinity Church, Brooklyn, expressed himself in print to the effect that in the last ten years our country had passed into a new social order and that the prejudice against pleasure as being intrinsically evil had broken down nearly everywhere. He recalled that up to twenty years before the new century there was hardly a place in the country where a grown man could openly set about to play without doing violence to established prejudice and without a sense of personal shame. While he might escape to the wilderness out of sight of man and disport himself with rod and gun, he could not frankly and openly set about to amuse himself; he did not dare! He ends his article with a suggestion that the golfer stop at the church, say a prayer on his way to the links; that, if he does, he will go out a better man, will find fuller satisfaction in his game, will treat his caddie with more consideration, and will count his strokes more carefully.[3]

In the year 1907 a Methodist bishop claimed that the New Testament was silent on the matter of amusements and that the church had no scriptural authority for its strict ban and was trying in vain to continue its enforcement. He asked, "Does the spirit of Christianity enjoin total abstinence from amusements? If not, how far may one use time or money on innocent sports?"[4]

In the same publication a Unitarian minister explained that the church should spend its moral force on permissiveness and help and that the church should have playgrounds and gymnasiums as well as sermons. He concluded by saying, "I claim the green fields on Sunday. . . . I insist on my right to take my rest with the games that discharge the blood from my brain."[5]

Another minister was quoted by one of his flock as saying that good wholesome recreation was first cousin to religion and that the refreshing of the body went a long way toward giving the soul a chance. He felt that, because the church had directed its energies toward "uplifting the whole man instead of a fraction of him," it had lost no whit of its spiritual power.[6]

An Anglican minister, in attempting to explain the church's attitude toward recreation, commented that, in ages past, solution to the problem of how to reform the world had been simple—emasculate it, it being much easier to let a thing severely alone or cut it off than to deal with it. But, if Christianity is a universal religion, it must recognize what is legitimate and universal in human nature. He makes a strong plea for the clergy to countenance dancing instead of placing it under a taboo, reminding them that David danced before the Ark and that Miriam came forth to meet Moses, beating time to her steps, even as the Salvation lasses do today.[7]

Theological schools recognize play.—In the theological schools a new generation of ministers was being indoctrinated with the philosophy that to minister to the bodies as well as the minds and the souls of men was a part of their work. A book entitled *The Minister and the Boy* was published in 1912 and contains a chapter on "The Ethical Value of Organized Play" which would need no revision to be consistent with modern mid-century practice. Attention is called to the conventional Christian ideal, "anemic and negative in the matter of recreation," and there is the suggestion that the minister can help by publicly indorsing and encouraging play movements and co-operating in their organization and management. The book goes so far as to say that the Decalogue itself cannot compete with a properly directed game in enforcing the fair-play principle among boys. The words of Martin Luther, speaking in favor of indulgence in "music and chivalrous games or bodily exercises, as fencing, wrestling, running, leaping and others," are used to provide a further persuasive argument.[8]

Nor is there concern only for the city boy. There are specific hints as to what the minister of the country church can do, especially during that part of the season when school is in session. It is suggested that he be on hand when school is dismissed in the afternoon, when the boys, after having been under a woman teacher all day, are glad to meet a man who will lead them in vigorous play. It makes little difference whether it be baseball, football, track work, or relay races, so long as the man is one who knows how, who is a recognized leader, and who can serve as an immediate court of appeal.

If the boys do not learn more about meeting the real struggles of life with moral and physical courage from this play period than from a "day's book-work in the average one-room, all-grades, girl-directed country school," then the minister must be a sorry specimen indeed.[9]

In another volume entitled *The Religious Education of Adolescents*, written by the director of the Department of Religious Education of Boston University, the question is asked as to whether or not there is sufficient realization of what a wholesome part physical training and athletics may have as time-fillers and outlets for otherwise aimless and unregulated energy. The author states that in the athletics of a well-conducted high school—that is, one where athletics are not only accepted but actually regulated by the school faculty—there is to be found a direct antidote for the soft sensuality of the age, a direct stimulus to school loyalty, a stimulus for scholarship, and a broadening influence by the travel, the business experience, and the sportsmanlike qualities which may be exercised in different ways through interscholastic competition.

The author also responds fearlessly and frankly to an oft-repeated criticism of the motives of the church.

The shameful trickery adopted by some workers in using a temporary or superficial play program as the means of baiting young people—drawing them within the range of the influence of leaders whose sole motive is ecclesiastical or institutional—stands exposed and condemned in the light of the true purposes of play. There are both legitimate and illegitimate methods of recruiting a church or a church school. . . .[10]

He repeated that play is not merely a recruiting device and that the church should supervise a program of play because of the physical, intellectual, social, and even religious benefits that it brings.

In the series of bulletins published by the American Unitarian Association, many are to be found which show a sensitivity to the recreational needs of the times and a forward-looking attitude as to what churches can do about the situation. The second in the series of bulletins is entitled *Working with Boys*, and Bulletin No. 10, written by Luther H. Gulick, is titled *Popular Recreation and Public Morality*.[11]

Thus it can be seen that, in the whole movement toward social reform which characterized the era of the muckrakers in pre–World War I America, the church was not entirely voiceless, and many such reform efforts reiterated the necessity for provision of recreation areas, for the right of children to play, and the responsibility of the churches in the accomplishment of these social ideals.

The church supports athletics.—Nor was all progress merely in the realm of the written or spoken word. In a discussion (dated 1907) of the history and role of the Amateur Athletic Union in the supervision of athletics, reference is made to Sunday-school athletic leagues and church athletic leagues functioning in and around New York.[12] And in 1910 there appears a discussion of the administration of playground, Sunday school, and social settlement athletics in Chicago.[13]

In 1909 there appears a story of a Catholic boys' camp operated by the Vincentian Fathers for the purpose of giving tenement children a chance for vigorous physical play in outdoor natural surroundings.[14] As early as 1912 there were 6,868 troops registered at the national headquarters of the Boy Scouts of America, and, of these, 90 per cent were associated with churches or Sunday schools. Eighty per cent of these were Protestant-sponsored (Methodist, 1,738; Presbyterian, 1,120; Baptists, 756; Congregational, 656).

In 1908 the Federal Council of the Churches of Christ in America came into existence through the action of twenty-nine co-operating denominations. In 1912 this body officially adopted the *Social Creed*, which, among other things, declared that the church stood for "the fullest possible development of every child; . . . the reduction of hours of labor to the lowest practicable point, and for that degree of leisure for all which is a condition of the highest human life."[15] The significance of the Council is that it furnishes a single organ through which the majority of American Christians can act together, and, while effective social action has been slow, a good beginning has been made.

THE CHURCH AND THE BOY SCOUT MOVEMENT

From the date of its chartering on February 8, 1910, the Boy Scout movement has had a powerful influence on hundreds of thousands of boys whose lives it has touched. The history of the Boy Scout movement in the United States, nonsectarian and secular in origin, is nevertheless closely allied with the church. As an organization, the Boy Scouts of America claims the support of all denominations, and this is not strange, since it recognizes religion as a most necessary and vital force in the development of a boy's character. The organization also states, unequivocally, that "the church of which he is an adherent or a member, should be the proper organization to give him an education in the things that pertain to his allegiance to God."[16]

The place of play in the Boy Scout program and the importance attached to play in the character-building process are based on two assumptions. First, that spontaneous play has inherent possibilities for physical development, intellectual growth, and social adjustment. Second, it is assumed that the changes which are brought about through Boy Scout play have moral implications for the growth of the individual scout's character.[17] The ideal scout program will offer opportunities for pleasurable participation in such activities as archery, athletics, canoeing, camping, cycling, hiking, horsemanship, and swimming.

In 1914 the Boy Scout National Executive Board passed a resolution creating a Department of Education. This department co-operated with prominent churchmen in securing the official indorsement of the major religious bodies. A Bureau of Church Relations was established in 1923 and expanded into a general Relationships Service in 1924. This bureau established several courses in scouting principles in church schools, church colleges, and universities. By 1926 such courses were being offered for credit in twenty-two seminaries and in thirty-seven colleges.

The Protestant churches created a Protestant Committee on Scouting in 1922. The Mormon church was the first to adopt scouting on a church-wide basis in 1913. It has consistently registered 65 per cent of its boys and leads all other churches. The Catholics used the Boy Scout movement early but not on a church-wide plan. Papal blessing came in 1919, and in 1923 the Knights of Columbus adopted scouting as the official program for boys. The Jewish co-ordinated effort in scouting came with the development of the Jewish Committee on Scouting in 1925 and 1926. Leading denominations have printed special circulars concerning their policies of co-operation with the scout movement. These include Methodists, Baptists, Congregationalists, Catholics, and Presbyterians.[18] The church was apparently well aware of the need for wholesome recreation for boys, and from its point of view the movement also offered a desirable stopgap between Sunday school and adult life.

The church had taken the lead in sponsoring Boy Scout activities in the early years of the century, but eventually other community groups and organizations began to assume a larger responsibility. In 1912, 90 per cent of the troops were church-sponsored, but by 1942 this percentage had dropped to 44. A variety of clubs and fraternal organizations could now be found sponsoring 21 per cent of the troops in the United States. There is much evidence that both the church and the Boy Scout movement have benefited from the excellent co-operation which has existed over a period of almost fifty years.

REACTION OF THE CHURCH TO CULTURAL
CHANGES OF THE TWENTIES

World War I and its aftermath really roused the church from its lethargy and brought about not only a greatly increased social awareness but a sense of humility in the face of the overwhelming cultural changes of the nineteen-twenties. In a period of less than eight years (1921–28) national income increased by over thirty billion dollars per year. Former barriers of time and distance were removed by the installation of six million more telephones, seven million radio sets, and the availability of an additional fourteen million automobiles.[19] Additional thousands of women joining the labor force of the nation, coupled with the increase in expansion of already overcrowded urban areas, brought living conditions which tended to weaken the family as a social unit and laid the groundwork for present and future delinquency.

It was a decade of experimentation, characterized by extremes rather than by moderation, by evidence of alternating unjustified optimism and cynical despair. In the midst of this scene of postwar confusion and spiritual insecurity, the American church, always conservative and slow in the matter of social reforms, struggled to retain a vital place in the life of the nation. Often confronted with indifferences and disdain from without, and with criticism and dogmatism from within, it was not an easy task. There is much evidence, however, of a deepening sense of responsibility for the immediate environment. There was a growth of effort to face the problem of applying the Gospel in the places where problems must be met and solved, in the places where men and women have their homes, earn their living, bring up their children, and seek their recreations. The growth of the institutional church is an exemplification of the attempt to extend the activity of the church to include every practicable form of ministry to the bodies and minds of men.[20] In the language of one minister:

He would be a madman, indeed, who thought that he had either the authority or the ability to tell the Christian world just how, in these times of flux and confusion, it ought to be applying the principles of Christian ethics to that way of living which is in the process of becoming. He would, however, be a blind man who did not see that the old ways of teaching ethics to Christian people and the old ways of comprehending ethics by those people are no longer vital.[21]

He develops his thesis in a positive way by declaring that the church should urge people to insist upon facilities for play being provided in every community for every child, and also upon such play being supervised. Further, that, if it is not done by other means, the church should do what it can to make such provisions. This constitutes an unequivocal statement of acknowledged approval and responsibility.

A publication entitled *Social Work in the Churches*, published in the early twenties under the auspices of the Federal Council of Churches of Christ in America, takes full cognizance of organized play as an aspect of church work and gives as one reason for this the fact that "young people learn some of their finest lessons in democracy and fair dealing in their associations of the playground."[22]

Architectural plans for churches more and more included provision for the recreational life of the congregation. One prominent church architect warned that care should be taken not to duplicate facilities already found in communities and that the maintenance of gymnasiums and swimming pools was not only expensive but, unless adequately supervised, had better be omitted.[23]

In 1921 the committee on conservation and advance of the Methodist Episcopal church approved plans for the erection of playgrounds and the organization of athletic teams and classes, the work to be financed from the $22,000,000 centenary fund of the church. A committee was appointed to visit all conventions of rural ministers for the purpose of giving instruction in the direction of games and calisthenics.[24]

The Catholic Boys' Brigade had been organized in 1916 and included in its program athletic meets, games, and contests. It was also the expressed desire of the National Catholic Welfare Council that pastors throughout the country introduce into their parishes the Boy Scout movement as a "real practical means of strengthening the nation's manhood and the church's valiant defenders."[25]

By 1927 a study of twenty-six Protestant city churches revealed the following services with regard to the sports life and physical recreation of their membership:[26]

	No. of Churches
Organized athletic teams	24
Boy Scouts or equivalent	23
Gymnasium instruction	19
Girl Scouts, Camp Fire Girls, or equivalent	18
Vacation farm or country property used for outings	11

The churches showed admirable zeal in their efforts to provide recreational opportunities; they were building and equipping gymnasiums, and the old-time repressive measures were everywhere disappearing. Many churches soon found, however, that they had not taken sufficient thought as to the problem of leadership. The growth had come so fast that the meager supply of trained personnel was not adequate, and many churches found themselves with nothing but mediocre leaders or untrained volunteers. An effort was made to compensate for the lack by publication of books and pamphlets which sought to explain how to construct a workable plan for play and recreation for church and parish.[27] La Porte's book, written under the auspices of the Methodist church, had the purpose in mind of providing elementary training for volunteer leaders.[28] It was not written as a substitute for thorough training but with the hope of inspiring some individuals to enter a good training school or university for a strong recreational leadership course.

The institution which supplied the greatest aid in providing leadership for church programs during the twenties was the YMCA. In 1922 the YWCA called a meeting of lay people and pastors to plan a program to make the YMCA a clearing-house for information, literature, and equipment for play and to help start church athletic leagues.[29] In 1923 the YMCA and YWCA and churches representing twenty-two denominations formed a General Counseling Commission with the purpose of bringing the organizations closer together. One of the major objectives was to enlarge the physical recreation program in churches through "Y" leadership. The group met annually, and a subsequent and substantial output of publications and surveys attests to their accomplishments.

The National Recreation Association was another organization which co-operated with the church in the solution of problems of leadership and program. Each year during the nineteen-twenties prominent churchmen were invited to speak at the annual Recreation Congress.[30]

A fitting climax to the decade seems to be the installation of the Sports Bay in the Cathedral of St. John the Divine. This ceremony probably marked the first time in American history that a portion of a cathedral was dedicated as a symbol of the relationship between religion and sport. Of the dedication, Bishop William T. Manning said:

Clean, wholesome, well-regulated sport is a most powerful agency for true and upright living. . . . True sport and true religion should be in the closest touch and sympathy.

Few things have done more harm than the idea that religion frowns upon sport or is out of sympathy with it. This notion gives men a wrong idea of religion and it puts religion out of touch with the life of the people. A well played game of polo or of football is in its own place and in its own way as pleasing to God as a beautiful service of worship in the Cathedral.[31]

CHURCH RECREATION IN AN ERA OF DEPRESSION

In the nineteen-thirties the church shared doubt, uncertainty, and economic reverses with all the various major social institutions in American culture. By 1936 an estimated twenty-one thousand rural churches, from Maine to California, had been closed or abandoned, and many more faced the same fate.[32] Forsaken by the young people streaming toward the cities, neglected financially by hard-pressed elders and members, and also hard hit by competition with automobiles and radio, some considered the plight of the rural church the number-one religious problem of the day.

In the cities the situation of the churches was not quite so desperate, but many social service and recreation programs which had begun so bravely were forced out of existence by lack of funds. And yet, so deep rooted was the fear of the church that its freedom might be lost through a misalliance with the government, that many times relief funds, although obtainable to help maintain their recreation offerings, were not secured. In the city of Chicago the WPA offered an annual sum of five million dollars to be spent through Chicago churches and synagogues for recreation work. It seemed a reasonable bargain, since the churches had trained personnel and facilities, which the government did not, but lacked the necessary funds to sustain their operation. A leading nonsectarian magazine editorialized on the possible danger of loss of freedom and urged nonacceptance of government funds.[33] When it was subsequently announced that other means would be found to use the money, the same publication wrote that the danger to Protestant church freedom had been averted.

As the millions of dollars of relief funds were poured into community recreation programs throughout the United States, the burden of responsibility for such programs was more and more shifted from the church to the government. Their splendid pioneer efforts in many places had borne real fruit, and, although the role of the government would continue to expand in the years that followed, the church would continue to supplement other community efforts and to make its own special contribution to the recreational life of the American people. That the church was still functioning in the provision of opportunities for physical recreation is indicated by the answers compiled from an entering group of physical education major students at the University of California in 1947. A question with regard to prior participation experience in physical education activities other than in a school situation brought out the following information: the larger percentage of both men and women had participated with Boy Scout and "Y" groups; almost half of the women in the group had received leadership experience with either one or more of the following groups: YWCA, church, Girl Scouts, or Camp Fire Girls. Forty per cent of the men had received leadership experience with the following groups: YMCA, Boy Scouts, church, and fraternal organizations.[34]

SABBATH LAWS AND SPORTS IN AMERICAN CULTURE

There is a very long history behind the religious and secular control of sports on Sunday. In the minds of many Americans of a generation ago the principal interrelationship of the church and sports was concerned with a policy of restriction and prohibition, particularly with regard to the Sabbath.

An interesting background to the Sabbath laws and their effect on sports is to be found in the issuing of the *King's Book of Sports* by James I in the year 1618. This action was so interwoven with both political and religious questions, with pressures and counterpressures, that a study of the circumstances surrounding its publication is of interest even to-day.[35] Some parallels with our own history are there, but there are many additional cultural factors in modern society —factors that inevitably doomed the legal enforcement of the old-time Sabbath to eventual failure. *The King's Book of Sports* proved so unacceptable to the church that it was withdrawn. However, the *Book* was reissued by Charles I in 1633 and continued to be the center of a storm of controversy. Finally in May, 1643, came an official order that all copies of the book were to be publicly destroyed. Persons having such books in their possession were required to bring them, by May 10 at twelve o'clock, to be burned.

While such repressive acts were the work of the Puritans in England, it is interesting to note that the first law enacted in America was not Puritan in origin but rather the result of the best thinking of a group of ministers in Virginia in the year 1610.[36] It can thus be seen that Sunday legislation was almost three hundred years old in America when the twentieth century began. The conditions under which such laws had been written were completely changed, and during this long period constant exceptions had been made to permit railroads, newspapers, food stores, and finally amusements to operate on Sunday. The breaches of law brought about by changes in our amusements or cultural preferences came later and were much more vigorously opposed. There were no Sunday motion pictures or *legalized* Sunday baseball in the United States until after 1919. There was, however, an ever growing desire for them, coupled with a rapidly growing interest in Sunday golf, tennis, driving, and other sports.

In 1906 the Reverend R. C. Wylie compiled a volume called *Sabbath Laws in the United States,* in which he remarked that in some states there had been developing "a pronounced antagonism to all laws protecting the first day of the week except such as would make it a mere holiday." His investigation revealed twenty-one states and two territories having strong Sabbath laws, two states and one territory (California, Idaho, and Arizona) which had no Sabbath laws, and twenty-two states and one territory having numerous exceptions or inherently weak Sabbath laws.

In the years prior to 1930 there was constant tinkering with the Sabbath laws, many of which were so antiquated as to be already annulled by custom. With the coming of the economic depression of the thirties widespread legislative action greatly liberalized the situation. Pennsylvania and New Jersey substituted local option provisions; Wisconsin wiped the laws off the books; Missouri legalized Sunday hunting; and Maine passed a bill permitting amateur sports on the Sabbath.[37] Observers at the time attributed this to many different reasons.

The churches had lost power by setting themselves over too wide an offensive in attempting to regulate things which the individual wished to decide for himself and which he saw no wrong in doing. The depression had brought a decrease in tax income, and there were taxes to be had from Sunday amusements. Furthermore, a new administration in the White House was less subject to pressures from the various church lobbies which had exercised such a powerful influence for so many years. The psychological effects of the depression, too, seem to have engendered a mood of realistic fact-facing which had not been evidenced in the previous carefree decade.

There was some fact-facing in the church itself. As one representative put it, the clergy was beginning to see that the alternative ways of spending Sunday are not churchgoing minus recreation or recreation minus churchgoing but rather churchgoing plus recreation and recreation minus church-going.[38] And another admits that the old conception of a Puritan Sabbath cannot be maintained in this country, since public opinion will simply not support it.

Many ministers were in favor of a compromise solution, that is, allowing various sports and other amusements to be held after 2:00 P.M. This method was used in the city of Baltimore, where in 1932 a municipal ordinance legalizing sports on the Sabbath (after 2:00 P.M.) received a majority of eighty thousand votes. Under this ordinance the fifteen sports allowed were carefully specified: baseball, football, golf, tennis, basketball, croquet, lacrosse, quoits, soccer, hockey, ice- and roller-skating, swimming, and track and field meets. [39]

Today there still remain a few pockets of prohibition in the United States, but the consistent trend is toward their total elimination. The impact of World War II, with its stepped-up industrial output, twenty-four-hour shifts, and seven-day-a-week schedules, had the effect of lessening any remaining restrictions. The tremendous mobility of both the civilian and the military population, with the necessity of seeking and finding recreation and amusements when and where the time allowed, was another factor. By the nineteen-fifties the question of Sabbath laws, for so many years the cause of so much controversy, had ceased to be a vital issue in most areas of the United States.

THE FUTURE ROLE OF THE CHURCH

More studies of the type done by Martin[40] and by Skidmore[41] are needed before the changing attitude and role of the church with regard to recreation can be seen in proper perspective. However, it is well to remember that the church has been a participant in the democratic experiment in the same way as other social institutions such as the school, labor and industry, and the home. Its progress and growth have been irregular and relatively unplanned. Its history is marked by sad failures and remarkable successes. When the Founding Fathers (and the church itself) insisted on a complete separation of church and state, the church forfeited the right to state support, assumed the responsibility for the formal religious education of the young, and declared itself competent to meet its own problems without outside aid. In view of the almost overwhelming cultural change in the world of the first fifty years of the twentieth century, the church has shown no greater cultural lag than many other social institutions. Without neglecting its primary task as bearer of the spiritual tradition through which a culture is made sensitive to spiritual demands, the church has greatly extended the services of religion as a stimulus to help individuals wrest from their daily living the significance that is there. By demonstrating a progressively more liberal and understanding attitude toward play and recreation as a valuable part of life, the church has established a greater rapport with people and with other social institutions within the culture. Interfaith contact and co-operation in the field of recreation have helped to purge the church of sectarian bias and have thereby gained an increased respect and confidence.

The future role of the church as actual provider of recreation facilities and leadership may be uncertain. As communities become more enlightened, it may be that the church will no longer be expected to do the work of the school and clinic and social club and that every needed facility for health, education, and amusement will be provided. Until this utopia comes, many churches will undoubtedly continue to make whatever contribution it is within their power to make. One thing seems certain—the twentieth century has seen the banishment of the dour, gloomy, unduly restrictive attitude toward clean wholesome physical recreation. As one minister put it, religion is coming to a new appreciation of the importance of physical well-being as an aid to soul culture. A hundred years ago churches were built on hillsides, surrounded by cemeteries; today they are built in settings of playgrounds, tennis courts, and swimming pools. Instead of preparing men for death, the new religion seeks to prepare men for life.[42]

8. *The Sports Page: An American Phenomenon*

GREAT NUMBERS OF AMERICANS LIKE THE SPORTS PAGE: THEY buy it, read it, talk about it, and argue about it. Whether or not they actually sit through a game, listen to a play-by-play description on the radio, or see the show on television, they still want to read about it. Since each fan considers himself an authority, it seems an indispensable part of the fun to compare his own opinions with those of his favorite expert and to dispute the judgment of those who disagree with him.

It may have been true in the early years of the century that the sports page sold newspapers largely to the *Police Gazette* audience, the outer fringe of literacy, although some doubt is thrown on this assumption by the following quotation from the *Atlantic* of April, 1908:

Friend, you who read the market page with its jargon of fractions and sudden whims, you who furrow the literary twaddle of book journals, or you, gentle lady, to whose nimble tongue wool batiste, challis, and pongee bishops and berthas are emotions and volitions, think of me and my likes playing the game an hour late and twenty miles away, watching as if before us the twists and turns and sudden emprises, the raps and wallops, miscues, pickups and swift fans of Nine against Nine on the levels of Parnassus![1]

Today the universality of its appeal presents quite a different picture. College alumni want the latest and most accurate information on the prospects of their school's teams, and the professional man often has an abiding interest not only in his own golf score but in the scores of the experts. The expansion in programs of industrial recreation has added to the host of readers whose interest is avid not only in their own organizational sports but in those same sports as played by others. The perennial interest in sports of the school- and college-age American finds an additional outlet via the sports page. It would be rare indeed to find many Americans who, during certain months of each year, were unaware of the current status of contending teams in the World Series.

Unlike the school and the church, the modern American newspaper is both a social institution and a business enterprise. Unless it is successful in the latter role, it fails to exist in the former. Even though one may prefer his ideal society to be one in which all men are preoccupied with an understanding of current affairs, if America does not represent that type of population, it is a little unrealistic to blame the newspapers and their editors.[2] Newpapers are social institutions, and their development will be shaped by all the social factors which impinge upon them.[3]

American newspapers are a mirror in which the nation is reflected in all its complex cultural diversity. Just so long as a free press can be maintained, they will continue to show the pride and prejudice, the weaknesses and strengths, the fads and fancies, of the American people.

ORIGIN AND EARLY GROWTH

In the middle of the nineteenth century sports news was covered to a very great extent by publications, mostly weeklies, which were devoted exclusively to the subject of sports. As early as 1835 several New York papers, notably the *Sun*, *Transcript*, and *Herald*, gave extensive coverage to prize fights, foot and horse races, as well as other sports. Although the *Sun* reported such bouts as the Williamson-Phelan fight at Hoboken in 1835, its policy was to condemn prize-fighting, calling it a European practice and better fitted to the oppressed classes of London than the enlightened republican citizens of New York.[4]

Henry Chadwick, who may (or may not) merit the title of original sports writer as well as "Father of Baseball," was reporting games of cricket between the United States and Canada in the eighteen-fifties for the *Times* and *Tribune* but was not getting paid for it, since few of the big New York dailies were giving much attention to athletics. Chadwick was finally hired by the *New York Herald* in 1862 to cover baseball games regularly. Henry Chadwick has been described as a quietly dressed gentleman in black plug hat and frock coat who might easily be mistaken for either a judge or the family doctor. To him baseball was an American form of cricket, and he tried vainly to transplant to America's unwilling soil the seeds of the English cricket spirit. He was saddened by the fact that the well-bred young men in mohair hats and cricket flannels were giving way to coarse young professional ball-players, many of whom he considered to be without breeding or any knowledge of proper behavior in railroad stations, in hotels, on trains, or in steamers. The venerable gentleman was doomed to disappointment and failure in his effort, for baseball was *not* cricket; it was essentially a poor man's game and essentially American![5]

What was probably the most important weekly concerned with sports in the United States appeared in New York in December, 1831, and survived until 1901, when it merged with the *Horseman* of Chicago. This was *Spirit of the Times: The American Gentleman's Newspaper*. Sworn testimony in a libel suit, at the time of the Civil War, gave a circulation figure of a hundred thousand, and only one weekly in America (excluding the religious press) had more. William Trotter Porter, editor and owner of the *Spirit*, encouraged cricket in the eighteen-forties and eighteen-fifties and indirectly helped to establish baseball. The *Spirit* was as thoroughly masculine as *Godey's Lady's Book* was feminine and was widely read by all classes of readers.[6] Daniel Webster was said to have subscribed at Washington while the Senate was in session

and at Boston when he returned home. Porter is credited with printing the first rules for baseball, the first scores, the first box score, and the first allusion to it as a national game. The *Spirit* gave much space to the first baseball convention of 1858, at which time the players voted to make nine innings a game instead of calling it when the first side had tallied twenty-one aces.

When William Randolph Hearst bought the *New York Journal* in 1895, he began to outdo his rivals in the matter of reporting sports news, and what emerged was the modern newspaper sports section.[7] Where rival newspapers were printing from three to seven columns of sports news daily, the *Journal* doubled, trebled, and quadrupled the space and also began the special Sunday issues of twelve pages. During the years 1896 and 1897 Hearst began the practice of signing up sports champions to write for his paper: Hobart on tennis, Bald on bicycling, Batchelder on wheeling, and Heffelfinger, the Yale hero, on football. Experts on his staff included Ralph Paine of Yale on rowing, Charles Dryden on baseball, and Paul Armstrong on boxing. It might be said that Hearst invented the present-day sports page makeup, since today the innovations of 1896 have become commonplace.

In spite of the fact that Hearst and other exponents of yellow journalism may have tainted the whole of American journalism with cheap and flashy emotionalism, the changes they helped bring about were not all undesirable. Such journalists attacked some of the oldest abuses of intrenched privilege; they reached an ever increasing proportion of the population and appealed to a greater variety of interests than ever before were touched by newspapers. Certainly it was the early exponents of yellow journalism at the beginning of the century who began really exploiting the sports page as a source of interest. Editors put some of their most talented cartoonists and writers to work on the sports staff, and the experiment proved so successful (and has continued to be throughout the ensuing years) that today hardly any major paper—be it ever so conservative or intellectual—goes to press without a sports page.

In the early nineteen-hundreds Will Irwin made a penetrating analysis of the sports page of the day.[8] He considered it to be a by-product of yellow journalism and to have successfully utilized the formula of the true yellow journalist— that is, to find the class of news which interests the greatest number of people—and this was sports for men and love and scandal for the women! He felt that power was man's business, the focus of his admiration, and that politics, wealth, and sports were all different manifestations of power. With prophetic insight he categorized the newspaper as the "most powerful extrajudicial force in society, except religion."

In tracing the story of the newspaper in general and the sports page in particular in the twentieth century, both the quantitative and the qualitative pattern can be understood only in the light of changes in the social environment of which it is a part. The needs of readers who formed the great mass of population in the emerging metropolitan economy were changing. The increasing *impersonal* quality of city life created a greater need for vicarious personal contacts and for humanized materials which would permit the illusion of sharing an emotional experience.

EXPANSION OF SPACE AND EXTENT OF COVERAGE

The expansion of interest in sports in the last two generations, and particularly since World War I, has brought about many changes in the technique of the newspapers in catering to and fostering this interest. From concentration on a few sports such as baseball, college football, horse-racing, and boxing, attention is now given to a tremendously wide range of activities. Following are but a portion of the sports activities covered by today's metropolitan newspapers: basketball, bowling, billiards, golf, lacrosse, cycling, wrestling, archery, lawn and court tennis, squash rackets, skiing, canoeing, motor-boating, rowing, swimming, diving, water polo, ice and field hockey, hunting, fishing, and all kinds of track and field contests. In bygone days a small sports staff was active in summer, but sometimes its writers were switched to the city staff for the winter. Today the sports staff is one of the busiest spots on the newspaper, with the ending of the season for one sport running into the opening of the other—when such seasons do not overlap or coincide.[9]

There has also come about a decided improvement in sports writing. Most newspapermen admit that sports reporting requires craftsmanship of the highest order and that the coverage of sports involves all the things that come up in general newspaper work, such as law, politics, economics, domestic relations, genealogy, dramatics, police, female fashions, and war.[10] To be successful, a sports writer must have the feel of the sport, experience its thrills, and understand the enthusiasm of its devotees. He must also know something of the history of the sport and of the leading personalities of both past and present and possess a sound working knowledge of the rules, traditions, etiquette, and customs of the sport with which he is dealing. According to newspapermen, both editors and reporters, no class of readers is more responsive and none demands a higher degree of accuracy than the sports fan. The baseball writer especially is writing for an informed readership, and, if he makes a mistake, both he and his paper will get a dozen letters in the next morning's mail calling attention to the fact.[11] A football story of today must include sufficient accurate description of the game's progress to satisfy a clientele whose grasp of technicalities may no longer be held in contempt.

There are uncounted examples which could be cited to show how a sports-hungry reading public has prompted invention and innovation in the processes of gathering and disseminating the news. It was in the year 1899 that the first story covered by wireless, *a sports event*, appeared. The inventor, Marconi, had been experimenting for four years and had arrived in the United States with his equipment packed in two trunks and eager to have his new wireless tested. The Associated Press hired Marconi and his equipment to report on the international yacht race involving Sir Thomas Lipton's *Shamrock* and the American *Columbia*.

By 1913 telegraph lines could be strung direct to the scene of most sports events, regardless of locale, and reports written by a sports editor and his small staff could go direct to newspaper offices. But it was the year 1916 that saw the real triumph in the transmission of the play-by-play story of the World Series. Even though the World Series had previously taken precedence over all other news, it had been customary to have the leased-wire circuits broken at strategic points to adjust the report for regional needs and relay. In the preparations for the 1916 editon of the World Series the Traffic Department of the Associated Press conceived the idea of delivering the play-by-play story direct from the baseball park to all points on the leased-wire system, without any intervening relay or delay.

Undaunted by the fact that such a thing had never before been attempted in either news or commercial transmission, a single circuit twenty-six thousand miles in length was set up to operate from the ball parks in Boston and Brooklyn into the office of every leased-wire member newspaper. This extraordinary feat so impressed the famous inventor, Thomas Edison, that he sent the following telegram to Kent Cooper, head of the Traffic Department of the Associated Press: "The Associated Press must be wonderfully well organized to be able to accomplish what was done in the ball games. Uncle Sam now has a real arterial system and it is never going to harden."[12]

The first time a complete newspaper page was transmitted by Associated Press Wirephoto from one city to another was on New Year's Eve, 1936, when the *Dallas Morning News* printed a special Rose Bowl Souvenir Edition on the presses of the *Los Angeles Times*. During the Tournament of Roses Parade and before the game between Southern Methodist University of Dallas and Stanford University, fifteen thousand copies of the paper were run off.[13]

The story of the growth of the American newspaper is also the saga of the sports page, since the increasing popularity and power of this section of the paper have kept pace with other developments. The early years of the century reveal a combination of sociological change and mechanical improvements, of the exercise of inventive genius and the struggle to meet the reader needs of a rapidly changing society. A part of the story lies in the fact that, between 1870 and 1900, illiteracy had been reduced from 20 to 10.7 per cent of the population and that the percentage of children attending public schools had increased from 57 to 72. Nevertheless, in 1900, the average American had received only five years' schooling. Showing comparable growth, the number of daily newspapers rose from 2,226 in 1899 to 2,600 in 1909. Figures on total daily circulation showed a stead gain: fifteen million copies in 1899, twenty-four million in 1909, and thirty-three million in 1919.[14]

The perfecting of the process of manufacture of low-cost newsprint from wood pulp is admittedly a basic factor in the rapid growth of the daily newspaper. In addition, there were further improvements in the cylinder press, which printed, folded, and counted newspapers at a tremendous rate of speed; the development of type-casting machines which almost eliminated hand-setting and made it possible for one man to do the work of five; and the farsighted policy of the federal government in allowing cent-a-pound rates on second-class mail, a policy predicated on the basis of encouraging the dissemination of current intelligence.

The boom of the twenties: boxing and baseball.—The nineteen-twenties saw the greatest boom of the sports page, and the factors which influenced this boom were more numerous and more complex than in previous years. Soldiers returning from war camps and active service had experienced more intimate contact with sports than ever before; colleges and universities across the nation were building stadiums to meet the public's demand to share the pageantry, color, and excitement of intercollegiate football; the country was experiencing a postwar economic boom and a postwar pursuit of pleasure which was in part at least a reaction to the grimness of the war just ended.

At this same time the sports world produced an unusually large number of competitors who were not only capable performers but colorful personalities as well: Babe Ruth, Bill Tilden, Helen Wills, Jack Dempsey, Bobby Jones, to name but a few. The same skill and shrewd promotion which went into selling cold cream, breakfast food, and automobiles to the nation also sold athletes and athletics to the American public. The excessive ballyhoo of sports in the twenties was but a part of the total picture of postwar disillusion, moral relaxation, the Prohibition era—all of which generated powerful and deleterious influences. The parade of heroes, the incredible gate receipts, and the general air of hysteria may have been an advance indication of the dizzier "golden age" of prosperity which followed.[15]

The case of pugilism, the championship boxing match, serves as an excellent example. On September 14, 1923, Jack Dempsey fought Luis Angel Firpo. Eight hundred sports writers were in New York and filed from the ringside 675,000 words by Western Union and cabled 12,000 words to South America, using seventy leased wires. Newspaper representatives from all important cities in the United States were present, as well as press delegations from the South American, Mexican, Cuban, British, Japanese, and French papers. This show was in turn dwarfed by the two million words from the ringside of the Dempsey-Tunney fight at Philadelphia on September 23, 1926.[16]

The genius of Tex Rickard in exploiting the business of pugilism is credited by some historians as being responsible for the tremendous amount of newspaper time and space given to boxing contests.[17] Endless psychological explanations have also been offered. One interesting theory advanced for the increased *respectability* of prize-fighting is that George Bernard Shaw wrote an eyewitness account of the Joe Beckett–Georges Carpentier fight in London in December, 1919. This was published in one of the intellectual British weekly journals and so widely reproduced in this country that, when Carpentier appeared here in 1920, the social status of the prize ring was established.[18] For whatever reasons, in America's inflated pre-1929 prosperity the championship prize fight—a spectacle that had been condemned and shunned by many twenty or thirty years before—became one of America's recognized First Nights!

By far the greatest recipient of newspaper space in the sports columns of the twentieth century has been professional baseball.[19] Baseball reporting is no longer seasonal; it is a year-round job. True, the playing season is from April to October, followed by the World Series, but the publicity goes on throughout the whole twelve months. When the football season ends, the various professional leagues begin daily releases of official averages, and the hot-stove season starts in earnest. All during November and early December the fans argue and talk about these figures, balancing a team's good hitting against its poor fielding, a pitcher's record of strike-outs against his total bases-on-balls, and so on ad infinitum.

In mid-December come convention time and the major- and minor-league meetings, at which most of the big baseball trades are arranged. This leads naturally into mid-February and spring training, which provides an apparently inexhaustible supply of material on the skill of the rookies and the general condition of the veterans.[20]

READER INTEREST DEMANDS FREE SPORTS PUBLICITY

In spite of the fact that the sports page sells the paper, the problem of a disproportionate amount of free space given to sports presents something of a dilemma. Newspapers have always been liberal with space for sports, in the belief that they were meeting reader interest and thus promoting circulation. As a consequence, American newspapers spend millions of dollars annually in sports coverage for which there is little direct financial return to the newspapers. The public interest has been stimulated to the point where it is almost impossible to stop. In the opinion of some they have built themselves a monster that consumes more and more space and gives little in return in either profit or gratitude.[21]

The sports page of the modern newspaper is the "softest" spot for the press agent. For instance, the winter resort owner who needs business does not buy advertising space; he stages a golf or tennis tournament or a swimming meet. Prizes large enough to entice first-rate talent are offered, and the free publicity begins. First the build-up, then the detailed progress of the event, and finally the results. A classic example is the popularizing of Sun Valley, Idaho, an unknown commercial venture, a thousand miles from nowhere and intended primarily to bring passenger fares to a railroad!

The manufacturers of bowling and billiard equipment advertise in the *magazines*, not in the newspapers, but it is the sports page that furnishes the publicity and is mainly responsible for making sports a profitable big business. It is the sports page that has put across professional hockey and professional football as well as fostering much of the interest in amateur sports.

Most major newspapers, with the exception of the *New York Times*, have at one time or another conducted and sponsored sports events of their own. Through the years literally thousands of all-star football, baseball, and basketball games, track meets, golf tournaments, skating matches, boxing contests, swimming meets, bowling tournaments, and roller-skating derbies have been promoted. Many newspapers have also conducted baseball schools for boys and basketball and football clinics for coaches. In the opinion of some news-papermen and from the point of view of the newspaper, the effort and space could be better applied to something else. However, the admission is made that such promotional efforts do serve a public good, even when costs are high. Such events stimulate interest and serve to widen opportunities for participation.

SPORTS PAGE REFLECTS THE SOCIAL SCENE

There is some evidence that the sports page has shown an increasing sensitivity to the general social scene and to social change, and this in turn has probably influenced, consciously or unconsciously, the attitudes, opinions, beliefs, and interests of readers. The findings of an unpublished study conducted at the University of California yielded some interesting information on the relationship of the sports page to the total culture.[22] Proceeding from the assumption that the sports page is one of the most widely read sections of the modern American newspaper, and granting the further assumption that a certain proportion of readers peruse *only* the sports page, the study attempted to find what effect this reading might have on the formation of reader opinion on social questions as a whole. An examination of two well-known sports pages located in opposite ends of the country (i.e., the *New York Times* and the *San Francisco Chronicle*), covering the period 1929 through 1935, showed that the following general problems of American culture were given rather extended discussion:

1. *The depression* and economic retrenchment: as shown through adjustments of admittance prices to the lowered income level and the staging of numerous contests for benefit and charity purposes.

2. *Race relations:* as shown by the protesting of the ban on Negro players and also the whole anti-Semitic feeling and sentiment involved in the plans for the 1936 Olympics in Germany.

3. *Public morality:* with relation to selling beer at games, athletic proselyting, and charges and countercharges of gambling in sports. There was also much lively discussion of the propriety of participation by women in certain sports and the suitability of costume—the "shorts" versus "skirts" controversy.

4. *Technological change:* as evidenced by the argument as to whether or not football games should be broadcast by radio and the whole question of "night" baseball.

5. *The basic American trait of helping the underdog:* in the case of the ex-convict "Alabama" Pitts and whether or not he should be allowed to play professional baseball.

The case of "Alabama" Pitts, sometimes referred to as baseball's first martyr, is interesting not so much because of the personnel involved but for the picture it presents of a basic American characteristic of sympathy and support for anyone the public thinks is being wrongly abused. In the year 1930, at the age of nineteen, Edwin C. Pitts was convicted of second-degree robbery in New York State and sentenced for a term of eight to sixteen years. He developed into a prize athlete at Ossining Prison in the next five years, starring on the institution's baseball and football teams and on the track squad. Since both professional and amateur clubs frequently played exhibitions at Ossining, tales of Pitts's ability were known to the readers of the metropolitan dailies.

At the time of his parole Pitts was offered a job playing professional baseball, but Judge W. Bramham, the little czar of the minor leagues, rendered a decision that Pitts could not play International League ball. This decision was reversed by Judge Landis, commissioner of baseball, but in the meantime quite a storm of protest had arisen. Charles Evans Hughes, Jr., New York lawyer and son of the former chief justice, wired Landis that anyone who opposed Pitts's plea was un-American! Clarence Darrow, the great Chicago criminal lawyer, objected to the decision, and the East Side Minister's Council of Buffalo framed a resolution urging that Pitts be given a chance to establish himself as a law-abiding member of society. Throughout the country sports writers and fans alike demanded not only a break for Pitts but justice to the underdog![23]

Public reaction to the sports page.—In attempting to assess the interrelationship of the sports page with the total sports life and tastes of the nation, it must be constantly kept in mind that the modern American newspaper is both a public institution and an extremely complex business enterprise. It must somehow arrive at a satisfactory compromise: to serve the public interest and still continue to sell enough of its product to make money. Each newspaper inevitably makes its major appeal to a special intellectual stratum in the total population and provides the kind of information in whch its readers will be interested. There is as much variation in the quality of sports sections as there is in editorial pages or general news coverage. A good sports section will exemplify the same news standards and ethical principles which animate the city staff or the foreign news service of a first-class paper.

The sports page has always been the center of controversy. It has been extravagantly praised and also deeply criticized and seems to have successfully withstood both approval and disapproval. In the opinion of partisan admirers it has produced the only genuinely original American literature of the twentieth century.[24] It is claimed to provide a welcome relief from the general heavy character of the news—wars abroad and murder and taxes at home. Critics of the sports page claim that it has had an incredibly vulgarizing effect on both the spoken and the written word and that it provides an easy escape, akin to the use of opiates, to a never-never land where all sense of proportion is lost and the average citizen is diverted from channeling his thoughts toward preoccupation with the state of his nation and the world at large.

A somewhat more realistic estimate seems to imply that the sports-page public is neither exclusively shirt sleeves and overalls nor business suits and tuxedos. In tapping all economic and social levels of American society, it represents a significant democratic phenomenon. It reveals the existence of a psychological common denominator with little relation to either education or economic status.

It is a truism with regard to the reporting of most news that the antisocial and undesirable aspects and events get the full publicity. Sometimes the hundreds of thousands of youngsters across the nation playing on school teams, fine honest sportsmen, seem forgotten in the sensational exposé of bribery and gambling charges brought against a handful of basketball players out of Madison Square Garden. Then the cry goes up from some quarters to abolish the whole thing! We hear no suggestions that the institution of marriage be abolished because husbands and wives are unfaithful and the divorce rate is high. We hear no voice raised to protest the continuance of the manufacture of automobiles, although the millionth American has met his death because of them.

There appears to be no particular magic about either the athlete or the sports fan that makes him immune from the foibles and temptations which are the lot of the rest of the human race. The valid hero and the unmistakable heel are probably as evenly distributed among this group as among any other group out of the total population. There is such a marked tendency to so overplay the heroic and to ignore the balancing side of the picture that, when the Achilles heel is discovered, the disillusion is even more painful and shocking than it might otherwise have been.

An interesting analogy seems to exist between the most distressing "scandals" in both professional and amateur sports and the most unsavory "scandals" in the conduct of government or in the culture as a whole. The "Black" Sox affair and the Teapot Dome scandals were contemporaneous. The Kefauver investigation and the basketball bribery as well as the West Point story all broke into print within a few weeks. The thoughtful reader can scarcely escape the conclusion that these are not *entirely* unrelated. A low level of public and private honesty and integrity at a given time in history inevitably permeates all levels and many aspects of the culture.

9. The Periodicals
Propagandize Sports

A SUBSTANTIAL PART OF THE TOTAL ANSWER AS TO WHY SPORTS
are such a vital part of American culture lies in the persistent
campaign of publicity, promotion, and propaganda which has
been carried on through the medium of the periodical press.
From its earliest days the United States has been prolific in the
matter of disseminating information and entertainment through
the medium of the printed word, both through newspapers
and through a greater number and variety of periodicals than
any country in the world has ever seen. The years from 1900
to 1930, particularly, represent an ideal period of time in the
nation's history for utilizing the periodical press as a mirror of
social, economic, and political history. The late years of the
nineteenth century and the first years of the twentieth century saw a new phenomenon in magazine publication—the ten-
cent magazine, bringing with it increased use of advertising
and marking the beginning of the mass-circulation magazine.

There seems to be no disagreement with the statement that
magazines have reflected and molded American tastes, habits,
manners, interests, and beliefs. In their capacity of reporting,
commenting, advising, and entertaining, directly through discussion of contemporary interests and indirectly through fiction and poetry, they have influenced the life of the nation and
of millions of individuals within the nation. They have at
times made their influence felt in government, commerce, and
industry by carrying on planned crusades to correct social
abuses. Magazines have stimulated the minds and imaginations
of Americans, helped form many of their ideas, fashioned their

ethical and social concepts, and influenced their clothes and their homes.[1] They also mirrored the growing interest of Americans in recreational pursuits of all kinds, and particularly all types of vigorous physical recreation, sports and games, hunting and fishing, reflecting an overwhelming nostalgia for an out-of-door life which seemed to be receding farther and farther into the past as cities grew and populations increased.

During the first three decades of the century the periodicals did more than attest to the bare literacy of the American public or its wish for easy entertainment. They offered a demonstration of the nation's appetite for information; of an irresistible urge to escape from provincial limitations, to acquire a sense of taste and style. Considered in this perspective, the periodical output gives an impressive exhibit of democracy at work.[2] It is clear, too, that the magazine-reading public was convinced that the world of sports and leisure was also a part of their heritage. Leisure-time activities were no longer the exclusive and envied property of the wealthy; workingmen and workingwomen experimented with the sports and sports costumes of the rich, gradually breaking down more and more social barriers.[3]

THE SPORTS SCENE AS PRESENTED TO PERIODICAL READERS

There is a discernible pattern of approach in each of the four general groups of periodicals in presenting the sports picture and a sports philosophy to their readers.

The women's magazines, notably *Ladies' Home Journal*, *Delineator*, *Good Housekeeping*, and *Harper's Bazaar*, accented the importance of play in the life of both the child and the growing boy and girl. Quite early in the century they came to recognize the importance and value of "camp" experience to children. The emerging realization that physical beauty had its foundation in abounding physical health and energy pointed up the role that sports participation could play in accomplishing this universal desire of all women to be considered attractive. The problem of suitable clothing for sports was given much attention and in a subtle way worked revolutionary changes.

The "quality" group, *Atlantic, Century, Harper's,* and *Scribner's,* with their appeal to a class that was supposed to combine wealth, discrimination, and literary taste, tended especially in the early years of the century to keep readers insulated from the stresses and tensions of common human experience. However, this audience included so many people who taught, edited, managed, and governed that their relationship to the operation of the total culture might be compared in importance to that of the ignition system in the operation of an automobile.

The pages of the "quality" publications give extended coverage to the pros and cons of intercollegiate athletic competition. The problem is more often than not approached from the *ethical* rather than the *practical* point of view, its advantages being praised with emotional fervor and its disadvantages attacked with moral indignation. This same approach, which incidentally is still applied in some quarters even today—and to the same problem—may well be a partial explanation of the gap that has never been entirely bridged between what is thought of as the "academic" point of view and the point of view of the vast majority of both participants and spectators. The average American has never actually acknowledged that there is anything intrinsically wrong in playing to win. In his judgment the team that isn't determined to win might just as well stay in the locker room! To him the only time criticism is justified is when the game is not played according to the rules. This average American will acknowledge that for every winner there must be a loser, but with characteristic optimism he will also say that there is always another game to be played!

The mass-circulation magazines, *Collier's, American, Munsey's, McClure's, Everybody's, Saturday Evening Post,* and others, "discovered the twentieth-century American-unintellectual and often half-educated, but wide-awake, intelligent, confident, and ready to spend his money freely."[4] Upon examination it is not difficult to understand why this type of magazine printed thousands of pages over the years devoted to athletes and their accomplishments, to articles on how to play the various individual sports and on how to be an informed and intelligent spectator, and to glowing descriptions of the great out of doors, of travel and adventure.

Take a growing population with a rising standard of living and increased leisure time—and remember that many have been debarred by city life from what had heretofore been the elementary adventures of life such as hunting, fishing, and hiking in the woods—and you get an uncounted potential audience who want to read about the out of doors, vacations, and adventures.

In the early years of the century it was not nearly so much the spirit of "keeping up with the Joneses" as it was the emerging concept of social mobility, the rising level of aspiration for millions of Americans. The dream precedes the reality, and for those millions of magazine-reading Americans golf and tennis and vacations at the seashore or in the mountains were still only a dream (as was the ownership of an automobile). Within another two or three decades they were to become a *reality*, if not for all of those who had the initial dream, at least for many of their children and grandchildren.

There is still another group of periodicals without which any analysis would be incomplete. Two outstanding examples of this group are the *Outlook* and the *Independent*. These had begun publication thirty and fifty years, respectively, before the year 1900 and eventually merged into a single publication in the year 1928. Both had been what might be termed "religious newspapers," a sort of weekly publication that had long flourished in America. By 1900, however, both had ceased to be religious periodicals and had become journals of opinion.

To many Americans, and particularly those closely affiliated with the churches, these publications brought tidings of change and paved the way for the rise of a movement of protest, exposure, and reform. They performed an invaluable service to their readers in cushioning the shock involved in the change from the moral and the religious to the sociological and political approach to the solution of cultural problems.[5]

The bound files of these two periodicals in the first two and a half decades of the century are among the richest sources to be found on the subject of sports and games as an integral and expanding part of American culture. Through their vigorous support of the playground movement, the conscience of the nation was awakened to society's responsibility to provide play space and play opportunities for underprivileged children. As with the mass-circulation magazines, impetus was given to the desire of Americans for vacations, for travel, for a share in outdoor life. The whole conservation movement was given much careful editorial comment, with the implication being stressed that it was the responsibility of the government to protect the natural beauty spots of the nation for all citizens and for the generations which were to follow.

The story is here, too, of the changing attitude of the church with regard to the physical recreational pursuits of members, the growing sensitivity to changes in the culture, and a realization of the implications inherent in the increase of leisure time and in changing standards of living. And, finally, the awareness that the church, as an institution, was in competition with many other forces in the culture for the time, thought, and energy of that most heterogeneous group of human beings who *were* America.

THE WOMEN'S MAGAZINES

There are many schools of thought with regard to the question of the pre-eminent and powerful role of women in American culture and many theories as to how it came about. Credit has been given to the invention of the typewriter and other business machines, which along with the establishment of universal primary and secondary education gave women a practical monopoly in the field of secretarial and office work as well as schoolteaching. Others claim that it was the long fight for the franchise and for equality in a legal sense. A broader view suggests it was both of these things, as well as many other factors within the culture.

Certainly a tremendously powerful area of influence would be overlooked if the part played by the women's magazines was not given adequate consideration. Through their pages a barrage of information and advice was aimed at the wives and mothers, the homemakers of the nation. In addition to the helpful hints on cooking, sewing, and house-cleaning, they were given basic and factual information on current problems of the day. They were introduced to the whole new world of thought with regard to the care and education of children.

The first twenty-five years of the century record a fundamental change in parental and educational attitudes and understandings with regard to child psychology, child development, and child care. During this period the child and the adolescent came to be recognized as *persons*, with problems, rights, and privileges, and not simply as adults in miniature. Such progressive views on the psychology of the child and the adolescent seldom neglected to emphasize the educational and therapeutic value of vigorous physical play. The readers of the women's magazines were the mothers of the generation of sports enthusiasts, participants and spectators, in the decades that followed.

The birth of sports clothes.—It has been said that no greater change in all time has taken place than in the lives of women during the past half-century, and nowhere has this change found more obvious and outward expression than in the clothing they wear, which has done so much to free them from the bondage of absurd and ridiculous convention.

Even before woman had obtained more than a semblance of

recognition in fields of economic or political endeavor, a few of her bolder sisters were fighting the battle for *all* through their persistence in participating in vigorous recreational pursuits, with each other and with the opposite sex. The gradual but relentless fight against the torso-distorting, action-inhibiting dress of the day, in the face of accusations of immodesty and worse, is worthy of the greatest admiration of all the women of today who enjoy the complete freedom of modern feminine dress. It is possible to trace, in the pages of the women's magazines, the detailed progress of this struggle. First the shy, almost apologetic appearance near the very end of the magazine of a half-page devoted to a very restrained description of the "Gibson Bathing Costume"[6] to the six- to ten-page spread devoted to sports clothes. So powerful and pervading was the influence that within the period of fifteen to twenty years revolutionary changes were brought about in women's apparel—both the outer and the inner variety.

Countless women who had never held a tennis racket in their hands and who could not positively identify a golf club if suddenly confronted with a specimen were enjoying the added freedom of shorter skirts, less bulky materials, more natural lines—so many items directly traceable to the early influence of the "sports" costumes.

In the early years of the century sports clothes were considered somewhat of a fad—an extravagance—but they became a firmly established part of fashion in the postwar period. In the middle twenties the fashion editor of one of the women's magazines wrote: "The sports feeling has almost totally usurped the daytime mode."[7]

An interesting commentary on the thorough Americanness of sports clothes is seen in the fact that fifty years of influence emanating from Paris, an influence which has several times in the last fifty years practically reversed and revolutionized certain women's fashions, has left relatively untouched the basic pattern and design of sports clothes. The garment which began life as a shirtwaist, symbol of independence and freedom for women—a costume without pretense or padding—still lives on in the modern blouses worn by millions of girls and women. The sweater-and-skirt combination, born on the golf course in the name of comfort and free-swinging, free-striding athletic performance, represents a tremendous proportion of modern ready-made clothing output. Successors to the early low-heeled and sturdy "walking shoes" are seen on every side. It is difficult indeed to conceive of modern Miss America minus her sports clothes!

Sports for health.—Concomitant with the increased approval of the participation of women in sports and the growing importance of the sports costume in milady's wardrobe was the emergence of the concept that beauty had its foundations in health. The women's magazine constantly reiterated that, in order to have a clear complexion, shining hair and eyes, and a good figure, it was essential to have a body in good physical condition. While sports participation was not claimed to be the *only* road to such salvation, it received considerable attention and discussion.

Emma E. Walker, M.D., was editor of a column in the *Ladies' Home Journal* entitled "Good Health for Girls." An examination of this feature during a single year (1902) presents a picture of how the theme of sports was closely interwoven with that of good health. In the March issue Dr. Walker discussed the latest fad among New York girls, the use of the punching-bag to solve the problem of indoor exercise. Through the use of this apparatus the stout girls grow thin and the thin girls grow plump. Its daily use will bring lightness of foot, graceful poise, and a springy step—to an even greater degree in fact than dance lessons.[8]

In May, Dr. Walker turns to golf and reminds her readers that one of the most valuable lessons to be learned from their English sisters is the benefit that comes from outdoor exercise. If the English girl feels a little below par in body or mind, she recognizes nature's signal, drops her work, and indulges in some vigorous outdoor game. Dr. Walker tells her girls that golf is better than medicine and that it will make over the poor tired body and fagged-out mind, and she concludes with a comment that, if as a nation we played golf more, there would be far less suffering from nervous exhaustion and depression—or, in layman's language, "biliousness" and "blues."

By June, Dr. Walker had turned to tennis, and, in addition to hints on how and where to build a court, she gives a few tips on the technique of play. She also advises a sensible costume: "The dress should be loose and of light weight, while the weight of the clothing should hang from the shoulder. The collar should be low and the sleeves loose."

The column in July is devoted to "Why Rowing and Canoeing Are Good for Girls"; in August, to "Swimming as an Exercise for Girls." Then in September a vital question of the day, "Side-Saddle versus Man's Saddle," is given full discussion, and the decision is reached that from the aesthetic point of view the sidesaddle is preferable!

The relative weight of such a series of articles as outlined above can more adequately be assessed in the light of the acknowledged leadership of the field of the women's magazines by the *Ladies' Home Journal* in this period. Edward Bok, who became editor in 1889, had succeeded in making the periodical an intimate friend to increasing hundreds of thousands of households. Whole books could be written on the influence of Mr. Bok, his ideas and his magazine, on the life of the American woman and the American home.

Furthermore, this particular periodical had no monopoly on such materials. *Good Housekeeping* had a regular department devoted to "Girls' Interests and Occupations" which contained many references to the benefits of exercise and sport. The *Delineator* announced with great fanfare in the January, 1902, issue that a series of illustrated articles entitled "Athletics for

Women" would begin in the February number, to run
throughout a full twelve months.[9]

The new approach to child care.—In these same women's
magazines mothers (and fathers) were besieged by experts in
child care, medical and otherwise, to recognize the right of
the child to bounteous, untrammeled outdoor play. The plea
was constantly made not to overdress the child and to let boys
and girls romp, play, tumble in the grass, and take part in
sports where their natural instincts could be exercised.[10] Arguments with regard to the older child were even more strongly
emphasized, it being pointed out that one of the most important parts of a boy's education was his learning to go about in
safety and to take care of himself. To accomplish this end
result, "he should know how to ride, to drive, to shoot at a
mark with precision of aim . . . to row, to swim, to climb, to
box, to do whatever a man may," in order that he may be prepared to take part with grace and skill.[11]

The president of the Mothers' Congress writes of the
"Twentieth Century Girl" and what is expected of her. She is
well developed physically, having inherited a fine constitution
from both parents. While she is not necessarily an athlete or
ambitious to be one, she can swim, row, ride a wheel, and play
golf and tennis.[12]

The women's magazines which did such a splendid and
essential job in the first twenty or thirty years following 1900,
inducting women as they did into the new century with its
miracles of science, technological development, and advances
in psychological and sociological thought, still flourish. While
retaining many of their special departments concerning fashions and the home, a larger proportion of the subject matter in
these publications has merged into a general table of contents,
offering material of equal interest to both men and women.
This seems to be another bit of evidence that the interests of
men and women are being brought closer together with the
passing of the years.

THE "QUALITY" MAGAZINES

While this group of periodicals has played a quantitatively less vigorous role in propagandizing sports, the part they have played in popularizing this area of American culture should certainly not be overlooked. In addition to the sizable group of classic controversial articles on football which have appeared over the years, the innumerable forums and discussions on general education seldom fail to include a discussion of intercollegiate athletics.[13] The problems and the possibilities inherent in sports as an integral part of campus life have captured the attention of college presidents and college faculties throughout the century and have been reported to the reading public through the pages of the "quality" magazines.

Of even greater interest, however, may be the more subtle campaigns which have been conducted along other lines. For example, when John Muir wrote in the pages of *Century* and *Atlantic* on the wonders of Yosemite and the big trees of California, his beautiful style and his enthusiasm for nature must have communicated to many of his readers a feeling of the urgent need of a crusade for the conservation of such natural resources and for the establishment of national and state parks.[14]

When Henry S. Curtis spoke to the readers of *Harper's* telling them that in his opinion the most notable movement in education in recent years had been the development of vacation schools and playgrounds in all the great cities of America, and the process by which such efforts were being taken over by boards of education to become a part of the regular school system, he was calling the attention of an influential group of readers to problems other than those of higher education.[15] And at the same time Jacob Riis was reporting to a *Scribner's* audience on the need for vacation schools and playgrounds in the economically less fortunate sections of New York City.[16]

The imagination and desires of readers for such recreations

as hunting, fishing, and mountain-climbing, for camping, motoring, and canoeing, could scarcely fail to respond to the siren song of such writers as Frederick Irland, Theodore Roosevelt, Ernest Thompson Seton, and many others whose exploits covered hundreds of pages of *Scribner's* and other magazines of this type.

The existence of the national game of baseball was not only acknowledged but given full credit for its many charms: "Man at his best and highest made baseball, it gallops gloriously to its sublime culminations, holds a nation spellbound from snow to snow, provides always the clash of player against player, and calls for combined exercise of muscles, brain, skill, and manly daring."[17]

The interrelationship of work and play in the life of man and child is given philosophical consideration, and the seeming fact that more people know how to work than how to play is lamented as a defect of education.[18]

The deleterious effect of too-rapid urbanization and resultant problems of lack of play space and juvenile delinquency was given a thoughtful exposition. A point of view was expressed which was to be given increasing emphasis in the years to follow, namely, that appropriations for playgrounds, recreation centers, boy's clubs, and other sports facilities would lessen future appropriations for detention homes and prisons.[19]

SPORTS, ADVERTISING, AND THE PERIODICAL PRESS

No one who would understand American culture in the twentieth century can ignore the important role of advertising. As has been stated, America is a literate nation and in the matter of accessibility of every conceivable type of printed material to the population has no near rival among nations. The question of how much of this vast mountain of paper is devoted to advertising need not be debated with the average citizen. He is at times both overwhelmed and appalled by the flood tides which sweep over him from all sides.[20]

It seems incredible at this point in history that the early

magazines did not welcome advertising. *Harper's* refused the $18,000 a year offered by Howe Sewing Machine for the back cover of the magazine. The reason given was that it was "a degradation of literature to allow monthly collections of *belles lettres* to be bound on one side by the announcements of trades people."

The advent of the inexpensive mass-circulation magazine was made possible by advertising. Most of today's leading magazines depend on advertising for the greater part of their income. It is advertising, in fact, which pays for the spread of public information through the press and by way of radio and television. By educating people to demand material and mechanical conveniences unknown to earlier generations, it has stimulated the production of these conveniences and in this way has been a primary force in raising the American standard of living.[21]

An examination of certain periodicals published during the early years of the century will sometimes reveal editorial comment that seems strangely aloof and unconcerned with contemporary life. This is certainly not true of the advertising pages! Here is found an authentic sociological history of the rise and fall of fads and of changing tastes and interests in food, clothing, and recreations. The editorials may indicate what people read, but the advertising pages show what they did and what they wanted to do! Here can be traced the growth of bicycling, climaxing in the nineties and dying out before the greater vogue of the automobile. The rise of tennis is reflected in the advertisements for balls and rackets for sale. The amazing popularity of outdoor sports, together with sports clothes— the only authentic fashions created in this country—all these and many more are depicted by the kaleidoscope of the advertising section of the magazine.[22]

Advertising techniques employ every possible approach to the problem of interesting the reader from logical persuasion to appeals to vanity, ambition, fear, snobbery, acquisitiveness, envy—in fact, to all human emotions. The appeal of sports has not been overlooked in this area of American culture.

The significance of the interrelationships of sports and advertising does not lie primarily in the amount of space devoted to the actual advertising of sports equipment. In fact, sporting goods do not appear as an individual "commodity group" in the list of accounts handled by a nationally known advertising firm until 1925.[23] In that year this "commodity group" represented only 0.24 per cent of their total business. There *is* a great deal of significance, however, in the use of sports pictures, sports language, and all manner of sports appeal in advertising copy.

For example, an advertisement for Coca-Cola first appeared in *Harper's* in 1905 and shows, most peculiarly, a young man in golfing costume carrying his clubs and a young woman dressed for tennis with her racket in hand. It is difficult to tell whether the rendezvous is taking place on the golf course or the tennis court, but then advertising writers *too* have improved in the last fifty years! Certainly both the advertising artists and the magazine cover artists helped deal a death blow to the frail feminine figure clothed in diaphanous robes and veils and popularized in her stead the vivacious, rosy-cheeked athletic girl.

Food, health, and athletic prowess.—A successful combination that has weathered more than fifty years of repetition to American consumers is that of food manufacturers' promotion of breakfast foods, employing many variations on the theme of health and athletic prowess. This has gone through several well-defined stages. The early efforts were aimed at parents and carried the implication that, if they wished their offspring to be healthy and to "make the team," this or that cereal should be eaten. At a later stage came the period when prominent athletic personalities were first being induced to sign testimonials for all manner of products from lemon juice to garters. Presumably both parents and children were intrigued by this appeal. A third and much more virulent stage was entered upon with the help of sponsored children's radio programs and still later the television shows, beaming their advertising and appeals straight at the youngsters themselves. In this era two box tops became a magic medium of exchange for a complete sports library, among other treasures. Eighteen different volumes were offered on varieties of sports from baseball to tumbling, each carefully written and prepared by a famous coach or headline athlete.[24]

An indication of the value of this audience of consumers to the advertiser and to the manufacturer is revealed in the time, thought, and care given to program preparation.[25] For example, an internationally famous psychologist in the field of child research evaluated and pretested the "Jack Armstrong" program for more than ten years.[26] He was responsible for making suggestions designed to produce a program that was educational as well as entertaining. He was also empowered to delete or change elements possibly harmful to the child's emotional life. "Wheaties" have been sold to the young audience by an overall healthful approach and by associating the product with championship performances of athletes.

The radio program is built primarily around three closely related motivations of children six to sixteen and amply demonstrates the successful appeal of sports material and sports ideals in this communication medium. This is particularly true in regard to the urge of the child to grow up, to lose his helplessness and become physically adept, strong, and clever. This means having heroes to emulate who have successfully accomplished this ideal. Furthermore, the growing child is in continuous conflict within himself in attemptng to reconcile the urge to do what he wants to do with what those in authority want him to do. He tends to identify himself with those characters in a story on radio or television who meet the challenge of danger and temptation, almost fail, but come out safely in the end. The sports story provides an endless repertoire of wholesome situations which permit such identification. Such programs illustrate the application of psychological and educational standards and strive to meet the approval of parents and pressure groups while at the same time they entertain the child.

Differences in presentation.—There are certain large areas of similarity and agreement with regard to the picture of sports as an expanding part of American culture which were presented to the magazine-reading public in the first twenty-five to thirty years following 1900. The institution and growth of the playground movement were given complete approval and sincere support. The virtues of outdoor living and the necessity of conservation measures to preserve the beauties of nature for all citizens were widely recognized. The importance of play as a part of the life and education of the growing child was acknowledged.

There is, however, an interesting difference in the way in which material on sports was presented as between the "quality" magazines and "journals of opinion" and the method employed in the mass-circulation periodicals. Such a statement, of course, must be understood to present a *generalized* view and is subject to many exceptions. However, when the former group discussed sports, it was usually the "good" or "evil" of the sport that was given chief consideration and not the sport itself. Articles on golf were prone to extol the character-building attributes of the game rather than the physical or recreational aspects. Articles on tennis deplored commercialization; those on football, the evils of hiring high-salaried coaches.

The more popular magazines, on the other hand, in writing of a given sport, dealt with the different aspects of the game itself, with the techniques required, with training for competitive matches, with stories of the lives of various outstanding athletes, with discussions of the value of different kinds of exercise, and with interesting facts about recreation in general.

Thus the periodical press of the nation, sometimes deliberately and sometimes quite inadvertently, did a magnificent job of publicizing, propagandizing, and popularizing sports as an indispensable part of American culture.

10. *Radio and Television Create Millions of New Sports Fans*

IN THE YEAR 1930 THE CENSUS ENUMERATORS ASKED THE QUESTION, "Do you own a radio set?"—a question which would have been completely irrelevant ten years before. These census figures revealed that 12,078,345 families in continental United States owned radio sets as of April 1, 1930. By 1932 the Columbia Broadcasting System estimated that this ownership had been increased to 16,026,620 families.[1] In the first decade of its existence the radio had become not only the great American toy but an important agency of mass communication. In less than three decades, 90.7 per cent of families had acquired radio receivers, or a total of some 33,998,000 families. Thus the growth and influence of radio broadcasting in the United States is one of the most dramatic chapters in the history of communication.[2]

SPORTS AND RADIO "FIRSTS"

WWJ, radio station of the *Detroit News*, went on the air August 20, 1920, with the announcement of the results of the year's World Series baseball games. This was before KDKA (the first radio station of the sort the public knows today) made its initial broadcast with bulletins of the Harding-Cox election on November 2, 1920.[3]

Perhaps this was an omen, forecasting the extraordinary popularity which the broadcasting of sports events has enjoyed since the first event came over the air. By the late 1920's it was a rare American radio-supplied home in which the pleasant voice of Graham McNamee had not been heard.[4]

One historian of the early radio days phrases it thus: "Sports-casting had no crawling or creeping stages. It jumped down from the obstetrical table, kicked its heels in the air and started out to do a job."[5]

One of the notable "firsts" in radio sportscasting was the Dempsey-Carpentier boxing match which occurred July 2, 1921. The first commercial station, KDKA, had opened a short year before, and nothing of the magnitude of such a broadcast had yet been undertaken. The public was hardly radio-conscious, and mass production of commercial sets had not begun. However, the man who was later to become the head of the National Broadcasting Company was so sure of an enthusiastic audience that he arranged for the attempt to be made.

The story is told that General Electric had in its possession a transmitter ordered by the Navy but not yet delivered. The Lackawanna Railroad agreed to let the broadcasters string an aerial between their towers in Hoboken. Special telephone circuits were installed to Boyle's Thirty Acres in Jersey City. A galvanized iron shack, which served as a dressing room for Pullman porters, was used for the transmitting apparatus. During the broadcast the equipment became hotter and hotter—it had not been built for continued service with the power that was being used. One tube exploded in the middle of the last round, and by the end of the fight the transmitter had begun to smoke. Shortly after the finish of the program it "resolved itself into a rather molten mass." Two hundred thousand persons were said to have heard the fight.[6]

Five years later the Jack Dempsey–Gene Tunney fight, on September 23, 1926, at Philadelphia, was carried on a nationwide hookup through N.B.C. stations. WGY of Schenectady relayed the bout by short wave to South America and England. Fans in Argentina, Brazil, and Panama, as well as Johannesburg and Cape Town, South Africa, heard the fight. One hundred and thirty-five thousand people crowded the arena to see the match. The following morning the *New York*

Times printed the verbatim radio account, one hundred column inches, plus a map of the United States showing the stations that participated in the broadcast. Fifteen million radio listeners are said to have heard the fight.

As an interesting sidelight, it seems that national temperament is reflected in styles of broadcasting, particularly in the field of sports. British broadcasting is considered by many American fans to be slow and stodgy, while British listeners feel that the booming method of many famous American announcers represents an emotional imbalance in description. One obvious point is that British fight announcers have much more latitude than is the American practice. They frequently voice their opinions as to who is winning and will also freely criticize the mode of fighting. American announcers ordinarily consider such comment the province of the appointed referees and judges.

The first World Series was broadcast in 1926 and today is considered the prize commercial program of the year. Behind this statement lies a story of baseball's stubborn resistance to radio. The major-league clubs always objected to broadcasting games at home, although they did not object when their teams were playing in other cities. The Yankees, Giants, and Dodgers had an interclub agreement until 1938 strictly prohibiting any microphone in the ball parks except for the opening games and the World Series.

By 1941 a single sponsor was spending more than a million dollars on minor-league broadcasts over ninety stations from Albany, New York, to San Diego, California. The unresolved dilemma of the probable benefits of radio broadcasting to the game of baseball and the dwindling attendance figures in many sections of the country is still debated.

The baseball fan is a hardy perennial and in many ways quite different from the ordinary sports fan. One world-famous sports announcer who has spent most of his life in broadcasting says that the World Series is the toughest sports job because "you're talking to the world's largest expert audience."[7] The confirmed baseball fan knows the background of the players and is familiar with the achievements of batters and of pitchers. He knows that every play has a direct bearing on the final outcome. A stolen base, a double play, a hit, an error— all these are factual aids which together with the verbal lift which the announcer gives complete the process of visualization for the listener. As one radio editor explained, "A fan can be wrong about what he sees but not the announcer."[8]

THE BATTLE OF THE NETWORKS

Among radio's most amusing feuds has been the intense rivalry of two national networks in scheduling the broadcasts of major sports events. This battle for exclusive right to sports events was at its height in the late 1930's. To give an example, N.B.C. had, in consideration of the sum of $10,000, secured from the AAU exclusive broadcasting rights to national meets for a four-year period. The contract, naturally, referred to broadcasts *from the stadiums*. The story of how C.B.S. pirated the broadcast of the annual National AAU Track and Field Meet held at Marquette Stadium in Milwaukee, not from the stadium, but from the roof of an adjacent church, is an epic in the history of sports broadcasting. This was followed by a turnabout mike-crash of an N.B.C. announcer at the National Open Golf Tournament at Oakland, Michigan, to which C.B.S. had secured exclusive rights.[9]

A climax in this sort of thing was reached at the time of the Braddock-Schmeling match, to which N.B.C. had exclusive broadcasting rights. A small local station rented an apartment overlooking Yankee Stadium, set up broadcasting facilities, and, armed with a powerful spyglass, their sports commentator gave a running story of the fight. Since the intruder in this instance was a very small station, it was relatively easy to overlook such piracy. However, when a rather large outfit (one that supplied news to a big list of stations) announced that they would supply a blow-by-blow account, it became obvious that steps should be taken. In this case a judge of the supreme court of the state of New York granted an injunction against the offender. The plan had been to have a man at the ringside equipped with a small battery transmitter through which he could short-wave an account of the fight to a near-by spot for rebroadcasting. Since the time of this incident, all fight tickets sold in the state of New York bear a notice warning the purchaser that broadcasting a fight or any portion thereof is illegal.[10]

EXPANSION IN LOCAL AND REGIONAL RADIO SPORTSCASTING

The years 1936-38 represent the approximate mid-point of radio sports broadcasting in twentieth-century America. Perhaps a look at the events of those years will give an idea of the scope of expansion in coverage which had taken place to that date and may also serve as a basis for comparison with the present day. Interesting as the developments were in nation-wide hookups for major events in the world of sports, these alone tell only a small part of the story of ever increasing coverage. The following are random samples taken from station records on sponsored sports, summer, 1937, to spring, 1938. These are broadcasts over individual stations or regional hookups and *not* national networks.

The program of a Tennessee radio station included forty-five college and prep football games, weekly wrestling, semi-monthly boxing, and weekly handball and bowling. A small station in Minnesota offered nine high-school and college football games, fourteen high-school and college basketball games, twenty hockey games, and twelve district and regional basketball tournaments. A station in Montana offered broadcasts of American Junior League baseball, college and high-school football, and fifty college and high-school basketball games. From one corner of Texas came sixteen baseball games, twenty-nine football games, and state high-school championships as well as the regular high-school basketball games. A small Pennsylvania station listed one hundred and forty baseball games, twenty high-school and one college football game, forty-seven high-school and professional basketball games, and regular broadcasts of amateur boxing.[11]

Among other sports activities listed by many stations as locally sponsored were tennis, swimming meets, hockey, Golden Gloves, track meets, softball, golf, sandlot baseball, table tennis, soccer, and marbles tournaments.[12]

RADIO, EDUCATION, AND COLLEGE ATHLETICS

From its very beginning radio planners were intrigued by the possibilities of using this new medium of communication for education purposes as such. By 1923 a well-known New York station had broadcast lessons in accounting, and experiments had been undertaken involving broadcasts to California rural schools. During the ensuing fifteen years many experiments were tried, with varying degrees of success. Individuals most intimately concerned were well aware that the over-all program was *not* an unqualified success. Speaking on a "University of the Air" series in 1938, one educator pointed out the central problem, which to a degree still remains unsolved. He predicted that not much would come of giving education the privileges of the air until a complete break was made with the old schoolmasterish methods, "the blackboard, the textbook, the outline, the examination—the whole miserable paraphernalia which has kept us in a strait jacket."[13] He felt the American people had a right to make a complaint against the current fare—that it was "monotonous, unvaried, unimaginative, drab, uninspired, tasteless."

This is given, not as a diatribe against education by radio, but by way of pointing out that the colleges might have been more alert to the use of radio sports broadcasts for the educational and public relations potential which they possess rather than the exclusive "pleasure and publicity" emphasis which such programs have assumed. The mistake of institutions in the early years of the century in shutting their eyes to the educational possibilities and allowing intercollegiate athletics to grow and expand without institutional support and control seems to have been repeated in the case of both radio and television. Undoubtedly sports competition is that phase of college life in which the greatest number of ordinary citizens has the most vital interest. It may have been that a golden opportunity was overlooked—an opportunity to present and interpret this phase of the college program to literally millions of Americans and to do it in the manner which was approved and with the philosophy of the educational institution dominating the situation.

Colleges and universities, in the process of fostering intercollegiate activities, have wittingly or unwittingly become engaged in the field of professional entertainment. Perhaps the time has come to recognize that, while intercollegiate athletics hold a vital and exciting place in our way of life, they do function under the banner of individual educational institutions. Although sports have an important place, they are an institutional auxiliary, and the prime aim remains a program of teaching and research.[14]

The situation may improve when and where athletics cease to be a fringe activity of the institution, tolerated but not fully accepted, and become a part of the educational picture, with all the rights, privileges, and responsibilities involved. To be successful, this would require a more honestly realistic approach than has sometimes been evidenced. It would require an acceptance of the fact that the program of intercollegiate athletics, with its many ramifications and complexities, cannot be operated on quite the same simple plan as the program of the department of philosophy.

The history of the relationship of intercollegiate athletic competition to the institutions responsible for such competition is a history of failure on both sides to achieve a common understanding. The personnel most directly involved with the conduct of athletics has sometimes failed to give due consideration to the underlying and fundamental educational aims of the institutions and to adhere to properly constituted administrative procedures. College and university administrators and faculties have also failed to provide sympathetic understanding of the problems and pressures to which the athletic department is constantly subjected. Most important of all, the fearless and aggressive leadership so badly needed has not been forthcoming.

The great American public has always seemed to feel that the sports activities of the schools and colleges somehow belonged as much to them as they did to the institutions that sponsored contests and the students who participated. This feeling may be classified as legitimate and even admirable interest, or as inexcusable interference, depending on the point of view. At any rate, it is a trend that has increased enormously over the years. Every modern agency of communication has contributed to its growth—the sports page, the newsreel, and radio and television. One thoughtful student of the problem puts it this way:

The last fifty years have observed a marked evolution in college athletics. Changes are no more alarming than in many other instances such as medicine, hygiene, business, economics or politics. Its conspicuity is the principal basis for a seemingly virulent overemphasis. In its modern form it is likely here to stay and must be woven into the fabric of modern education in some balanced pattern.[15]

In the year 1937 there was a wide variation of reaction and policy on the part of colleges and universities to the problem of radio sports broadcasting. A large Midwest university stated that it did not feel it "advisable to broadcast our football games at this time."[16] Two of the Ivy League eastern universities had steadfastly refused to sell radio rights, but a third had sold its six home games for $20,000.[17] Both the Pacific Coast Conference and the Southwest Conference had arranged with large oil companies for exclusive rights to broadcast all their inter-collegiate athletic contests.

All such details were remote and of little interest to the sports fan who was simply happy to have more and better coverage of such events for his listening pleasure. The wide-spread radio broadcasting of such collegiate sports has engendered a new species of alumni, the radio alumni, many of whom have never been within a thousand miles of the campus of their choice. Among this group are to be found the nation's most rabid football fans. As an audience they demand the strictest impartiality in reporting and are apparently insatiable in the matter of sidelights on the game, the players, and the general surroundings.

TELEVISION AND SPORTS

There is every indication that televised sports will enjoy the same widespread popularity that radio sportscasting has enjoyed since the first event came over the air. A baseball game between Princeton and Columbia at Baker Field furnished the first telecast in the United States. It was later reported that the players "looked like so many bounding four-limbed insects" and that, if it hadn't been for the voice of the announcer, the televiewer would have had difficulty knowing what was going on.[18] By 1952 the nation-wide televising of the World Series demonstrated beyond doubt how many of the early technical difficulties had been successfully solved.

The Nova-Baer encounter in June, 1939, was the first televised boxing bout, and the floodlighted arena proved to be an excellent scene for the camera to cover. Viewers were furnished with thrills quite as stimulating as though they had occupied front-row seats. Boxing continues to enjoy tremendous popularity on television but is probably overshadowed by the professional wrestling matches. In fact, the enjoyment of these shows by a strangely heterogeneous group of the population is, to many, a truly strange and unexplained phenomenon of the present era.

Football has proved very successful as a television sport. It somehow invites audience participation in a way that is not true even for the spectator in the stands. At the stadium the spectator knows the game is separate; he is sandwiched in the crowd, and the players are out on the field. By way of television the contest is in the living room. The spectator in this case stands with the coach at the sidelines, right beside the white lines that run over the grass!

A sports poll of sixty-four TV stations, taken in the year 1949, revealed the highest proportion of time devoted to sports as 35 per cent, the lowest as 4 per cent, and the average as 16 per cent. More than twenty different sports were televised, with the following five sports showing by far the highest percentage of time: football, boxing, baseball, wrestling, and basketball.[19]

THE QUESTION OF CONTROL—AND OF
INFLUENCE ON ATTENDANCE

The concern over the effect of various forms of public communication on attendance at sports events has a long history. Serious attention was once given to excluding newspapermen from the ball parks. The newspapers in turn resisted the invasion of radio, and not only the newspapers, for the Eastern Intercollegiate Association passed a resolution in 1932 banning the broadcast of football games. In 1949 professional football banned "live" telecasts in the home area of the team playing, and in 1950 the Big Ten banned "live" telecasting for that year.

By January, 1953, the most important business before the forty-seventh annual meeting of the NCAA, from the standpoint of the general public, was the solution to the question of what should be done about televising football games. In spite of strong opposition from Notre Dame and Pennsylvania, the vote was 172 to 13 in favor of continuing strict controls on the televising of football games. The question as to whether or not there is a violation of antitrust laws involved remains to be settled and may eventuate in the necessity of a Supreme Court decision.

Regardless of the eventual outcome of the controversy as to the benefit or harm to actual attendance, television sportscasting has demonstrated a positive as well as a negative effect.[20]

1. Television sports have a growing audience among women as well as men. Social and cultural unity is promoted when a greater area of interest is enthusiastically shared by men and women, by parents and children.

2. Television has shown a definite potentiality for educating the public to a new enthusiasm and a keener interest in sports by making all sports more accessible and by bringing to the attention of the public sports that have hitherto had a much more specialized audience.

3. The complete enjoyment of a complex sport presupposes an understanding of its rules and strategy as well as the skills and qualities required of its players. There are two ways of acquiring this basic knowledge: a considerable period of active participation or a spectator apprenticeship which involves watching the game while someone explains it. Television puts each viewer in the front row with an expert at his side.

II. *From Bicycle to Automobile*
Modern Man with the World
at His Wheels

IT HAS BEEN SAID THAT NO SOCIAL FORCE IS OF GREATER CONSE-
quence than improved transportation and communication. A
brief list of major effects of the automobile in twentieth-
century America confirms this statement. In addition to
revolutionizing methods of transportation and distribution of
goods, the automobile has brought into being metropolitan
areas, with the accompanying change in real estate values;
it has fostered huge industries involving oil and rubber and
automobile repairs, as well as the era of the small hotel and
tourist camp; it has contributed to the appearance of the
consolidated school and to the disappearance (almost) of the
little red scholhouse; it has necessitated a change in the structure of homes to include the indispensable garage; it has helped
in the centralization of government functions, bringing federal
and state police; it has changed tremendously the national
mores with regard to family relationships and habits of courtship; and, most of all, it has emphasized the pursuit of pleasure
as opposed to the more puritan virtues.

The essence of modern American living is mobility. As
nowhere else in the world the economic, social, and recreational life of the population depends upon the mobility afforded by the automobile. It would be strange indeed if such
fundamental changes did not also transform and revolutionize
the sports life and recreational habits of the populace.

By the year 1900 the United States had developed the most

extensive railway system in the world, and the principal lines as they now exist had been completed. By this time, too, Americans of all ages and both sexes were pedaling ten million bicycles, and three hundred manufacturers were producing them at the rate of more than a million a year.[1]

Bicycle-racing was the sensation of the time and was given proportionately as much coverage by newspapers as football and baseball are today. When the members of the American World Racing Team of 1897 returned from Europe with honors won throughout the Continent, they were given a heroes' welcome. The League of American Wheelmen, organized in 1880, had conducted a vigorous educational campaign for better roads, which led to legislation for state aid to counties and eventually to federal interest in legislation for road improvement.[2] But the story of the first half of the twentieth century is really the story of the automobile!

THE AUTOMOBILE—A VEHICLE OF SPORT

An eminent anthropologist has pointed out that "inventions motivated by play impulses are fairly common."[3] Certainly the automobile began life essentially as a vehicle of sport, luxury, and recreation. In this it paralleled the history of the bicycle, which was originally purely an instrument of sport. It was not until much later that either vehicle began seriously to be used as a means of getting around on business.

Every cultural innovation, whether it be in the form of a mechanical invention or a new and revolutionary idea, is confronted by resistance from certain segments of the culture, particularly those to which the status quo represents a thoroughly satisfactory state of existence. This resistance to change was well demonstrated in the case of the early automobile. Investigation reveals that one of the most successful pressures which helped to break down this resistance was that exerted by the pioneer sportsmen, the racers and the seekers after adventure who tackled and overcame obstacles and problems in a manner which seems almost heroic from the perspective of mid-century.

Racing was the first and foremost attraction of the automobile in the days when its usefulness for any other purpose was very seriously questioned. Readers of the sports page were familiar with the names of the drivers, and eventually spectators became a problem beyond the control of the management. On one memorable occasion the starter turned a high-pressure hose on the crowd so that he could send the first car on its way. The third running of the Vanderbilt Cup Races on October 6, 1906, was witnessed by three hundred thousand spectators, said to be the largest crowd ever to attend a sporting event in America.[4]

Denounced, endured, embraced.—It is sometimes forgotten that the American motorcar in the early days of its introduction made many enemies as well as friends. The majority of a generation geared to the quiet and tempo of a horse age found it too noisy and too fast. One writer in 1902 considered the automobile an invasion of public property and an encroachment upon the liberty of men, women, and children, to whom the roads belonged.[5] The farmers were especially bitter about the new "devil wagons" that terrified their horses and filled the air with noise and pollution.

Throughout the land there was a hue and cry against the automobile as "a disturber of the peace, a breaker of quiet and bones, and an agent of unrest."[6] Laws and ordinances were enacted which reflected the antagonism of the time. A small town in California had an ordinance requiring the driver of an automobile to come to a complete stop within three hundred feet of every passing horse; and Vermont was attempting to enforce a statute which required every motorist to employ "a person of mature age" to walk ahead of his vehicle one-eighth of a mile, carrying a red flag in his hand.[7]

The medical profession found itself on both sides of the question. While some of the country doctors were among the first to adopt the automobile as a means of transportation, certain of their colleagues were busy denouncing it heartily. One practitioner likened the indulgence in speed to that of indulgence in tobacco and alcohol, and another pointed out that automobiling had an unfavorable influence on pregnancy.[8]

Together with golf, the automobile was frequently denounced from the pulpit as one of the deadliest enemies of the church. So thoroughly was this done that it seemed as though "cloven hoof, forked tail, and horns had been supplanted by golf bag, pneumatic tire, and windshield."[9] Banks refused to loan money if such funds were to be used for the purchase of an automobile, and yet the first vehicles, made almost entirely by hand, were very expensive and beyond the reach of most citizens. Thus the early automobile was half-feared by its owner and detested by the populace; "reeking of gasoline and wealth," it flouted class distinction in a most offensive manner.[10]

There were, however, other powerfully influencing factors in the culture—factors more than sufficient to counteract this disapproval. America was committed to a progressively more mechanized civilization. The fascination of new mechanical inventions, of increasing speed and fast motion, was in the air. With all sorts and conditions of men, women, and children, there has always been an irresistible fascination for speed.[11] What else could so well explain the urge for racing —horse-racing, yacht-racing, foot-racing, boat-racing, bicycling, and all the many "chutes," "loops," and "roller coasters" that fill the amusement parks? The automobile simply represented a possibility for greater speed than man had ever known before.

In view of the above, and with all due respect and credit to inventors, investors, and manufacturers, it may well be that some homage is due to that small group of bold pioneers, real sportsmen all, who risked the hazards of bad roads, erratic power, and embattled farmers in the first decade of

the motorcar's introduction in America. The automobile did
not wait for good roads but multiplied in the face of obstacles.
This era of nonacceptance came to an end with the advent
of the mass-produced, inexpensive car, and in less than two
decades (1909–29) fifteen million Model-T Fords were traveling American roads. Following World War I, a newly mature
generation showed a very different attitude with regard to
the automobile. It was no longer regarded as a toy, a luxury,
or even primarily as an instrument of recreation but rather
as an indispensable convenience, a day-and-night, year-round
utilitarian necessity. The few experimental cars known to
be in existence in 1895 had increased to 55,290 in actual use
in the year 1904; by 1910 there were 468,500 registered motor
vehicles, by 1920 there were 9,239,161, and by 1949 there
were over 43,000,000 registered motor vehicles on the road.[12]

MODERN TRANSPORTATION AND AMERICAN SPORTS

In Chapters 8, 9, and 10 an attempt has been made to show
some effects of improved means of communication on the
sports life of America. This chapter will attempt to discuss,
from among the infinite variety of forms of physical recreation and sport, a few which have been most directly influenced by the advent of the automobile: winter sports, golf,
school and college sports, camping, attendance at national
parks, hunting and fishing, and spectator sports.

Winter sports.—The origin of skiing as a means of travel
is buried in antiquity. It was in 1856, according to the records,
that an intrepid Californian carried the mail some ninety miles
between Placerville and Carson Valley wearing a pair of
Norwegian skis. In the Midwest the influx of Norwegian,
Swedish, and Finnish immigrants brought many ski enthusiasts.[13] A New York City sports store advertised skis in 1902,
and the Sears, Roebuck catalogue for 1905 contained a statement which indicated that a number of manufacturers were

making them: "We consider ash better adapted for work of this kind than any of the cheaper woods used by various manufacturers."[14] The Dartmouth College Outing Club was founded in 1910 and held its first winter carnival the following year. From a handful of members this organization has developed into one of the world's most influential ski organizations, its ski teams and winter carnivals being internationally famous.[15] During these early years skiing was confined to exceedingly small groups of participants. There were no such things as chair lifts, racing trails, snow trains, or automobiles that could drive through the snow-laden roads.

It was following the Olympic Winter Games of 1932, held at Lake Placid, that skiing came of age in America. Between the years 1932 and 1942 the "new" sport grew at an unbelievable pace. In ten years it had become a two-hundred-million-dollar industry and was rivaling other sports as one of the largest participant sports in the United States.

All this would have been impossible without modern transportation facilities. The first "snow train" left Boston's North Station in 1931, and four years later such trains were pulling out of New York's Grand Central Station with thousands of apartment dwellers on board, intent on spending two days in the snows of New England. The lower mountains of the East and Midwest mean traveling farther distances north, and a well-organized snow-train service has made this possible. The Union Pacific Railroad is responsible for the most lavish of all winter sports resorts, Sun Valley, Idaho. The enthusiast in the Midwest, in the Chicago-Milwaukee area, has a choice of several overnight snow trains or the "snow boat" from the Milwaukee dock, where he and his car are transported on a lake steamer to within easy driving distance of Sugar Loaf or Otsego.

The farther west in the United States, the greater is the reliance on the automobile for ski transportation. Many cities are located close to high mountains, and most of the skiers drive to their play. Denver is within two hours of four excellent ski resorts, Salt Lake City is just twenty-three miles from Alta, and Reno is but eighteen miles from Mount Rose Bowl. Skiers in Portland are seventy miles from Mount Hood and Timberline Lodge,[16] and enthusiasts in Seattle and Tacoma have a wide choice of mountains within one hundred and twenty miles.

Yosemite National Park lies halfway between San Francisco and Los Angeles and has been called the "Lake Placid of the West." Northern California and Bay area skiers have Donner Summit and a dozen places there within a ten-mile radius. Los Angeles has San Gorgonio within one hundred miles. Both Arizona and New Mexico have ski clubs and good skiing!

Organized skiing can be found today in twenty-nine of the forty-eight states.[17] The spectacle of approximately four million Americans and their enthusiasm for skiing is somewhat of a mystery to the average non-skiing citizen. When the thing began, it was dubbed a "craze" and compared to the miniature golf and mah-jongg fiascoes of an earlier time. Apparently the critics and the doubters are wrong. The sport survived the critical war years and is currently growing and expanding.

To the millions of devotees there is no mystery; it is the doorway to beauty, excitement, and fun! The sport has a sizable group of competitive skiers of all ages, but the *millions* are recreational skiers who are not jumpers and who do not compete in races. They are a peculiarly American crowd and have developed a mass sport that is as different from St. Moritz skiing as Coney Island is different from Cannes.[18] There are school and college students and city dwellers snatching a week end or using up the two weeks' vacation hoarded from the summer months. So long as the snow-covered mountains continue to be accessible by train, by car, or by plane, apparently the skiers can be depended upon to keep them occupied.

Golf.—If any man doubts the democratizing influence of sports as they function in American culture, let him study the history of golf as it has developed in the United States. Here is a game which began as the sole property of the wealthy and near-wealthy, nourished in the atmosphere of exclusive country clubs, and ridiculed by the penny press as pastime for "dudes." Within a half-century all this was changed. Municipal golf courses, intercity tournaments, professional golfers, the rise of caddies to the rank of top-flight players—all this signified that the "four million" had definitely taken over the game from the "four hundred."

Improved transportation facilities were only one factor in this total development, but in many instances it was a rather important one. The early golf courses were laid out in the wealthy commuting towns near big cities, such as those in Brookline, Massachusetts, and Morristown, New Jersey. Availability of transportation by road, railway, or trolley was quite often one of the determining factors in the choice of a site. It was the question of distance and transportation which helped to bring about the initial break with tradition in the matter of selection of golf-course sites. In England and in Scotland, where the game of golf had a three-hundred-year history, the ideal links were along the seacoast. In fact, the word "links" originally meant a chain of grass-covered sand dunes. Since the Atlantic seacoast was not only unsuitable but quite inaccessible, Americans went about hewing golf courses out of the forest. Hills and streams, lakes and rivers, were appropriated, and there were always plenty of trees. The Scotch and English doubted that golf could ever be played as it should be played on America's inland-type golf courses.

There was another reason for this development of the inland golf course in the early days. The country club, that peculiarly American institution, had come into existence before the popularity of golf in this country. With the coming of this sport, it was natural that courses should be built around or near existing country clubs. Eventually it was the game of golf that would perpetuate the name of "country club" in practically every city, town, and village in America.[19] By the year 1900 the list of golf clubs totaled one thousand and forty, and every state in the Union had its golf course, from Maine, with thirty-three, through New York's one hundred and sixty-five, to Illinois's fifty-seven, to California's forty-three.

In the year 1895, at Van Courtlandt Park, New York, was constructed the first public golf course in the United States. A group of players petitioned the park commissioner to lay out a course, not because they were public benefactors, but because they hoped to establish a private club. Upon being told that a public park could not be used for private amusement schemes, a compromise was reached whereby this particular group had exclusive use two afternoons a week.[20] Transportation was ideal, since the New York and Putnam Railroad started at One Hundred and Fifty-fifth Street and ran right beside the park. It became a favorite rendezvous for writers, artists, actors, doctors, and lawyers who came early in the morning and played a round before going to work for the day.

An eminent social historian has called the development of golf between 1898 and 1914 "the unique feature in the history of American sport during these years."[21] In addition to the men and women of great wealth, there was an expanding middle-class group who were finding leisure for sport, and golf seemed an ideal answer to their need. But 1914 was barely a beginning. The prosperous twenties brought a great increase in land values, and this in turn forced the building of courses at greater distances from business and residential sections. The continued growth in numbers of participants would not have been possible without the concomitant increase in automobile ownership.

By 1930 Metropolitan New York had seventeen municipal golf courses, all within forty miles of Times Square. The Chicago district had ten municipal courses, and Los Angeles and San Francisco ranked third and fourth, respectively, in municipal golf. Today it is estimated that there are between two and three million golfers in America, a group which spends some two and a half million dollars a year in traveling costs, transportation, and hotel bills.[22]

The consolidated school.—The growth of the one-room rural school under frontier conditions was one of the miracles of American education in the nineteenth and early twentieth centuries. The extension of free transportation to rural youth, making possible the consolidation of many one-room schools into larger units of administration, is one of the major developments of the twentieth century. The magnitude of the accomplishment can be better understood by examining official estimates for 1947–48 which show approximately five million children transported to school each day in ninety thousand buses, which travel three million miles.[23]

The consolidation of small schools into units which have sufficient taxable wealth to provide adequate buildings, equipment, and transportation and better-trained teachers has had a profound influence on all areas of the curriculum, but particularly in the field of physical education and sports. The four-year high school with an enrolment of fifty pupils or less (and there were 2,429 such schools in the United States as late as the year 1946)[24] simply cannot offer to its students the opportunity for participation in team games and athletic contests or for expert instruction in various sports skills. This lack of opportunity may result in a cultural loss to the individuals concerned and to the community as well. A study of rural society reveals that the school, and more especially the high school, is the most important and decisive single factor in determining town and country community solidarity and in defining community areas.[25] There was ample evidence in the study that joint enthusiasm and responsibility such as is involved in the staging of athletic contests or evenings of dancing and group games often eliminated differences due to residence, occupation, class, or creed and made of the community a working group.

The automobile has also helped bring about the growth of regional and state championships in high-school athletics and, with the attendant increase in publicity, has done much to stimulate the interest of ever greater numbers of citizens in sports and athletics.

The extent of the interdependence of competitive school athletics on availability of transportation (for both participants and spectators) became obvious with the advent of tire rationing in 1941–42. At that time an informal survey was conducted by the Athletic Institute to ascertain the number of miles actually traveled by buses transporting high-school teams for purposes of athletic competition. Figures ranged from 386 miles in Illinois to 10,760 miles in New Mexico.[26]

Camping.—The value of camp experience in the lives of youngsters, and particularly those growing up in crowded urban areas, has long been recognized by parents, educators, and others interested in the welfare of children. The first formal meeting to be held for a discussion of camping was in Boston in 1903, with an attendance of about a hundred men and a handful of women. By 1949 the American Camping Association had a membership of more than four thousand, representing all regions of the United States.[27]

Pioneers in the field of camp work may still remember the days when boys and girls were delivered to them by farm wagon after an exhausting trip from the railroad station. They may also remember the almost insuperable difficulties involved in transporting food and equipment. The development of the low-cost automobile and the construction of good roads has made possible a tremendous expansion in all varieties of camping for both childern and adults.

In addition to a vast network of private camps which are to be found in every part of the country, there are many organization camps operated by the Boy Scouts and the Girl Scouts, the YMCA and the YWCA, the Camp Fire Girls, the 4-H Clubs, and many others. All such camps include sports as a part of their program of activities.

Recreation departments throughout the country are conducting a variety of camping programs ranging from the in-town day camp, the overnight or week-end camp, to the vacation camp where families spend a week or more. Many such camps are being used throughout the year in sections of the country where winter sports may be enjoyed.

Currently there is great interest in school-camp development. Three states (California, Michigan, and New York) have provided specific legislation which permits schools to maintain and operate camping facilities outside their immediate school districts.[28] A great deal of the credit goes to the W. K. Kellogg Foundation for demonstrating that school camps can be conducted as public enterprises. The developments in this regard in the state of Michigan in the years since 1940 serve as a model for other states and communities.[29] Another noteworthy accomplishment in the promotion of school camps has been at San Diego in California's Pilot Project in Outdoor Education.[30]

The development of the school camp is one of the significant developments of the twentieth century. It represents a consciously planned cultural adaptation, an attempt to provide educational experiences from which many individuals are debarred by reason of lives spent in industrialized urban communities. Basic to the idea of the school camp and to its success are those modern vehicles of transportation, trucks and buses, which so faithfully carry the campers to and from their new adventures in outdoor living.

National parks and the National Forest Service.—A goodly part of the whole project of conservation of natural resources in the form of national parks and national forests is an outgrowth of the basic American concept that outdoor living with attendant physical recreational activities is a fundamental, essential, and desirable part of the national culture. As was pointed out in an earlier chapter, an extensive campaign to educate the general public was carried on by the periodical press in the early years of the century. That these early efforts were successful in building a firm foundation is evidenced by the fact that today the National Forest Service administers the use of one hundred and fifty national forests, comprising 180,000,000 acres of land and located in forty states, Puerto Rico, and Alaska.

The magnificent development of the national park system and its widespread enjoyment by millions of Americans would have been literally impossible without the automobile. Some idea may be gained of the contribution of the existence of these areas to the sports and recreational life of the nation by a brief review of some recent figures. In addition to an estimated twenty-eight million persons who drive over the national forest roads and highways to enjoy the scenery, there are accommodated annually more than eighteen million visitors who enjoy hunting and fishing, camping, boating, swimming, horseback riding, and all types of winter sports, including skiing, skating, and tobogganing.[31]

Prior to 1916 national parks were valued principally for the majesty of their scenery, although a trend toward greater use of such national park areas for active recreational purposes was under way as early as 1915 and was commented on by a writer in the *Overland Monthly*, who said that first and foremost a park should be a *playground*, not merely a showplace where things are to be seen.[32]

The National Forest Service now has two hundred and fifty-four winter sports areas spread over 51,000 acres that will accommodate 156,000 people at one time. In addition, there are three hundred and eleven organization camps operated by such organizations as the Boy Scouts, 4-H Clubs, or cities, and a total of 168,000 miles of improved trails for those who enjoy hiking.

Hunting and fishing.—Hunting and fishing are the classic American sports. Since the earliest settlers indulged, more sometimes for food than for fun, the enthusiasm for these recreations has never dimmed. Progressively in the twentieth century, as urban populations increased and cities and towns multiplied, the importance of rapid and inexpensive transportation has had an ever closer relationship to the extent of opportunity for fishing and hunting.

When more than eighteen million hunting and fishing licenses are issued each year, it becomes a prime concern of government to protect and nurture the fish and wildlife resources so that these sports may continue. It is estimated that the conservation program of the Fish and Wildlife Service affects the recreational pleasures of forty million people.[33]

It is one of the miracles of America that, in spite of a high degree of industrialization, there remain vast protected areas devoted to the rod-and-gun enthusiasts. Americans, more than any other urbanized people in the world, have been a race of hunters and fishermen. The expenditures of this group of sportsmen (a sizable amount of which goes for transportation by both automobile and boat) represent a not inconsiderable proportion of the nation's annual expenditures for outdoor recreation. The automobile, and with it the building of roads, has made hitherto inaccessible hunting and fishing areas available to an ever widening group of citizens of all social and economic levels.

Spectator sports.—Nothing could have pointed up more dramatically the dependence of spectator sports on adequate transportation than the events following gas and tire rationing in World War II. By 1943 attendance at big-league baseball games was suffering noticeably. The National League had cut off 34,600 miles of traveling and the American League 35,000 miles. Race tracks in Florida and California were closed due to poor attendance, and many college football schedules were either dropped completely or continued on a local basis.[34] When the war ended, the year 1946 brought a record-breaking year for attendance in organized baseball—forty-seven million spectators and gate receipts of approximately forty-eight million dollars.[35]

Sports have benefited more as a result of the automobile than any of the other forms of spectator entertainment. The motion-picture theater, the concert hall, and the opera are usually located in easily accessible areas of the city, while the baseball park, the football stadium, or the race track are more often a greater distance from the residences of their prospective spectators. While improved public transportation and the automobile have made it possible for millions to witness sports events, currently the parking problem is one of the most difficult with which management has to cope. Many sports facilities were originally constructed without adequate preparation for the enormous traffic they are now expected to handle. In the battle for spectators which is being waged between football conferences, baseball club owners, radio broadcasters, and the television interests, the difficulties of traffic congestion and inadequate parking facilities may prove a decisive factor.

Epilogue.—It would leave incomplete a chapter on the effects of transportation on the national sports life to neglect some discussion of air travel. In his book *The Social Effects of Aviation* published in 1946, Ogburn predicted that the recreational life of people would be affected in various ways by the increased availability of this most modern of all means of transportation.[36]

1. That outdoor recreation might be definitely stimulated

through making good hunting and fishing areas more accessible.

2. That the exceptional sports spectacle could be expected to attract greater attendance, particularly from more distant places.

3. That there would be a definite increase in the radius of sports; intersectional games of both college and professional teams in such sports as football and basketball.

4. That international competition in sports might be aided by air transportation and promote a greater familiarity with the outstanding athletic personalities of other countries.

Today there is evidence that these predicted effects are already noticeable in the American sports scene.

12. *The Increasing Concern of Government for the Welfare of the People*

THE EMERGING ATTITUDE OF GOVERNMENT REGARDING THE physical recreation of its citizens is the product of changing cultural conditions in the United States. It may well go back to the phrase in the Constitution which says "promote the general welfare." As the culture has accented the importance of physical recreation in the out of doors, so government has accented its efforts in that direction. Operating on the premise that recreation is one of the basic human needs, government at all levels has steadily developed and implemented its philosophy since the act of Congress in 1872 created Yellowstone, the first national park in the world.

The Role of the Federal Government

A review of the work of the various agencies which in one way or another provide facilities and sponsor programs involving sports and physical recreation clearly indicates a deep concern on the part of our federal government with an area of life of vital importance to the welfare of the nation. This deep concern has been brought about by cultural change. Urbanization and leisure produce needs on the part of the people to get out in the open, enjoy the out of doors, do the things for which there is no provision at home—to hunt, to fish, to hike, to camp, to live the rugged life.

In the early part of the century, along with President Theodore Roosevelt's enthusiasm and drive for conservation of natural resources, came the idea that play was an important part of the life of the child and that the experiences gained in an out-of-door life, even for a week or a few weeks a year, were vital in the child's future outlook. There can be little question but that the exposure of children to outdoor experiences during the first decade of the century had a considerable influence upon developments by the federal government in the twenties. Though it cannot be said that the whole conservation movement was based on the use of lands for recreational purposes, President Roosevelt never neglected that aspect of it. Since his time the acquisition and maintenance of public lands for recreational use is the one function of government in this regard best understood by the general public. He was aided in no small measure by the dissemination of information regarding the natural wonders and beauties of America. The periodical literature in the early part of the century is replete with stirring articles on the beauty spots of America—Yosemite, the Grand Canyon, Yellowstone, and the like. Among the more prominent men and women whose articles had much to do with creating a desire for the out of doors may be listed John Muir, John Burroughs, Stephen M. Dale, Bradford Torrey, Harriet Monroe, Maurice Thompson, and many others.[1]

There can be little doubt that in the reading public there was created a desire to see and live in the great open spaces. *Sell enough people on the idea, and you can sell the government.*

FEDERAL AGENCIES AND RECREATION PROGRAMS

The various agencies of the federal government which offer recreation programs fall quite naturally into two general categories: (1) those which have to do with land and facilities used for recreation and (2) those which act in an advisory capacity, disseminate information to local agencies and groups, and administer funds which are given to state and county agencies. The primary function of the federal government, through various agencies, is to help people obtain and enjoy recreation.[2]

In the first category there have been created the following services:

The National Park Service, among other things, provides for the people both recreational facilities and activities, including hiking and riding trails, fishing and camping, boating, and ski runs.

The Fish and Wildlife Service recognizes the desirability of providing facilities and services for physical recreation, and its national wildlife refuges assure "millions of hunters the perpetuation of the sport of hunting."[3]

The Forest Service, wherever possible, develops the facilities necessary for recreation in a forest environment, including such activities as camping, swimming, riding, hunting, fishing, hiking, and skiing.

The Bureau of Reclamation gives special consideration to the development of recreation areas in all its investigations of reservoir projects, with the co-operation of the three agencies just mentioned.

The Corps of Engineers, in doing its job in the improvement and maintenance of rivers and other waterways, creates many and varied opportunities for recreational enjoyment. New and enlarged water and reservoir areas are being utilized for such activities as fishing, sailing, canoeing, and boat-racing.

The coming of the automobile offered the opportunity for millions of Americans to spend vacations and week ends in national parks and forests and literally "forced" the federal government into a road-building program the like of which was not dreamed of in the early part of the century.

Under the second category come the Extension Service of the Department of Agriculture, with its emphasis on recreational programs for 4-H Clubs; the Office of Education and the Children's Bureau of the Federal Security Agency, with specialists on call to assist in improving school-community relations regarding recreation and securing recreational opportunities for children, youth, and families. Over the years minor contributions to the recreation resources of the nation have been made by such agencies as the Public Housing Administration, the Bureau of Indian Affairs, the Bureau of Land Management, the Soil Conservation Service, the Public Roads Administration, the Bureau of Community Facilities, the National Capital Park and Planning Commission, and the Tennessee Valley Authority.

THE DEPRESSION

President Theodore Roosevelt's drive for conservation in the early nineteen-hundreds was not well received by Congress, but President Franklin D. Roosevelt had the stage set for him in relation to conservation as it applies to recreation. To be sure, he was motivated by the possibility of large-scale employment, but the fact remains that he embraced the opportunity to make a contribution to the public welfare in the form of recreation as against another possible type of public welfare. He undoubtedly was aware, as were our leaders in recreation, that unemployment tends to produce a loss of spiritual power, that an opportunity for recreation is as important as an opportunity for work, and that a loss of morale may be more serious than the loss of a job. Stimulated by such considerations, it is not surprising that the leaders in Congress agreed with President Roosevelt's proposals and that the federal government was ready and willing to support his recommendations. In all probability the relief activities of the federal government during the period of the depression advanced recreation twenty-five years.[4] Among the agencies created to assist our national morale by various provisions for recreation are the following:

The Civilian Conservation Corps involved about three and a half million young men and was concerned with the building and improving of roads, picnic areas, camp grounds, hiking and riding trails, swimming and boating facilities, and many other types.

The National Youth Administration provided part-time employment for needy youths some of whom either served as leaders of recreation or were engaged in the construction of facilities of various types in parks and recreation centers.

The Public Works Administration administered vast appropriations for public works of all kinds, including the building of recreational facilities of many types.[5]

The Work Projects Administration, among other things, had projects involving the construction and repair of recreatonal facilities and areas as well as the employment of recreation leaders to supplement already existing programs and to provide for small communities their first recreation program.[6]

WORLD WAR II

Just prior to and during World War II the federal government embarked on a new recreation venture and created the Division of Recreation in the Office of Community War Services, Federal Security Agency.[7] This agency, with a field staff of eighty, was particularly concerned with war-impacted communities, and its recommendations for Lanham Act funds reached hundreds of communities.

One must not forget the Office of Special Services, Veterans Administraton, which, among other things, has an extensive program of physical recreation in hospitals.

The principle of associative activity operates in government as well as in other aspects of our society. Witness the voluntary organization in 1946 of the Federal Inter-Agency Committee on Recreaton, established to bring about co-operative planning for recreation.

During World War II, also, an attempt was made to make recreation a part of the daily life of every serviceman. The idea of recreation, built up in the minds of ten million men, was bound to have an influence on the attitude of the federal government and, though indirect, must be given due consideration in the picture of over-all cultural change.

The Role of State Government

The state's responsibility in the field of recreation has grown markedly in the past half-century, just as has its responsibility in the fields of education and health, the improvement of working conditions, the expansion of means of communication and transportation, and the concern for the delinquent and defective members of its society. The welfare of its citizens is of prime importance in many regulatory controls which have been established, such, for example, as public utility agencies, insurance boards, and banking commissions. It is not surprising, then, with the increase of leisure time and the coming of the automobile into pratically every home, that the state should give a considerable amount of attention to the promotion of recreation as one of the important aspects of public welfare.

Of special importance in the state's concern for the recreation of its citizens are provisions for participation in physical recreation and sports. Before 1900 only one state had a state park system,[8] whereas at mid-century the majority of state governments had set aside lands for recreational use totaling some thirty-five hundred parks with an expanse of over eight million acres.[9] While the activities within state parks include many not directly associated with physical recreation, provision is made in most for sports and games, camping and hiking, and in areas where water facilities are available there are provisions for swimming, fishing, boating, and sailing. Winter sports available in many states include skiing, tobogganing, and ice-skating.[10]

STATE LEGISLATION RELATING TO RECREATION AND SPORTS

The state's concern with the provision for and regulation of recreation in various forms might seem to be very minor. One thinks immediately of laws relating to fishing and hunting licenses, of the provision in state parks for the leisure-time use of citizens, of enabling legislation permitting a municipality to conduct a recreation program with tax funds, and of certain state agencies which have a role in the development of recreation services.[11] However, the ramifications of the state's concern in sports and physical recreation extend far beyond these aspects, important as they are.

Cultural pressures of one sort or another which have been exerted in all the states usually result in state legislation which in the long run will benefit the general welfare of the people. What is commonly called *service legislation* gives recreational functions to such agencies as the state department of education, the state park department (or the department of natural resources), the fish and game commission, and the youth authority or commission. For example, in most states, the state department of education is authorized by law to (1) exercise general supervision over courses in physical instruction and athletic activities of the public schools; (2) promote and develop athletic activities; (3) encourage the use of school facilities for community recreation; (4) establish standards for recreation and play area space; and (5) co-operate with youth-serving groups in their programs, including physical recreation. Though state recreation commissions are to be found in only three states (North Carolina, Vermont, and California), there appears to be something of a trend toward establishing by law a state recreation authority whose major function shall be the promotion and development of community recreation.

Special project legislation is sometimes required for the construction of certain kinds of recreational facilities, as, for example, in California, by the special legislation creating Mount San Jacinto Winter Park (1947) to be developed for winter sports and summer recreation areas.[12] Examples of *regulatory legislation* include the maintenance of standards relating to public health and safety, the regulation of commercial amusements, and the supervision of professional boxing and wrestling matches by state athletic commissions.

FEDERAL AND STATE LEGISLATION REGARDING
PROFESSIONAL (SPECTATOR) SPORTS

The two spectator sports which have drawn the greatest "fire" from the people of America have been boxing and baseball. For one reason or another, when sports such as these become embroiled in either federal or state legislation, it is clear that their regulation carries great cultural implications.

Boxing, as a professional sport, had been merely tolerated before World War I. At the turn of the century "prize fighting" was legalized in only five states—New York, California, Louisiana, Nevada, and Florida—but in 1900 the old "Horton Boxing Law" in New York State was outlawed. Only four-round bouts were legal in California until the early twenties.

It could well be that the training every serviceman received in boxing during World War I and the tremendous spectator interest which was aroused both in this country and in France had much to do with its tremendous following in the twenties. So widespread did boxing become in this decade and thereafter that by 1943 it was legalized in forty-two states and regulated and controlled by appointed commissions.[13]

Since the early years of the century, baseball has been close to the hearts of the American public. The formation of the American League in 1901, which was set up to compete against the well-established National League, brought into being the World Series, probably considered by all the premier sports event of America.

One of the first, if not the first, legal actions involving baseball was instituted in 1915 by the newly formed third "major" league, the Federal League. It asked the court to declare illegal the operating system known as organized baseball, to dismiss all suits brought against players who had "jumped" contracts to join the Federal League, and to restrain major-league clubs from instituting any more such suits. The case was set for Chicago in the United States District Court for Northern Illinois, January 5, 1915, and brought into great baseball prominence Judge Kenesaw M. Landis, who was later to become baseball's high commissioner. The case dragged on for almost a year without a decision and was finally dropped by the Federal League in a peace settlement effected with the other two leagues. There is no question but what Judge Landis used stalling tactics, but, in doing so, he probably saved organized baseball from complete chaos.[14]

The sequel to this case came in 1922, when a decision was handed down by the United States Supreme Court. The Baltimore Club of the Federal League had brought action against organized baseball under the Sherman antitrust laws for $900,-000 and court costs. The case had dragged on for nearly seven years from lower to higher courts with what appeared as favorable consideration for the Baltimore Club. "The Supreme Court ruled that baseball was a 'peculiar business,' that the games were played by personal effort, and therefore nothing is produced, that baseball is not a commodity, and therefore trust laws were not violated."[15]

The famous "Black" Sox scandal involving eight of the Chicago White Sox players in 1919 broke during the final weeks of the hot 1920 American League pennant race. The Chicago grand jury brought in indictments against these eight players and several gamblers for conspiring to throw the 1919 World Series between the Cincinnati Reds and the Chicago White Sox. Although all were acquitted in the grand-jury investigation and a subsequent trial, the players involved were banished from organized baseball forever.

The Chicago grand jury in its final report brought out the cultural implications of baseball.

The jury is impressed with the fact that baseball is an index to our national genius and character. The American principle of merit and fair play must prevail, and it is all important that the game be clean, from the most humble player to the highest dignitary. Baseball enthusiasm and its hold upon the public interest must ultimately stand or fall upon this count.

Baseball is more than a national game; it is an American institution, having its place prominently and significantly in the life of the people.[16]

When Justice McDonald said that the Chicago grand jury had purged baseball for a generation to come, his words were merely a hope.

In 1924, when Judge Landis thought he had gambling stopped, another scandal reared its ugly head involving Dolan and O'Connell of the New York Giants, who offered a bribe to one of the Philadelphia players. The testimony in this particular investigation, amounting to twenty thousand words, was printed in several of the New York newspapers and caused considerable furor throughout the country as well as in the two major leagues, particularly the American League.[17] Both Dolan and O'Connell were barred from organized baseball, but the gambling interests still operated in certain sections of the country.

The legal actions of the early nineteen-fifties in relation to "fixes" in college basketball served to indicate the recurrent and serious nature of the problem of gambling—in sports, as well as in other aspects of human life. Since sports do not exist in a vacuum but are closely related to all elements of the culture, they are exposed to the same sorts of temptations and pressures which are present in our business, social, and political life. Constant vigilance is the price of preserving democracy. It is also an essential in maintaining high standards in the conduct of sports.

STATE RECREATION AND ITS CULTURAL IMPLICATIONS

1. The provision for recreation as a service comparable with education and health, largely because of the demands of citizens, coupled with the changes in the pattern of living dur-

ing the last fifty years, has become a responsibility of government at the state level as well as at the federal and local levels.

Public interest in state-supported recreation resources came into being shortly after the turn of the century. Millions of people, needing relief from effects of urbanized living, brought a demand for areas reasonably close at hand where they could enjoy the freedom afforded by the out of doors. Gradually, state governments accepted the will of the people by establishing state parks, forest areas, fish and game preserves, and other areas which could be used for recreational purposes. The coming of the automobile greatly accentuated demands of this sort and taxed the nation with provisions for highways.

A reasonable proportion of this life in the open resulted in physical recreation of one sort or another. Hunting, fishing, hiking, camping, boating, and swimming were popular because of the provisions made available, and today winter sports have been added to these provisions. Out-of-door life is conducive to an interest in many types of vigorous activities which hold an appeal for people when they must return to the cities. Because of our modern means of transportation, week-end life in the open is increasingly sought, and year-round vigorous recreation becomes a habit rather than a passing fancy during vacation periods.

2. States have had to be concerned with recreational resources involving the misuse of waterways within the state boundaries. Streams and rivers, lakes, bays, and sounds, often become undesirable for recreational purposes because of polution. The refuse of industries and the sewage from cities polute these waterways and make them undesirable for recreational use in such activities as swimming and fishing. Unhealthful conditions of this sort may affect areas far removed from the source and make it necessary for the state to provide for controls protecting the interests of all citizens.

3. Recreational developments in one area, established by a local authority, often attract people from other areas and

crowd out local citizens who have been taxed for these developments. This happens within a state and sometimes between states where the recreational development is near the state line. There is need then for larger units of government (states) to pass legislation which will help to correct this difficulty or to make special provision for broadening recreational opportunities in a given area. Such action by a state may apply to the conduct of municipal recreation in a state park located near a city and should include a provision for the use of such state area for a definite period of time to protect the investment of the municipality.

4. For the welfare of all and in order to lend uniformity on a state-wide basis, regulatory controls must be set up which affect alike the people of all communities. These controls refer largely to health and safety regulations in the use of specific facilities for physical recreation. They apply to private and voluntary agencies as well as to public agencies.

5. The interrelationships of state control in education with the promotion of physical recreation in various forms has many ramifications. First, in all probability, should be cited the state laws requiring the teaching of physical education in all public schools. Forty-one states, covering 94.6 per cent of the population, have laws or state regulations requiring the teaching of physical education in the public schools.[18] The exposure of millions of children to the acquisition of physical skills is unquestionably one of the greatest services rendered to physical recreation by the state. Many states, through employed personnel in state departments of education, offer consultation service to communities in matters pertaining to school physical education programs, athletics, and recreation. State enabling legislation permits and encourages the use of school buildings for all types of community recreation including physical recreation and use of school facilities for out-of-school athletic teams. In general, the schools, aided by state

authority, have assumed a measure of responsibility for community recreation as part of the total process of education.

6. State recreational facilities attract out-of-state visitors. The multiplicity of advertisements appearing in magazines regarding the recreational potentialities of numerous states indicates that physical recreation is of prime importance in attracting the vacationing public. In some states the tourist trade is considered one of the leading industries, and, while it is true that private agencies benefit greatly from such trade, it is also true that the state in general reaps indirect benefits. Thus, the provisions made by the state for the recreational welfare of its citizens can be and are directly related in a sense to industrial expansion. State and local chambers of commerce are increasingly aware of the wealth which is brought to a state having vast recreational resources.

7. The need for co-ordination of state responsibility in recreation has led a number of authorities to believe that there should be established in all states a recreation commission similar to those which have been set up in North Carolina, Vermont, and California. There is evidence that many states have given more than lip service to recreation as a state function.[19] Authority given to existing state agencies in a number of phases of recreation and the formation of state interagency committees for recreation are significant steps in the direction of recreation by a single state authority. In the event that this happens, recreation as one of the aspects of our culture will be put on the same basis as public education, public health, and public welfare. In any case the constructive use of an ever increasing leisure has advanced to a position of prominence as a state concern.

The Role of the Municipalities

In the early years of the century two influences were prominent in the cities which contributed to the growth of sports in America. One involved civic pride and a drive for city beautification. The other was a concern on the part of philanthropic individuals and organizations for the welfare of underprivileged youth—keeping children off the streets and away from physical and moral dangers.

THE DRIVE FOR CITY BEAUTIFICATION

Crowded living conditions in the larger cities, the development of slum areas, the lack of consideration by public officials—all these and more were enough to arouse a public opinion favorable to the beautification of cities. The people wanted some place where they could get out in the open, where there were trees, flowers, green grass, and shade, where there was a place for the children to play aside from the streets and dirty vacant lots—in short, where there were provisions for the enjoyment of living. They wanted to recapture, if possible, the conditions of rural life which had disappeared for a large percentage of Americans since the advent of the city. The recreational needs of city dwellers became an important item in their lives, and stress by civic leaders was placed on the benefits to be gained in increased health by seeking exercise in the out of doors and by participating in pleasant outdoor sports.

During the first decade of the twentieth century there was a rapid extension of parks in and around the big cities.[20] Boston, New York, Chicago, Cleveland, Washington, St. Louis, Philadelphia, Seattle—these serve as examples of a park movement which swept the country. In the smaller cities and towns civic organizations of various sorts and notably the women's clubs worked unceasingly on campaigns for beautification, for children's playgrounds, for parks where families could go on holidays and Sundays and play together. "Keep-off-the-grass" signs soon became intolerable, and, though many park officials were displeased, public sentiment became too strong to buck.[21]

As early as the end of the first decade of the century, landscape architects exerted their influence on groups interested in city planning and pointed out the necessity of providing recreation facilities in any program of city planning.[22] They urged specific sizes for playgrounds and parks and pointed out the need for athletic facilities in every city.[23] The vacant lots, they said, were gone from the scene, and the average citizen could not afford to belong to a country club.

The small town is not forgotten.—While the spectacular development of parks and playgrounds in the large cities of the country, involving millions of dollars, was featured in the periodical press, a considerable amount of space was given to needs and developments in small cities, towns, and villages. These smaller communities were urged to act on the park and playground problem while the city was still small, and it was pointed out that the "plenty-of-vacant-property" argument was not valid in any long-range plan. Here again landscape architects urged small cities to set aside areas indispensable for public recreation.[24] Nolen, for example, pointed out that

one of the chief fallacies concerning play and recreation is that it is only necessary for the public to provide for it in slum districts or, at least, in closely built-up sections where there are no private yards. . . . Country children often know less of good games than city children, and they often show less of the play impulse. They sometimes actually do not have so much opportunity to swim and skate and enjoy conveniently other outdoor sports.[25]

He then goes on to show what should be done in the recreational development of Wayland, Massachusetts. First of all, it should accept the Park Act in order to make provision for young and old. In addition to fields for games, certain river, brook, pond, and hill areas should be acquired by the city and developed for maximum use. It is especially fortunate, says Nolen, that "the town may still secure open land for play in direct connection with the public schools."[26]

THE PROBLEM OF JUVENILE DELINQUENCY

The second early important urban influence on sports in America came as a result of the provision of playgrounds by philanthropically minded individuals and organizations. As a result of these ventures, particularly during and after World War I, playgrounds were "sold" to the public on a basis of reducing juvenile delinquency, and a large number of recreation leaders and municipal officials attested to the fact that the provision of playgrounds had greatly reduced the incidence of delinquency. One writer even stated that five years of supervised amusement had reduced juvenile crime in Binghampton, New York, by 96 per cent.[27] The assumption was that, if children are kept busy in a supervised recreation program, they will have little or no time to get into trouble, that idleness and unwholesome surroundings form the basis for misconduct, with the presence of undesirable commercial amusement as a contributing factor.

Truxal, in an attempt to evaluate recreation in relation to juvenile delinquency, made a study of Manhattan play areas.[28] He concluded that a certain amount of association exists between the provision of recreation areas and the absence of juvenile delinquency but that, on the basis of the evidence, no easy generalization can be made which assigns the presence of recreation spaces as the *controlling* factor in the prevention of delinquency.

In connection with the problem of supervised recreation as an aid in the prevention of juvenile delinquency, attention should be called to the comprehensive study made in Chicago which convinced the Chicago Recreation Commission that more supervised recreation was necessary in the high-delinquency areas, with special consideration for outdoor recreation.[29]

It has aptly been pointed out by a noted authority that delinquency is not confined to the city. The country child's need for activity is just as great as that of the city child, and, if given no wholesome outlet, he may well find release in undesirable ways.

Unwholesome community influences and lack of constructive recreational facilities are no less potent destructive forces in rural communities than in cities. The bleak homes of the tenant farmer and the mill hand, the monotony of life in some small towns with nothing to do for the young folks in their spare time but "just sit" —such situations are seed-beds for undesirable behavior.[30]

INFLUENCE OF THE PLAYGROUND ASSOCIATION

The influence on municipal recreation of the Playground Association of America[31] (established in 1906) was felt in all sections of the country. It solicited and secured the hearty support of professional and lay personnel everywhere. The fact that Theodore Roosevelt was honorary president of the association from the time of its organization until his death in 1919 added a great deal of weight to the attempts of its leaders to secure co-operation in many high places relative to financial support for the ideals associated with the worthy use of leisure time. Gradually, municipal enthusiasm for supervised recreation programs was built up until in 1914 over 350 cities in the United States had established recreation programs. This figure mounted to 945 in 1929 and to about 1,300 cities in 1937.[32] Now approximately 2,000 cities spend annually over $100,000,000 on public recreation.

During World War I the work of this association, then called the Playground and Recreation Association of America, did much to show cities the potentialities of a recreation program. Under its leadership, the War Camp Community Service organized over six hundred communities close to military camps and instituted recreation programs with ample provision for sports and games.

CITIES EXPAND RECREATION SERVICES

During the first decade of the century the general attitude of a large percentage of the taxpayers, including city, state, and federal officials, was that the provision of facilities for play, while a proper function of charitable organizations, was

not a fitting use of public funds.³³ However, a great stimulus
was given to publicly supported recreation all over the country by Chicago's action (1903) in passing a $5,500,000 bond
issue for the establishment of additional parks and the erection
of fieldhouses in the South Park system. Of equal importance
was the creation in 1904 by Los Angeles of a board of playground commissioners.³⁴ Here was the beginning of an idea
that was later to receive the attention of hundreds of municipalities, namely, the creation of a new department to which
was assigned this important function of government rather
than forcing the work on some existing department as a side
issue where it might be neglected. Almost immediately, the
Los Angeles commission gave its attention to the provision
for special recreation facilities for the working young men
and women and the adults, and a recreation center was erected,
thus indicating the demand from a sizable group, other than
one of school age.

The provision for special recreation facilities grows.—An interesting development stressed in the second decade of the
century was the provision for special recreation facilities.
Swimming pools headed the list of these facilities. Among
the municipal baths or natatoriums opened from 1900 to 1904
were those in Syracuse, Kansas City (Mo.), Albany (N.Y.),
Newark, Chicago, Milwaukee, Pittsburgh, and Boston.³⁵ After
1910 most of the city recreation developments included swimming pools, some rather ingeniously devised and financed.
The pool at McKeesport, Pennsylvania, for example, was
conceived as a part of the city water purification and softening
plant and was operated in connection with the plant. From all
accounts it changed a dumping ground of a soft-coal mining
community into a beautiful area. As in so many other cases
of large pools (150×240 feet), it was used as a skating rink
during the winter months.³⁶ The operation and maintenance
of swimming pools were discussed in some detail,³⁷ and even
night lighting was given consideration.³⁸

Provision for skating also came in for a good deal of consideration. In Pennsylvania, Reading's open-air municipal skating rink used for roller-skating in the summer was supposed to have been the first of its kind.[39] Minneapolis rather boasted of maintaining free skating rinks in most of the parks;[40] Chicago could accommodate twenty thousand at one time on a pond in Lincoln Park;[41] and the supervisor of recreation in Portland, Maine, reported on the flooding of certain streets by the fire department to be used for skating and coasting.[42]

The development of water-front areas and beaches was also given consideration in the whole matter of city planning, and provisions were made for canoeing and sailing as well as swimming.[43] At Rye, New York, a farm of thirty-seven acres was purchased by the city to save the Long Island beach for its citizens.[44]

Cities pointed with pride to their accomplishments in the establishment of parks, playgrounds, municipal golf courses, swimming pools, bathing beaches, water-front areas, and later to the establishment of war memorials, which almost always provided facilities for vigorous recreation. During the first fifteen years of the century (certainly not more than twenty), municipalities throughout the nation were thoroughly convinced of their duty in providing sports facilities for adults as well as children, and the developments which have taken place in the past thirty to thirty-five years offer the best proof of what American citizens desire.

EXPANSION IN THE TWENTIES

The decade of the nineteen-twenties was one of great expansion in athletics on publicly owned areas. Not only was there a tremendous increase in the acquisition of park areas by cities but city officials discarded the idea that parks were places for the "quiet enjoyment of well landscaped, wooded areas" and emphasized the fact that parks should be used by the people as playgrounds for active games and sports.[45] With the growing demand for outdoor recreation came the provision by municipalities for many types of athletic facilities including baseball diamonds and football fields, tennis courts, soccer fields, and golf courses.

Municipal golf and winter sports.—In the municipal recreation programs during the past half-century there has been a very significant growth in the provision for golf and winter sports.

Steiner reported that in 1910 there were only twenty-four public golf courses in operation.[46] This figure is corroborated by the statement of a Chicago golf architect in 1916 that golf courses in public parks were to be found in considerably over 25 cities in the United States.[47] In 1923, 89 cities reported municipal courses;[48] in 1928, 185 cities, some with more than one. The number of municipal courses rapidly increased through the nineteen-thirties, the highest number being reported in 1944 as 409. It should be remembered that these are reported figures and may fall considerably short of the actual number. Public demand for a game within the pocketbook range of the average citizen has certainly been reflected in municipal provision for golf. People of both sexes, young and old, have thus been given an opportunity to learn and play a game which has a peculiar fascination for millions.

In the early years of its existence municipal recreation provided only for a summer program. As public pressures commenced to be given consideration, there was gradual acceptance of the idea that provision must be made for the sports life of youth and adults in the winter as well as in the summer months. In a period of twenty-five years, from 1921 to 1946, the cities reporting a year-round program rose from 144 to 568.[49] Of the demands for activity in the winter months, one of the most insistent was for winter sports—skating, tobogganing, and skiing. In 1922, skating areas were provided in 143 cities; in 1930, in 291 cities; and, in 1939, there were 2,968 skating areas in 427 cities, with a participation figure of sixteen and a half million on slightly more than half of the number of areas. In planning for winter sports, cities have given serious consideration to the multiple use of facilities. Tennis courts, for example, if provided with a six-inch curb, may be flooded and put into use as ice-skating areas. Wading pools also can easily be made suitable for ice-skating areas, and many natural depressions in parks can be flooded for use in winter months.

Nature, hiking and bridle trails may become trails for skiers in the winter. Hillside areas in parks and golf courses may be adapted for coasting and simple skiing without interfering with their major use. . . . Even the natural bowl of an outdoor theatre has been used as a coasting area. In one city a band shell serves as the take-off point for a small children's slide.[50]

Even ski-jumping has been relatively successful in a number of cities. In 1939, 64 cities reported 116 ski jumps. In the same year the National Recreation Association reported 301 toboggan slides in 114 cities, with a participation figure of over seventy thousand on only 120 of those slides.

The co-operation given by municipal recreation agencies to industrial organizations sponsoring sports teams of various kinds has been good for both groups and has tended to swell attendance figures reported by cities and to make the twenty million who now participate in industrial recreation of all kinds conscious of the provisions made by cities in behalf of the sports life of the communities. Many of the large industrial plants have sports facilities of their own, but in the main industries use facilities which exist in the community.

During the early depression years and before the federal government began to subsidize municipal recreation there was a sizable drop in public support. In 1930, for example, 917 cities reported an expenditure for recreation of 38.5 million dollars, while, in 1932, 914 cities spent slightly less than 28.1 million. The high point of government subsidy came in 1938, when, of a total of more than 60 million dollars, over 31 million came from federal funds. It is impossible to indicate the percentage of funds chargeable to a sports program. Some experts believe that vigorous activity constitutes 60 per cent of municipal recreation, and, if so, the amount spent for sports by local government out of what was appropriated in 1948, namely, 93.8 million dollars, represents a sizable sum.

CURRENT DEVELOPMENTS

The contribution which a public recreation department can make to the sports program of America is well summed up in the following statement:

It serves all the people in the community, young and old, male and female, regardless of skill, nationality or any other factor. Its sports program is based upon the recreation interests of the people, includes indoor and outdoor activities, and is carried on throughout the year. In its hands, in a very real sense, lies the opportunity to insure to every member of the community the means of participating in a varied sports program and the leadership which such a program demands.[51]

In recent years a number of community studies have been made in an attempt to indicate the sports interests of adults as well as children. The National Recreation Association, in a study of the leisure-time activities of five thousand adults in twenty-nine states, found that the five most desired activities were tennis, swimming, boating, golf, and camping. In another study conducted by the National Park Service, swimming was the most popular, followed by fishing and boating. In a Los Angeles study involving seventeen thousand junior and senior high school boys and girls it was found that

sports held an overwhelming place among the activities engaged in and preferred. Seventeen out of 23 leading boys activities were of this type, and 12 out of the 20 leading girls activities. . . . Sports desired by the boys in rank order were swimming, archery, boxing, tennis and wrestling; by the girls, swimming, tennis, archery, hockey, and paddle tennis.[52]

A number of significant sports trends in publicly supported recreation have been noted by various observers in recent years.

1. *An increasing emphasis upon sports for all the people rather than the development of a few champions.*—Such a trend is not peculiar to community recreation, since the schools have vigorously supported intramural sports for a long period of years. Trained leadership in community recreation has increased the opportunity for instruction in sports skills on the playgrounds, thus adding to the satisfaction gained from participation.[53]

2. *The promotion of co-recreation sport activities.*—Particularly during the period of the depression and the World War II years has there been vigorous promotion of sports in which both sexes can engage together. These would include skiing, bowling, badminton, figure skating, table tennis, and paddle tennis and were listed by one observer as among the ten fastest-growing sports in the summer of 1940.[54] Such a growth is indicative of an increased emphasis on activities which can be continued over a long period of years.

3. *The rapid expansion of winter sports.*—A considerable amount of attention has been given to winter sports by community agencies, owing in part to the expansion by private agencies of suitable areas for their conduct and the fact that more municipal recreation agencies have placed their program on a year-round basis.

4. *Night illumination of sport areas.*—This is becoming the custom rather than the exception and may stem in part from the necessity of making provision for the conduct of wholesome sport at night and thus reducing delinquency. Then, too, the demands of employed young men and women for participation in sport have had a growing influence on these provisions.

5. *A more widespread participation of girls and women in sport activities.*—In this connection it should be pointed out

that there is a considerable difference of opinion regarding the standards set up for school sports and those in use by recreation departments.

6. *Recreation for oldsters.*—One of the comparatively recent trends initiated by municipal recreation agencies has been that of recreation for oldsters. This has a very definite cultural connection because of the fact that the proportion of people in the United States over sixty-five has about doubled in the last fifty years and that the absolute numbers have almost quadrupled. There are now more than eleven million people in this country over sixty-five years of age.[55]

One of the ways of meeting the total problem of the aging is through the provision of facilities for recreation. It is surprising to find the large number of cities in which such provision exists. Among the most popular physical activities are dancing, lawn bowling, horseshoes, and shuffleboard.[56] Cities report that horseshoe and roque courts are standard equipment on playgrounds, that oldsters take part in hiking associations, that fly-casting clubs are popular, and that volleyball is played by many older people.[57] One interesting experiment in modified softball has been conducted at Columbia, Missouri, in which a total of two hundred and fifty games were played under the lights by twenty-two organizations composed of middle-aged men from fraternal orders and business establishments.[58]

Softball in St. Petersburg, Florida, is one of the activities of the Three-Quarter Century Club which affords a great deal of fun to both players and spectators. A story is told of an unforgettable incident in one of these games. The young gentleman in question was eighty-four:

He just barely missed scoring a home run because he stopped half-way between third base and home plate to pick up something. When the umpire jumped on him for stopping, the player yelled, "Well, damn it, I dropped my teeth!" Imagine the kick that 5000 roaring fans got out of that classic! It even made the newsreels.[59]

A considerable number of cities all over the country have oldster clubs of one sort or another, and many are sponsored by municipal recreation departments.[60] It is apparent that physical activities (sports, if you please) are not neglected in the over-all program of recreation for older people. Much of the club organization is confined to cities, but one writer indicates that some thought has been given to recreation for older people in rural communities. Among other things, she points out that "for men, fishing and hunting knows no age limit."[61]

13. *Sports and Physical Recreation on War Front and Home Front*

The Changing Attitude and Procedures of the Armed Services with Regard to Sports and Physical Recreation for Their Personnel

IN TWENTIETH-CENTURY AMERICA THE ARMED SERVICES HAVE played a major role in the sports life of the nation. With the exception of the public school and the public playground, the various branches of the service have provided one of the greatest *single* means through which a maximum number of individuals have been exposed to active participation in sports programs. The extent of spectator participation has also been a significant factor.

A comparison of the methods and personnel employed in the first World War with those in the second World War in making provision for sports and physical activities as a part of the training and the recreational life of service men will clearly indicate the transition in attitude and in degree of importance attached to such efforts. Josephus Daniels, then Secretary of the Navy, speaking in 1919, paid one of the most sincere (and prophetic) tributes to the role of sports in war that appears in the record. He began by saying that the war had taught the lesson that any authority, taking charge of a man's whole life, from sunrise to sunrise, must provide all the essential requirements that go into that life—food, sleep, work, education, and play.

There has never been in all history a more convincing demonstration of the value of play and recreation than has been achieved

by the American army at home and abroad. The demonstration
has been so clear and the influence so striking that there can never
again be organized a military program in America or anywhere else
in the modern world which will not contain provision for supervised, organized recreation, entertainment and play.[1]

Another result of experiences in World War I was a major
reorganization in the curriculum at West Point. Douglas Mac-
Arthur's tenure of service as superintendent was marked by
an expanded athletic program and the recommendation that
the director of athletics be appointed in the same manner and
with the same standing on the academic board as other professors. Following World War I sport and physical training
became as much a part of the cadet's training as a study of
physics, chemistry, or a foreign language.[2]

PRELUDE TO WORLD WAR I

As late as the eighteenth century an army could be described
as representing a nation in almost the same terms that a football team represents a college. The civilian population supplied
the funds, prayed for victory, and cheered from the sidelines,
but it took little active part in the game. War in the modern
world means not simply an army to be mobilized but a nation:
mine and factory, farm and home, school and laboratory, all
become essential parts of a single machine.[3] August, 1914,
the year the great powers of Europe began their general war,
marked the end of an era in human affairs. The prelude to
America's entry into international affairs as a world power,
economically and militarily, was being played—but so softly
few could hear. This, the first World War, was to bring to
an end war as an activity for hired mercenaries or professional
soldiers or as an exercise for the young and adventurous few.
It was to introduce war as a desperate and horribly destructive
test of the whole fabric of civilization.

It is not strange that the declaration of war in April, 1917,
found the United States Army without an organized or adequately manned plan of physical training and recreation. The

army of the first decade of the century was an organization of 4,388 officers and 70,250 enlisted men, "slowly awakening after a slumber of nearly fifty years which had been only briefly disturbed by the absurd confusion of the Spanish war."[4] Approximately one-fourth of this army was on duty in outlying possessions, the Philippines, Hawaii, Alaska, the Canal Zone, and Puerto Rico. The National Guard, which represented a force of some 125,000, was still forty-eight little armies under the jurisdiction of forty-eight states and with as many standards of training and equipment.

Between 1912 and 1917 several things happened which pointed up the necessity for reorganization. The problem of maintaining neutrality with Germany was constant and difficult in the face of divided cultural pressures for "peace," on the one hand, and "preparedness," on the other. The task of patroling the Mexican border had proved too much for the small regular army, and the entire active militia of the states (the National Guard) was mobilized and three-fourths of it sent to the Rio Grande. Eventually there were a hundred thousand men in service in Mexico or on the border.

The sending of an expedition to Mexico and the massing of large numbers of troops on the Mexican border were tests of the preparedness, or lack of it, in the American army. There was another outcome of this expedition which is of particular interest in the story of the changing attitude and procedures with relation to the sports life and recreational needs of armed service personnel. In the summer of 1916, Raymond A. Fosdick, a civilian, was sent by the War Department to investigate conditions in communities where American troops were stationed, with particular reference to their leisure-time pursuits. The investigation disclosed that thousands of troops had absolutely nothing to amuse them except a few saloons and a very well-run red-light district.[5] Thus an examination of the leisure-time problems of these soldiers was to aid in the solution of similar and greatly enlarged problems of this nature in World War I.

HOW THE JOB WAS DONE IN WORLD WAR I

The magnitude of the task of supplying physical training, sports, and recreational activities to the armed services, with the attendant problems of equipment, facilities, funds, and personnel, can only be understood in relation to the magnitude of the total problem of mobilization. War was declared on April 6, 1917, and within eighteen months two million American soldiers were in France, two million more were in camps and cantonments in America, and twenty-four million men had been registered and classified under Selective Service.[8]

The War Department set up the Commission on Training Camp Activities, known as the Fosdick Commission, which authorized the YMCA, the YWCA, the Knights of Columbus, the Jewish Welfare Board, the Salvation Army, the American Library Association, and the War Camp Service to provide recreational, educational, and religious activities for all servicemen. Within three months the Navy Department had taken similar action, and Fosdick was selected to head both commissions. Out of the organizational work of these commissions came the division of physical training and athletics for both army and navy, the former headed by Dr. Joseph E. Raycroft of Princeton University and the latter by the famous athletic coach, Walter Camp.

Programs of competitive athletics in training camps.—The zeal with which these two men attacked their responsibilities soon resulted in mass programs of competitive athletics under the direction of civilian camp athletic directors aided by divisional military athletic officers. The YMCA had placed a physical director in each camp, and, in spite of some confusion and rivalry, a great deal of constructive progress was made. Each of the "Y" directors was supplied with initial equipment costing around $200.00, and additional equipment was obtained through the co-operation of individuals connected with professional baseball and through tennis and golf associations, and there was also a "company" box of athletic equipment provided by the commission.

Military authorities gave hearty support to the mass sports program because of the increased physical efficiency shown by the troops in training and because observers testified to the importance of habitual athletic participation in preventing the development of shell shock.[7] Important for the later development of sports in the culture, it was felt that "men who are accustomed to take part in athletics will continue to do so; and thousands who have never taken part in athletics before will begin now."[8]

The YMCA, sports, and the American Expeditionary Forces. —While a large share of the responsibility for conducting the physical activities for army personnel within camps in the United States fell on the shoulders of the YMCA, practically the total responsibility for such activities in the AEF was carried by this organization. Probably no agency active in World War I was subject to more concerted and more deadly criticism than the YMCA. This criticism was not, however, with regard to their efforts in providing sports and physical recreation. The operation of the post exchange (or canteens as they were then called) was a thankless job, given to the "Y" to get it off the mind and out of the hands of the army, which needed men desperately elsewhere. In the operation of these canteens the "Y" was often violently criticized for deficiencies in supplies for which it was not responsible.[9] As to the charges of religious bigotry, sectarianism, and a tendency to overemphasize religious work, it seems inevitable that among 12,022 persons (the total the "Y" sent overseas) there should be some who were of this type, but they were weeded out when discovered.

On the positive side, the work of the YMCA physical directors in France received high praise from General Pershing and other army commanders at the various fronts. Two million, two hundred thousand dollars were spent abroad by the

YMCA for athletic equipment of all types and in amounts which run into fantastic figures with such items as boxing gloves, baseballs and bats, basketballs, volleyballs, and the like. Nor did the "Y" stop with equipment. They assisted in establishing great army playgrounds such as the one at Saint-Nazaire, where seventy-five baseball diamonds were laid out. Physical directors accompanied the men to the front lines and took athletic equipment with them, as, for example, in Belleau Wood, where basketball was played. Behind the lines in the humdrum Service of Supply, where there were four hundred thousand men, organized athletics did much to keep up morale and physical condition.[10]

The Armistice, demobilization, and the Inter-Allied Games. —The grand finale of the YMCA's athletic endeavors for the army came with the staging of the Inter-Allied Games in Paris, June 22–July 6, 1919. This was to be a love-feast, with no nation named as winner, a means of "bringing diverse peoples together in friendship upon the field of sport." There were other excellent reasons to justify the building of Pershing Stadium, on ground donated by France, with funds contributed by the YMCA and through labor furnished by the American Army. The signing of the Armistice and the cessation of hostilities plunged the army into one of the most trying periods which the AEF had to face. The battle was over, and two million men wanted to go home, *right now!* The first General Order (No. 236) issued after the Armistice, concerning what was to be done about the soldiers' newly acquired leisure, provided for eight hours' military drill a day. The roar of protest that arose was louder than the sound the big berthas had made!

General Order No. 241, dated December 29, 1918, resulted from a series of conferences between GHQ and the YMCA Department of Athletics and very cannily provided a modification of the drill order. General Pershing directed the attention of all concerned to the importance of "encouraging the development of general and competitive athletics, for the purpose of keeping up the morale, fostering and developing organization *esprit de corps*."[11] Commanding officers were ordered to excuse from all military training, in excess of four hours a day, men of their command who took part actively each day in any of the athletic sports approved by the divisional or unit athletic officers. The army realized that men could not be ordered to play, but, when presented with the opportunity as an elective alternative to drill, there was little doubt as to the outcome. This incident probably represents one of the world's outstanding examples of mass motivation!

Eighteen of the allied nations out of the twenty-nine invited joined in the Inter-Allied Games. Approximately 90,000 people attended the Dedication Day ceremonies, although 110,700 persons were transported to the area. In all probability during the course of the games a total of 800,000 persons watched fifteen hundred athletes competing in fourteen different sports.[12] Following the Armistice the overseas papers began to give more space to "baseball and boxing matches between regiments and divisions than to war reminiscences, the Peace Conference, or vocational problems facing the soldier."[13] Certainly the sports activities and enthusiasms of the army were the brighter side of the coin of war, helping to take the sting out of military training, to democratize and to humanize it.

DIFFERENCES IN ATTITUDE AND PERSONNEL
BETWEEN WORLD WARS I AND II

The Selective Service Act, passed in September, 1940, increased the strength of the armed forces from 425,000 to nearly 2,000,000 by December, 1941, when war was declared.

America was not the same nation when it faced war in 1941 as it had been in 1917. And the millions of young men who were to be inducted through selective service were almost as different as the country itself. Nowhere was the difference more obvious or more pronounced than in their recreational life. Here was the first American generation to reach maturity with a background of participation in sports on the public playgrounds, required physical education (heavily tinged with sports) in the school, and widespread familiarity with the field of sports through movies, radio, the sports page, and the periodical press. The Puritan tradition of play as "sinful" formed no part of their heritage. The memories of sandlot baseball games, of school basketball and football teams, of days at the beach or swimming pool, of pleasant evenings in the bowling alley, of interminable discussions about the relative merits of the Dodgers and the Yankees—all of these were as inextricably woven into the pattern of their life as the routine of eating and sleeping.

Of the six million servicemen who were overseas in 1944, it was reported that 33 per cent came straight from school, 20 per cent had been out of school one year or less, and 15 per cent from one to two years. The World War II army provided millions with their first real job, building not upon the basis of vocational maturity but upon "the carefree base of high school and college days."[14] It was a better educated army than that of World War I; 11 per cent college men as against 5 per cent; 25 per cent high-school graduates as against 11 per cent; 33 per cent who had not gone beyond grammar school as against 80 per cent whose education stopped in grammar school prior to 1917.

Cultural change had also effected marked differences of attitude in the armed services, where it was obvious that the thesis had been accepted that morale is a primary function of command, and the army and navy were prepared to implement their own prewar programs for the general well-being of members of the armed forces as they had not been in 1917.[15] Army Special Services and the Welfare Division of the Navy came into being, using their own trained presonnel and demonstrating through their programs full recognition of the superior value of sports and recreation over military drill in establishing and in developing morale.

ARMED SERVICE PROGRAMS IN WORLD WAR II

The War Department's basic field manual states quite bluntly that a man does not become an effective soldier simply by taking an oath and donning a uniform, that the transformation from civilian to soldier must be accomplished by training. A vital part of this training is *physical* training.

One of the best methods of motivating participation in the more formal physical training activities is to combine them with athletics. Conditioning exercises, guerrilla exercises, grass drills, log exercises, and running are activities about which soldiers are not particularly enthusiastic, but they will engage in them conscientiously and vigorously if they are followed by stimulating, competitive sports and games.[16]

The sheer numbers involved in the army of World War II made the compulsory mass sports in the training program of the first World War an impossibility. It was not a question of the merit or demerit of sports, but the very practical question of space requirements. For everyone to compete in team games such as football, baseball, or basketball was literally impossible in a camp of fifty thousand men. Aside from the equipment involved, to develop adequate play areas for such a group would involve from one to two thousand acres in each camp in addition to large indoor areas. Obviously the *army* sports program had to be put on a voluntary basis.

Programs carried on in colleges and universities, such as the Army Specialized Training Program, the Pre-Meteorology Program, the Navy V-12, and others, offered college men in uniform a sports program whenever and wherever conditions warranted. At most institutions the type and extent of the activities were dependent upon the facilities and personnel available and the desires of the commanding officer. In some institutions sports participation predominated, while in others physical fitness activities formed the major portion of the program.[17]

At the preflight schools and naval aviation bases sports flourished under what was popularly known as the Hamilton program. Here, competitive sports were considered to form the basis of a program in which "a sports for sports sake philosophy is replaced by the more utilitarian plan of using sports for what they will contribute to the war effort in general and to flying cadets in particular."[18] Such a program was possible because of relatively small numbers of men and of site selections lending themselves to areas for team-game operation. Athletic equipment was provided in quantities which would have been impossible in a program involving large masses of men. Leadership for this program (i.e., commissioned officers) involved approximately two thousand athletic coaches and physical education teachers.

World War II saw the armed services for the first time directly concerned with feminine personnel in uniform, a profound example of cultural change in the twentieth century. The distinguished record of the Women's Army Corps and the Women's Reserve of the United States Naval Reserve, better known as the Wacs and the Waves, is something of which all citizens may be proud. The physical training and sports programs of these two branches of the service were conducted by specially prepared women officers and displayed an admirably judicious combination of physical fitness activities and sports of many sorts.[19]

The Welfare Division, Bureau of Navigation, with personnel drawn largely from the field of community recreation, worked toward providing physical recreation for the navy both in continental United States and in areas outside these limits. Through the co-operation given by commanding officers, attention was directed toward providing gymnasiums, bowling alleys, outdoor areas for courts and field games, and indoor recreation areas.[20]

The President's Committee on Religion and Welfare in the Armed Forces reported under date of February 28, 1951, and recommended three phases of a free-time program: (1) indispensable, (2) essential, and (3) desirable. The attention paid to sports facilities and leadership in this report is an indication of their worth to the serviceman in his free time and represents recommendations made after careful study.[21]

There is abundant evidence of the part sports may play in the life of a serviceman in the informal conversations and undocumented letters which came to many citizens on the home front. The authors' sons have contributed a wealth of personal reminiscences as to how soldiers and sailors continue to play in spite of war; how the executive officer of a destroyer can break his leg in a friendly touch football game between officers and crew; how divisional basketball championships can be held in Germany; how dreary occupation duty can be lightened by swimming in the beautiful bay at Trieste or skiing in the adjacent Alps; and how a Korean rice paddy *can* be used—but, wet or dry, it undoubtedly makes the toughest, roughest baseball diamond anyone ever imagined.

War Brings Change and Development on the Home Front

It is easy to look back from the vantage point of mid-century and to be appalled at the lack of organization, the fumbling, and the mistakes that characterized the first year of America's entry into World War I. It is not always remembered that, contrary to the circumstance as it was in 1941, the country had not passed through a depression in which the total manpower and resources of the nation had been examined and where the federal government had ceased to be an outfit in Washington and had become an intimate and daily part of the life of most citizens. By contrast with the situation of some twenty years later the federal government was woefully ignorant of the recreational potential, needs, or assets of the nation and its citizens. In view of these circumstances, an eminently sensible action was taken; the job of mobilizing for recreation on a national scale was turned over to the organization best fitted for the task.

WAR CAMP COMMUNITY SERVICE, WORLD WAR I

The Playground and Recreation Association of America, with a background of experience dating from 1906, was asked to assume the leadership in the War Camp Community Service. At this organization's Recreation Congress, which had been held the previous year (1916), questions of preparedness for war were very much in the air. Secretary of War Newton D. Baker spoke to those attending and made a plea for the organization of leisure through recreational activities "which develop health, vigor, team play and good citizenship."[22] The national interest aroused in this congress was evidenced by letters received from ten state governors, a congressman, and a senator. Advocates and opponents of universal military training met and discussed their varying points of view, and it appeared to be the consensus that the essentials of military training are "best developed, not by gun drill, but by games, athletics, and physical education."[23]

It was not the purpose of the WCCS to go into any community and take over the recreation program. Its personnel was to supply the expert knowledge, the techniques of organization, and the enthusiasm which would unite the forces and co-ordinate the efforts of each community to meet its own particular problems. Perhaps one of the greatest effects of this program on the home front was the awareness it brought and the stimulation it provided with regard to the possibilities inherent in the use of sports in such an undertaking and in the fact that community leaders in at least two hundred and seventy communities had to familiarize themselves with sports activities and facilities.[24] Many thousands of women were active in WCCS organizations, and the knowledge about sports which they acquired as a result of their work created an interest which was to become important to the growth of sports following the war. Short as was the actual war period, the WCCS, with a staff of some twenty-seven hundred leaders, helped organize recreation accommodations in more than six hundred communities located near military posts and in fifty industrial districts.

A nation-wide "Patriotic Play Week" was held during the first part of September, 1918, based on the popular slogan, "Happy play for children keeps up the morale of the Army and of America." This was a joint enterprise of the Children's Bureau of the United States Department of Labor and of the Women's Committee, Council of National Defense, with the hearty co-operation of the Playground and Recreation Association. Eleven million women were asked to organize ten thousand communities.[25]

Juvenile delinquency was estimated to have increased between 30 and 60 per cent during World War I, and civic groups intensified their efforts to provide facilities and leadership for sports as a counteracting force. Judges in juvenile courts in various parts of the country testified to the importance of playground facilities and leadership in reducing the number of delinquency cases in courts. "Give a boy a chance at football, baseball or basketball; give him an opportunity to perform difficult and dangerous feats on a horizontal bar, on the flying rings, or from a diving board, and the policeman will need a gymnasium himself to keep his weight down."[26]

Although some advances had been made in providing recreation for industrial workers before the immediate World War I years, the imminence of war spurred employers and employees alike to a more serious consideration of the situation. Provisions made by certain of the large corporations, United States Steel and Goodyear Tire and Rubber, were followed by others. Industrial athletic leagues were organized and maintained, and the sports program was built on the premise that personnel would be healthier in mind and body as a result of participation either actively or vicariously and that the sports program developed a type of morale of great importance in industrial team play.[27]

THE MAJOR CULTURAL EFFECTS EXTEND
INTO THE NEXT DECADE

Actually the major problems, economic and psychological, were to be solved in the postwar, not during the period of this war that had started and terminated so abruptly. The surrender of Germany and her allies left a million and a quarter men who had had a taste of trench warfare, but it left nearly three million who had been steeled for a long hard struggle and who were to have no battle experience. The government was left with uncompleted contracts, huge factories and power plants—designed for war purposes—were half-completed, "and a nation which, having just passed through all the stages from apathy to profoundest enthusiasm, had no appropriate outlet for its emotions."[28] In the decade that followed the end of the war many millions of Americans found a partial outlet in sports. Professional sports, spectator sports of all kinds, had been drastically curtailed during the war, but its end found not only the returning soldiers but the whole nation eager to play.

The most notable theme running through the sports pages of papers such as the *New York Times* and the *San Francisco Chronicle* in the years following the first World War was the remarkable comeback sports made.[29] Cultural change as a result of war was forcibly demonstrated in several instances. The prestige of professional baseball had been enhanced by the splendid war record of many volunteers from its ranks, and, with the signing of the Armistice, everyone seemed eager to get baseball players out of the army in time for spring training. The War Department, while it did not make a policy of releasing baseball players ahead of other servicemen, did help locate players, and, since they had their old jobs waiting for them, commanding officers strove to effect a discharge where military efficiency would not be injured by such action.[30] The battle for Sunday baseball was also fought and won in the year 1919, in spite of organized and articulate opposition from opponents who sincerely believed it meant a desecration of the Sabbath.[31]

The Sunday baseball controversy was only a skirmish compared to the fight against the rising popularity of boxing. The criticism of the churches was met by a rebuke from the army, navy, and civilian board of boxing:

The government made boxing an integral part of the training of soldiers for war, which resulted in a great revival of the sport. . . . If you will pardon us for saying so your opposition is half a century behind the times. We consider those who are opposing this match are incurring grave responsibility, as such opposition can only react to the detriment of religion in the minds of millions of men who can see no harm in the exponents of the highest skill in a given sport, engaging in a contest for supremacy.[32]

Following the war, football made a comeback that had not been anticipated by the wisest experts. Fear had been expressed that the game might be marred by rough tactics, since many players had been exposed to brutality in their war experience, but quite the contrary was true. The season was outstanding for clean play and good sportsmanship.[33] Interest in the game continued to increase and was generally attributed to the following four reasons: a better understanding of the game and its rules, more open play on the part of the teams, an increase in intersectional contests, and the building of new stadiums or the enlarging of old ones, permitting more enthusiasts to attend.[34]

COMMUNITY PROBLEMS ON THE HOME FRONT
WORLD WAR II

Fortunately, America's plans and programs for recreation were in high gear and proceeding full speed ahead long before war was actually declared. Here, as in many other areas of the culture, a business-like resourcefulness and efficiency characterized the nation's approach to the second World War.

The comprehensive preparations for defense, and later for the successful winning of the war, shifted literally millions of workers from one section of the country to the other, uprooted families, and hurried adolescents into jobs. The social and economic upheaval created not only intricate technological problems to be solved but human problems as well. For many on the home front the war meant adjustment to jammed cities, the pinch of shortages, and strain on family ties. Childcare centers had to be provided for the preschool-age children, the best of such centers being really schools for social play, for manual and bodily skills, and creative activity. Plans had to be made for the recreational life of school-age children of working mothers. Many such children were sent to school in the morning with a key tied about their neck and with instructions to come home from school and let themselves in. The teen-age problem in many localities was most serious of all. The number of high-school-age boys and girls employed in full- or part-time jobs increased from nine hundred thousand in 1940 to nearly three million in 1944. It would be impossible to say how much the growth of the teen-age canteens, or teen towns, helped to curb the delinquency rate in this group. However, the energy and enthusiasm which were diverted into the organization and operation of the some three thousand such canteens which were functioning by 1946 were obviously important factors.

Division of Recreation, Office of Community War Services, Federal Security Agency.—In February, 1941, the Division of Recreation was established in the Federal Security Agency. On the last day of June, Congress passed the Community Facilities Bill, under which federal funds could be used to build recreation centers in defense areas. Of the total appropriation of $150,000,000 to cover such essential facilities as schools, hospitals, clinics, sanitation systems, and water lines,

$17,000,000 was secured for the construction of recreation buildings.

A sound and constructive organizational policy was set up. In any given community the primary responsibility was to rest with that community. All agencies, national and local, public or private, including the National Recreation Association, the WPA, and the USO, were to render their services when called upon by the local community. The Federal Security Agency field representative acted as official government co-ordinator of all recreation services and was the channel through which supplementary aid from national and state agencies, both public and private, reached the community. By 1942 the Division of Recreation, working in co-operation with local defense recreation committees, had established a functioning community program in 541 cities across the country. Sports were always prominent in such programs. As of April, 1942, 267 federal Defense Recreation buildings were made available under the Lanham Act at a cost of more than sixteen and one-half million dollars. The figure of numbers of war-impacted communities rose rapidly, and by April, 1943, there were reported to be twenty-five hundred.

In many cities municipal recreation departments gave special attention to programs for war workers and their families in vigorous physical activities and also made provision for newcomers to have the opportunity to get better acquainted with their neighbors.[35]

The swing-shift workers were not neglected; in fact, special provisions were made for them.[36] Organized swing-shift leagues were given appropriate competition hours by local recreation departments, and provisions were made for all-shift teams on week ends. The YMCA and the YWCA were particularly responsive to the needs of war workers on all shifts, as were also commercial recreation enterprises such as bowling alleys and roller-skating rinks.[37] The swing-shift worker could swim, dance, play badminton, bowl, and roller-skate often up to 4:00 A.M. or could play golf in the early afternoon. Mixed-group activities (for both sexes) were very popular, as can be seen from the number of articles on the subject in one volume of *Recreation* magazine.[38]

Industrial recreation and World War II.—Beginning in 1939 with increased production and consequent increased employment due to Lend-Lease orders, and continuing at an ever increasing tempo through the period of America's entry and participation in the second World War, industry was called upon to perform tremendous feats of production.

With the rapid expansion of plants and personnel, the need to sustain workers' morale became urgent. As war towns boomed, living conditions grew more overcrowded, and towns themselves became alarmed at the problems such an influx of strangers might bring. A phenomenal growth in programs of industrial recreation was one solution to the problem. This proved a sufficiently potent factor in influencing worker preference from one plant to another that quasi-competitive programs were installed in the labor-short industries for attracting employees. Since factories were operating under controlled wage ceilings, attractions other than wage increases were required to get new help and keep them interested.

The program of the Lockheed Employee's Recreation Club was termed a proving ground for industrial recreation on a gigantic scale. Originating in 1934 as an outgrowth of the baseball team which played on Sunday and passed the hat to cover expenses, the club moved through various stages of expansion until in 1944 a compilation revealed the amazing total of five million man-hours of participation each year, in an average of sixty definitely organized activities.[39] These activities included eighty-two softball teams, over three-hundred bowling teams, seventy basketball teams, five thousand employee's children in various organized activities, and golfers and tennis players in the hundreds. The program was organized on a day-and-night, twenty-four-hour basis and covered the eight Lockheed plants.

SPORTS ON THE HOME FRONT, WORLD WAR II

The sports world presented a miniature of how the world conflict affected the country as a whole. There were problems of inflation, manpower shortage and transportation, black markets and wartime profiteering in athletic commodities, and a tremendous boom in those sports least handicapped by wartime conditions. The scarcity of rubber and gasoline made the school, college, and professional teams as well as the average citizen rely on public transportation. Hence sports events in areas away from cities were practically eliminated.[40] Certain national classics such as the Indianapolis Speedway Race, the Poughkeepsie Regatta, the golf championships, and such tennis fixtures as the Davis Cup, Wightman Cup, and Wimbledon were temporarily abandoned. The $100,000 Santa Anita Handicap was canceled, and by 1943 it was reported that a dozen horse-racing plants had closed.

Professional baseball, which sent more than four thousand men into the services, lived on a day-to-day basis. Night baseball was drastically curtailed by power conservation and security measures, and this fact, together with travel restrictions and the manpower shortage, caused many minor leagues to go out of existence. There were some shouts of disdain early in the war every time a ballplayer was rejected by his draft board, but, as the numbers going into service increased, the noise diminished.[41] In May, 1943, a Gallup poll showed that 59 per cent of the nation thought professional baseball should be continued.[42] A Spokane Athletic Round Table found that 99 per cent of 38,000 sailors and 93 per cent of 95,000 soldiers wanted baseball to continue. The War Department showed an approving attitude toward the game in many ways: by assigning star players in service to teams which went from camp to camp to entertain the fighting men and as morale boosters and by arranging to have World Series games broadcast to all fighting fronts. It was estimated that 75 per cent of the news cabled overseas was concerned with sports.[43]

Golfers and fishermen were hard pressed for equipment, and ammunition was not available to the sports hunter.[44] Military demands for individual and team sports equipment caused athletic supply houses to hang out the "not available" sign.[45] However, despite curtailments in sports equipment and supplies, the participation in vigorous sports actually increased.[46] This was due in part to the provision of facilities by the federal government as well as local authorities and industry. Add to this the widespread propaganda for physical fitness which included sports participation and the drastic reduction of spectator sports due to a variety of reasons, and conditions were presented which required sport lovers to use their ingenuity in developing possibilities for physical recreation.

14. *The Widening Opportunity for Sharing the Sports Life of the Nation*

AS THE PEOPLE OF A NATION BECOME INCREASINGLY SUCCESSFUL in their struggle and preoccupation with merely keeping alive, a larger proportion of their time becomes available for expenditure in other ways. In modern America the per capita amount of leisure is probably greater than in any other known industrialized society. Such surplus time is not now and very likely never will be evenly distributed over the total population. But the difference which existed at the beginning of the century between the leisure time of a very small proportion of the society and the great lack of such leisure in the very large proportion does not exist today. The millions of Americans who have elected over the years to spend increasing amounts of their time and energy participating in, watching, and reading about sports and physical recreation have placed such activities in a central position in the culture.

If the manner in which people spend their leisure time reflects the values held by the culture, and if the uses of leisure bear a direct relationship to the smoother functioning of the culture as well as to the greater efficiency of the individual, then the role of sports and physical recreations assumes a place of vital importance. Recreational activities which individuals choose in their leisure also provide important clues to the kinds of pressures and strains inherent in their "working" lives.

The most unusual and unique feature of the development of sports and physical recreation in the United States has been the trend toward inclusiveness: sports for all, rich and poor, young and old. All the various forces and institutions within the culture have aided in the process of making the opportunity for participation in sports and the outdoor physical recreations of the country available to an ever widening group of the total population. The story of this transformation both underlies and is intertwined with each of the chapters of this book.

It has been estimated that in the years between 1820 and 1930, a period of one hundred and ten years, the immigration to the United States totaled twenty-seven million persons. This influx represented a conglomerate of all sorts and conditions of people and not a transfer of an established class with any self-conscious status. While the immigrant who was without resources or special skills did not find the streets "paved with gold," he did find a pay scale, a freedom of movement, and a hope for his children that he had not experienced before. To those who arrived in the years of the twentieth century the available free schools, the lack of outward distinctions of class among those with whom he came in contact, and the increasing opportunities for recreation for himself and his children were among the important elements in the general process of assimilation.

The cost-of-living charts and statistics on the widening diffusion of income in the population as a whole cover only a part of the progress that has been made in the general standard of living and in the enormous growth of play opportunities and recreational outlets for the average citizen. A history of the United States in the twentieth century, written in terms of the average citizen's opportunities to share in the sports and recreational life of the nation, would include the story of each of the following significant landmarks: the increase in educational opportunity, which at the beginning of the century found one out of fifteen individuals of high-school age actually in high school, by 1930 found one out of every two such individuals enrolled; the efforts on the part

·of the church to enrich and enlarge the leisure-life of its members; the work of the manifold agencies of government which have been concerned with making available recreational opportunities to those citizens quite unable to obtain them through their own individual efforts; the effects of the major and minor wars of the century which have brought sharply into focus the necessity for recreation and sports for increased morale and for the greater physical efficiency of citizens in and out of the armed services; and the splendid record of labor and management in helping the worker to achieve fuller stature as a human being in his off-the-job living.[1]

CONTRAST BETWEEN 1900 AND TODAY

By comparison with the picture as it is today, 1900 presented a very meager offering of sports and recreational outlets for the poorer classes of citizens in the large urban centers of population, and only slightly better for the middle-class citizens. None but the very rich could afford the luxury of golf and tennis or secure the means of transportation for hunting and fishing trips. Places to swim were scarce indeed, and winter sports were an unknown thing to the millions of city dwellers. The great chains of national and state parks and forest preserves had not been set aside for public use, and, even if they had been, the average citizen had not the remotest chance of getting to visit such places and to enjoy their beauties and benefits. The movement to provide playgrounds for children was just getting under way in widely scattered parts of the United States, and in the meantime they swarmed the city streets and alleys, untaught and unsupervised, but playing nonetheless in the manner which all children have played everywhere and always.

The wealthy minority, who had long ago discovered the delights of play, gradually found their sports and pastimes being usurped by this ever growing group of quite ordinary citizens. By mid-century little more than polo, yachting, or fox-hunting, with their involved requirements of paraphernalia, remained beyond the reach of large numbers of people. Opportunity became sufficiently widespread that a taste for sports had become less a matter of income status than a matter of personal temperament. And it was frequently as possible to explore the more rewarding depths as it was to skate the surface.

Sports as an aspect of the "good life" have today become so firmly established that a share as spectator and participant has become a "right"—a citizen's right, evolving from the idea that society is a co-operative enterprise in which all are concerned and from which all should receive benefit. It represents a share of the total good of a culture to which its individual members are entitled. This has come about both in a permissive form, where each man could obtain such opportunities for himself, and in an enabling form, in which the culture helps him to obtain it.

Writing of "The Big Change" in the Centennial Issue of *Harper's*, Editor Allen says:

Whenever I think of this change, I think of something I saw the other day in New York City. A street was being torn up for repairs, and while the workmen were standing waiting for the arrival of new equipment, one of them, who had in his hands an iron rod presumably used for prying off manhole covers, was enjoying a little relaxation. I looked twice to see what he was doing with that rod. He was practising a graceful golf stroke.[2]

Among the participant sports golf presents perhaps the most outstanding example of how an activity was transformed from the exclusive possession of a small minority of individuals representing wealth and leisure to the favorite pastime of millions, representing an extremely diversified background in income and social status. Writing in the *Overland Monthly* in the year 1900, a contemporary observer gives an amusing sketch of the reaction of that day:

As in other parts of the United States, the game has been taken up almost exclusively by the rich, and is consequently regarded by the "Average American" with that air of tolerant and half-contemptuous amusement with which the sports and vagaries of his wealthy fellow countrymen are commonly viewed.[3]

In the nation's capital President-elect Taft was warned by Theodore Roosevelt that his popularity with the people might be damaged by his public indulgence in a game associated with "dudes" and "snobs." Fifty years later President-elect Eisenhower, following a tremendous victory at the polls, announced that he would go to Georgia for ten days of golf and relaxation, a course of action most heartily approved and well understood by citizens everywhere.

During the nineteen-twenties the game of golf expanded so rapidly that it was estimated there were two million Americans who spent "part of every summer in a sand-pit." The total value of golf real estate was placed at a billion and a half dollars, and the *New York Times* estimated that a half-billion dollars were being spent annually on greens fees, new equipment, lawn-mowers, caddies, and lost balls. The days when golf was considered a game for elderly professors and presidents of banks were gone.

It seemed preposterous then to believe that great armies of lawyers, jewellers, hardware men, and drygoods merchants in the cities and smaller towns could ever be persuaded to take golf seriously, let alone with ecstasy. As for the sporting crowd that followed baseball and the prize-ring; golf was glorified croquet for dudes. Times have changed considerably. To-day the very gods of baseball and the prize-ring have gone in for golf, and the rotogravure sections bring us home-run kings and heavyweight champions wearing tassels at their knees.[4]

Courses ranged from the thirty-six-hole offering at the five-million-dollar Westchester-Biltmore Country Club at Rye, New York, to the nine-hole course in the town of Gaylord, Kansas, with a total population of 356.

The period of overexpansion, of lavish spending on country-club buildings and de luxe courses, came to an end with the nineteen-thirties, but golf survived the depression, and in the twenty years following 1930 there was a perceptible readjustment of values and the emergence of a more common-sense attitude toward the game in general.

The important role of municipal golf facilities and promotional efforts in bringing opportunities to play within reach of ever increasing numbers is discussed in other chapters. An additional and very significant development at mid-century is the growth of golf as a favorite sport in the program of industrial recreation. Many fine golf courses are now maintained for industrial players. Among industrial people who have courses of their own are RCA at Lancaster, Pennsylvania, as well as United States Steel, Goodyear, Firestone, IBM, Endicott-Johnson, and others. It has been well demonstrated, however, that lack of ownership of a course has proved no great handicap in the face of enthusiastic desire to play.

Aluminum Company of America employees play on the course of Purdue University in Indiana,[5] and the game is played by the Heintz Manufacturing Company of Philadelphia on the facilities of a country club just a five-minute drive from the plant.[6] Undaunted by the increase in golfers and a shortage of playing facilities, employees at Lockheed Aircraft in southern California organized a twilight golf league. Courses at Griffith Park, largest city park in the nation, had customarily been closed to the public at 3:50 P.M. to allow maintenance crews to begin sprinkling at 4:00. Arrangements were made to have the watering deferred to 4:30, thereby allowing competing teams one-half hour for teeing off, to coincide with the maintenance schedule.[7] Employees at Tennessee Eastman Corporation have constructed a "hole-in-one" layout where they can practice their swings during the noon hour or have hole-in-one tournaments.[8] In another area of the country enthusiasm bubbles over to include the younger generation. Horton Bristol Manufacturing Company of Connecticut has inaugurated a "Subteen Golf School" for the nine- to twelve-year-old sons of employees, more than half of whom are enthusiastic golfers.[9]

The Sixth Annual Midwest Industrial Golf Championship held at Notre Dame Country Club, South Bend, Indiana, in 1951, had some three hundred individuals competing, representing more than fifty industrial concerns. Competition is open to all companies interested in entering four-man teams comprised of players employed by the sponsoring concerns.[10]

The Eaton Axle Division Company of Cleveland, Ohio, is a three-shift plant employing two thousand, and since 1943 it has operated a successful golf league of more than one hundred players. In the words of the company's recreation director:

Long ago golf was considered a rich man's game. Now that concept seems almost quaint; golf, like democracy, is for everyone, regardless of race, color, creed or even financial status. And unquestionably an important factor in the extension of golf to all economic levels has been the industrial recreation program, which has helped fill the need for organized golf competition.[11]

EFFECTS OF INCREASE IN INCOME

From all the multitude of factors which have influenced the narrowing of the gap between that portion of the citizenry who enjoyed everything in the way of play opportunities and that portion who enjoyed practically none it is possible to distinguish certain trends which seem to have had the greatest degree of relationship.

First consideration might be given to the increase in income, the rising standard of living of ever greater numbers of people. The United States, in common with all other industrial nations, operates on a money basis. A man's opportunities and accomplishments, his ability to obtain and maintain a satisfactory and happy life, are often intimately tied up with the question of income. As much as this may be deplored, it is nevertheless true. There has been much greater progress in accomplishing a more equitable income distribution in the second half of the fifty years since 1900, and indications are that this will be a continuing trend. Studies in the field indicate that there is an extremely high correlation between gross personal income and the amount of money spent on recreation and also that individual sports participation correlates very highly with personal income.[12]

To some it may seem strange to include sports in a discussion of living standards. But if those standards are to measure the full life possible for modern man, certainly sports have their place along the yardstick. Admit over-emphasis on sports on the part of our schools and colleges, grant the absurdities of the mass glorification of games and their players, and still you must confess that the current concern with sport is on the whole a healthy sign.[13]

THE PRODUCTS OF INDUSTRIALIZATION

The second item for consideration, and bearing very close relationship with the question of increased income, is the availability of the products of industrialization. Household equipment of all sorts did much to emancipate men and children, as well as women, from untold hours of drudgery. Not only the mechanical household conveniences but the time-saving and labor-saving involved in the advent of processed and packaged foods contributed to ever expanding leisure. The invention and widespread distribution of radio, phonographs, and television equipment are of such importance in this regard that they are treated more extensively elsewhere.

What has been aptly termed the "logic of mass production"[14] coupled with the philosophy of high wages as a basis of wider purchasing power have been indispensable components in the process of narrowing the gap between rich and poor. There was inescapable evidence, especially following World War I, that it pays better to produce substantial products within reach of a great many income levels than luxury items for a few and that a nation of workers relatively free from oppression or acute poverty is a nation of consumers. That there was an awareness of this, even in the early years of the century, is well illustrated by a quotation from an issue of *Outing* dated September, 1900, in which the future of the automobile in America was being discussed: "The American maker believes that there are more people who have $300 to spend for a luxury than there are who have $3,000 for the same purpose. This means that here we will see machines turned out by thousands, where abroad they have been slowly produced by scores."[15]

Perhaps more than any other of the many products of industrialization, the automobile has served to enhance the sense of power and freedom of the average man and to render him, psychologically, as good as another. It may be nearer to accomplishing equality than the right to vote or to hold office, since it wipes out an age-old and conspicuous mark of social inequality, the difference between he who walks and he who rides.[16] The owner of the $75 jalopy and the $4,000 new car have the same rights on the highway and access to many of the same facilities, whether they be a ball park, a bathing beach, a football stadium, or a national park.

The automobile is an extraordinary machine and toy in which the American genius finds most complete expression. It is the vehicle through which is most amply demonstrated the passion for size, distance and speed, engineering, for play, and, above all, for democracy and fellowship. It is the most costly and elaborate plaything ever devised by man, and it is impossible to find in history a comparable instance of a nation spending so large a share of its earnings on a single form of entertainment. This is not to deny the practical and utilitarian aspects of the automobile, but its central role in the culture has from the beginning been associated with its actual and potential contribution to the play life and recreational pursuits of the average citizen.

CLASS LINES ARE ELIMINATED WHEN THE NATION WEARS SPORTS CLOTHES

Third on the list is an item which is too frequently overlooked but which has had great influence in lessening the definite line of demarcation between rich, middle class, and poor, as well as between town and country. This is an increasing standardization in clothing and is exemplified most definitely and most frequently in sports clothes. The sweater and skirt, the sport shirt and slacks, the bathing suit, the tennis shorts—what identifying marks of wealth or caste can shine through such uniformity as these offer? Even in such a specialized area as the costuming for winter sports, the very rich may buy their skiing equipment from Norwegian makers and their ski clothes in London or Paris, while the middle class are buying their equipment and clothes from Sears, Roebuck.[17] It takes a surprisingly short time for the most expensive and exclusive models to be duplicated and to become available to a great section of the total population.

THE CHANGING PATTERN OF LIFE

Fourth consideration might be given to the change in the pattern of life which has been brought about by shorter working hours and yearly vacations. An old and time-worn difference between the outline of living for the man of wealth and for the worker is gradually disappearing. It may even be that the man who owns the business has less actual carefree leisure than his employees. Ordinarily the workers shed the responsibility of the job outside the prescribed eight-hour day, five-day-a-week routine, and their vacations are both a right and a privilege which are seldom interfered with. In addition, there is the really magnificent job of providing recreation and sports opportunities for industrial workers which has been done by both management and labor and which sometimes supplies a more balanced and rewarding pattern than that achieved by the self-employed individual.

PUBLIC EDUCATION AND THE RECREATIONAL USE
OF SCHOOL FACILITIES

A fifth consideration would include the increased availability of public education. Universal public education is so much an integral and accepted part of the American scene that the arguments which were being advanced against public tax-supported schools less than a hundred years ago are almost forgotten. The equalitarian process which is the pride and hope of the nation would certainly not have been possible if such arguments as these had triumphed:

Public schools make education too common and will educate people out of their proper position in society.

Public schools will tend to break down long-established and very desirable social barriers.

The industrious will be taxed to educate the indolent. Citizens having no children should not be taxed for schools.

It took more than a generation to overcome such prejudices and to awaken the public conscience to the need for free and common schools in a democratic society. If an educational system had been established on the basis of the parents' ability to pay, the public schools would not have become the most important institution in our national life working for the perpetuation of a free democracy and the advancement of the public welfare.

It became the task of the public school and the public playground to take the millions of immigrant children and transform them into acceptable American citizens. One measuring rod for the social progress of the new racial elements is familiar to everyone—the new names on school and college athletic teams. Following World War I, the sons of the new immigrants came into their own, and by the mid-nineteen-thirties Columbia University was defeating Syracuse University with the aid of Richavich, Coviello, Ciampa, Wurz, Hudasky, and Brominski. In the Midwest, Notre Dame played Army, using Schiralli, Michuta, Viaro, Bonar, Melinkowich, and Elser. The cynical explanation for this was simply that football coaches went into the mining regions to hire husky young coal-diggers, truck-drivers, and ice-peddlers to come to college and play football. Without arguing this point, it could only mean as well that the sons of the Central European immigrants were *already in high school*. The Slavic tinge on school and college football teams and the impressive Italian contribution to professional baseball are evidence of the part the school and the playground have played in making fame and fortune available to many boys and young men through the medium of their sports skills.[18]

It was the deservedly famous Rochester Experiment in 1907 that provided the first real impetus to the community use of schoolhouses in the United States. The successful functioning of this plan brought a fuller realization to social workers, parents, teachers, and others interested in community problems as to the potentialities of the school as a neighborhood center. Schoolhouses have been used throughout the country for various community purposes, and, if recreation activities have been chiefly emphasized, it has been because they have met the need of the greatest number of people.[19] The movement to make the schoolhouse a community center was not born of the need of the economically and socially self-sufficient citizenry. It was the direct result of the necessity of providing educational facilities for those beyond the years of formal schooling, for the immigrant struggling toward understanding and status in a new country, and also of providing recreational facilities for people in isolated rural districts and for residents of the crowded districts of large cities. Over the years the recreational phase of school-center work has developed to a greater degree than any other. It would seem evident, since this has come about as a result of the demand of the people, that the leisure-time activities thus provided have helped to break down barriers between people of different creeds, nationalities, and social and economic strata by providing means of friendly contact among them.

A FREE PRESS AND OPEN CHANNELS OF COMMUNICATION

Sixth on the list of considerations is the tremendous increase in the last fifty years of newspaper circulation and periodical publication and in the last twenty years of radio and television ownership. All these channels of communication brought information to the economically underprivileged as to other ways of life and proved a powerful stimulant to their desire and determination to share in the "good things of life." Occupying a prominent place in the list of such things to be attained was ever greater opportunity for recreation, for sports, for vacations, for an active part in the play life as well as the work life of the nation.

The twentieth century has seen not only a furious advance of industrialism but a disciplining of industrialism; a growth of counterforces which have transformed the trend from one which made the rich richer and the poor poorer to one which has consistently narrowed the gulf between rich and poor.[20] The rebellion against the way things were going, and the mockery which was being made of democracy in the process, began in the late decades of the nineteenth century. But more powerful and articulate voices took up the battle in the early years of the present century. Jacob Riis and Jane Addams exposed the unlovely picture of slum life; the muckraking journalists uncovered the sordid business deals and political corruption of the day; liberal spokesmen from the ranks of organized religion espoused a "social gospel" which concerned itself with the physical and material aspects of man's welfare; political progressives like Theodore Roosevelt fought the forces of monopoly and exploitation. World War I climaxed this era by pointing up, as perhaps nothing else could have done, the truth of the matter that a minimum standard of physical health, education, and satisfactory mental and emotional adjustment is a basic requirement for *all* citizens if any nation is to achieve its full stature.

Thus in these early years foundations were laid in philosophy, in attitude, and in assumption of responsibility—foundations which undergird our present-day programs, plans, and facilities for the recreation and sports life of the nation. Jane Addams at Hull House in Chicago and Lillian Wald's House on Henry Street in New York demonstrated what could be done by providing playgrounds and kindly and intelligent encouragement and supervision to the children of the city streets. The success of these experiments and many similar but less well known efforts in other cities, and the widespread publicity they were given, aroused the compassionate interest of men and women throughout the country and led eventually to the establishment of a nation-wide playground movement. These early efforts form the background for the modern concept of recreation as an essential phase of social planning and for what has been perhaps the greatest development of this century: the entry of all divisions of government—city, county, state, and national—into a concern for the recreational life of all citizens.

YOUTH-SERVING ORGANIZATIONS CONTRIBUTE
TO THE WIDENING OPPORTUNITY

The social and economic gains of parents are very naturally reflected in the increased privileges and opportunities which they in turn can provide for their children. In addition to the operation of this principle on the level of the individual family, there has been a tremendous amount of time, money, and energy expended by various groups within the culture, working toward widening opportunities for all youth. Chambers lists 320 national nongovernmental associations classified as "youth-serving organizations," and the inclusion of sports and other varieties of physical recreation is standard operating procedure in most youth-serving agencies.[21] Often without realizing it, such organizations have played a rather prominent role in developing sports as a part of American culture.

A number of well-known organizations for boys and girls and for youths form a familiar and important part of the picture of youth welfare in America. Among these are the American Junior Red Cross, the Boy Rangers of America, the Boy Scouts, the Boys' Clubs of America, the Camp Fire Girls, the Girl Scouts, the YMCA and the YWCA, and many others.

In addition to the old-line and long-established youth agencies, there is another group which might be called quasi-commercial and which has been and is now very active in the sponsorship of competitive athletics for boys and sometimes girls of elementary- and junior-high-school age. Certain of their programs have not received the approval of important professional organizations in education, recreation, and related fields because such competition is considered to be physically, emotionally, psychologically, and educationally harmful for this younger age group. The question as to whether or not children and youth are exploited rather than served by some groups providing athletic programs is one which bothers many thoughtful persons who are interested in the problems involved.

A brief sampling will illustrate the extent of participation in some of these programs. Little League Baseball records 776 sanctioned leagues in 1951 operating with 3,333 teams composed of 60,000 boys between the ages of eight and twelve.[22] The 1952 estimate on the number of boys involved in Little League Baseball is 250,000. Biddy Basketball for boys between the ages of nine and twelve is gaining in strength under the indorsement of a number of individuals well known in the sports world.[23] Its junior counterpart, Iddy-Biddy Basketball for children five to eight, has already been organized.[24] Pop Warner football leagues, sometimes called "midget football," have been organized in many sections of the country and in some two hundred communities. The total participation figure in 1952 was estimated at 50,000. Boys must be thirteen years or younger and weigh 110 pounds or less. The 1952 season ended with four "bowl" games—the "Pony Bowl" at Las Vegas, Nevada; the "Santa Claus Bowl" at Lakeland, Florida; the "Toy Bowl" at Birmingham, Alabama; and the "Milk Bowl" at Rosenberg, Texas.[25]

Other youth programs include the American Junior Bowling Congress, the Junior Olympics, the Carnation Milk Company Tennis Clinic, and various athletic programs sponsored by the United States Junior Chamber of Commerce, not to mention a considerable number of programs in various cities throughout the country.[26]

American Legion Junior Baseball is an extensive program for older boys up to sixteen, with 1949 reports showing 15,912 teams and over half a million boys participating.[27] The United States Golf Association sponsors a national Junior Amateur Championship and has a Chick Evans Caddie Scholarship Fund to aid deserving caddies in obtaining a college education.

The important fact, culturally, is that such enterprises engage the enthusiasm of millions of young persons and often profoundly influence the tone of their subsequent careers. Since it is impossible for either parents or teachers to insulate children from the currents of public opinion and reaction or from community activity, the situation would seem to call for a maximum of understanding co-operation. Even if a sponsoring group has as *one* motive the advertisement and sale of a commercial product, or the gaining of publicity for a locality or an organization, it may still have as its highest aim the welfare of the individuals concerned. A statement by Chambers seems to point the way to a more rational estimate of one aspect of the situation.

At any rate, if the absence of propaganda is to be the test of an acceptable youth organization, none will be acceptable. Even those societies of youth which are ostensibly free of any affiliation with adult pressure groups often conspicuously, though perhaps unintentionally, operate to indoctrinate their suggestible members with definite patterns of social and economic prejudice. In this matter of propaganda, it is plainly appropriate to invite him who is without sin to cast the first stone.[28]

15. *Some Interrelationships of Sports Ideology and Sports Language*

THE LANGUAGE OF SPORTS

EVERYONE IN AMERICA WHO READS OR LISTENS IS EXPOSED TO sports expressions by means of newspapers, magazines, books, radio, and television. As a result even those unfamiliar with most games inadvertently employ in their daily speech words and phrases which have been absorbed from reading and conversation and which have their source in the field of sports. The sports writer has become an important contributor to the growth and development of the language. The best evidence of this fact lies in the many sports terms, of slang origin, which have attained the level of colloquial speech and the number of such terms which have moved through the colloquial stage and become standard English.

It has been said that any speech which is true, natural, real, and which provides the most effective expression, arises out of the immediate social relations of man with man. Since the field of sports offers one of the commonest possible mediums for the furtherance of those relationships, it is only natural that this area of the culture would provide for an enrichment of the vocabulary of action with many new verbs and verb phrases. Language is a living, growing thing, and, if everyone followed standard speech alone, there would be no innovation, no development. The sports page has developed many interesting devices for heightening the impact of language—striking metaphor, sometimes shocking yet effective simile, and lavish alliteration. Although there are many regional differences and peculiarities in the United States, the tendency is toward a more or less universally standardized sports jargon.

Many sports terms will never achieve the level of true standard speech, but all usually justify themselves in their particular realm (and many times in other fields) by accomplishing their purpose—that of securing a satisfactory and unhindered transmission of thought.[1]

The quality of sports writing has shown a marked improvement over the years of the twentieth century since its infancy as a distinct branch of American letters. After passing through an era of luxuriant verbiage, "when no spade could be called a spade," sports writing went on to a period of disillusionment and debunking, some of which it still retains. This particular approach sometimes represents a healthy attitude and sometimes degenerates into mere exhibitionism. At mid-century the two wings of the craft, sometimes identified as the "Gee whiz!" and the "Aw nuts!" branches, seem headed toward intelligent reporting and writing, the ancient, simple test of newspaper excellence.[2]

Earlier in the century the magazine *Nation* had expressed itself as puzzled as to why, in the matter of sports reporting, the language must stand on its head and try to convey meaning by waving its hands and feet instead of speaking sanely. The magazine recommended the services of a psychiatrist as well as a philologist! This unfavorable reaction was not wholly shared by the sports fans of the day as was proved by an experiment conducted by the *Chicago Record-Herald*. The newspaper ran two stories, side by side, one in straight English reporting and one in "baseballese." Of the many letters received as a result of this printing, the majority favored retention of the more colorful presentation. One astute observer commented that the real genius is the one who can introduce all the enjoyable piquancy possible within limits which enables the ordinary reader to understand what is being said. It was admitted that a distinction should be drawn between graphic description and hysterical slang.[3] It would be unfortunate indeed if the newspaper had to print a glossary after the sports page to make it intelligible.[4]

This chapter, however, is not devoted to a discussion of sports language as such but rather to pointing up the numerous instances of persistent infiltration of sports language and modes of expression into many other areas of thought and action in the culture and to the ideational and conceptual values which underlie this transfer. Many illustrations may be found in such widely diverse fields as child-training, education, and American art; in the conduct of government and of public affairs and in the pursuit of war; and in the personal and public lives of the men who have been President.

CHILD-TRAINING AND SPORTS

The usefulness of sports language and sports analogy in the difficult job of child-training, whether such training be concerned with physical, ethical, or social development, has been amply demonstrated. The play spirit forms the major part of a child's life and is an integral and important factor in his education. American parents and teachers have learned to translate the most sacred and important concepts of life and living into the vocabulary of children at play.[5]

Every parent soon discovers that the young child has no sportsmanship and no generosity in his games. He will take advantage of his opponent and cry loudly when he loses. It is only by a long process of painful experience, patient teaching, adult example, and other social pressures that such reactions are modified. In the opinion of one psychiatrist it may be counted as one of the major achievements of the human race that the contestant in a game or sport can forego an accidental advantage and the spectator cheer him for it, and the loser in turn can smile and congratulate his vanquisher.[6]

An important part of the role of parent and teacher lies in transmitting to the child the basic beliefs and understandings, as well as the rituals and modes of conduct, which are a part of the society in which the child is to live. Thus indoctrination in the idea of being a "good sport" begins at a very early age, and to be able and willing to "play the game according to the rules" will be an ideal toward which he is expected to strive throughout life.

From one point of view an American is more easily identified and understood as a cluster of ideas and ideals than as a definable or describable racial type. And an inseparable part of this cluster of ideas and ideals is woven about the spirit of sportsmanship and a deeply ingrained habit of fair play. In this cultural connotation being a "good sport" is not a matter of definition or formula. It is rather a spontaneous quality that rises to opportunity and to emergency. Its greatest inspirations may come from disaster and disadvantage. The spirit of sportsmanship becomes not so much a set of rules to be followed as an attitude of mind. By way of illustration, the belief is widely held that the humor and sportsmanship in American business assure standards better than anything Congress could enact or the Department of Justice enforce. And if this tendency to regard politics and business as a game suggests immaturity, it also implies a wholesome willingness to abide by the rules of the game, acquiesce in decisions, and accept defeat cheerfully.

In America sportsmanship is considered a form of enlightenment and sometimes as an acceptable substitute for the rule of love, which so far in history has proved much too hard a doctrine to live by. The Christian ideal of brotherly love, of the Golden Rule, has not been achieved. But progress has been made, and making the rule of sportsmanship a rewarding and respected pattern of behavior in the culture, from earliest childhood, has accomplished much of this progress.[7]

EDUCATION AND SPORTS

Education in America has escaped both aristocratic and ecclesiastical control and has never been simply a means of formal instruction. The program is frequently fashioned not so much by teachers as by the society which teachers serve. The broad social aim is the teaching of common habits necessary to American life and a common political and national faith. This is the supreme test by which the American experiment of universal education must be judged. The millions of youngsters who have been products of this school system, coming as they do from the most varied ethnic, social, and economic backgrounds conceivable, are living evidence of America's belief in itself and in the future.

It is this aim and this success that justifies the lavish buildings of the local high school; not merely the classrooms and the laboratories, but the gymnasium, the field-house where basketball can be played in comfort in the depth of the bitter winter, the swimming pools in which the summer heat can be endured.[8]

Sport in American schools has proved an important influence in uniting parents, children, and the community in a common interest. A definite reflection of this is shown in a study of *Newspaper Editorials on American Education*, in which study it was discovered that following World War I the yearly averages showed an increase in editorial comment on athletics of over 250 per cent.[9] This period coincides with the institution of required programs of physical education in public schools, as has been discussed in another chapter.

The compulsory physical education programs in schools have provided an impetus to sports participation and enthusiasm, but they have also demonstrated a negative influence. The nonathletic youngster who is compelled to participate, often with those more generously endowed with ability, may emerge with his body unbruised but with his ego very badly damaged by a sense of his own inadequacy. The zeal of the sports instructor is sometimes only to be compared with that of the fanatical missionary who must convert or perish in the attempt. This may well be the background and source of many confirmed spectators, who emerge from the painful experience of their "required" program with a firm resolve never again to expose themselves to the humiliation and discomfort which the whole process involved.

In his autobiography James Thurber describes some of his reactions.[10] Thurber was, even as a youth, extremely near-sighted, and he was not allowed to play games with his glasses on, and yet he was almost totally unable to see with them off. As a consequence he spent much of his time in the university gymnasium bumping into professors, horizontal bars, agricultural students, and swinging iron rings. Thurber claims he would never have graduated (since learning to swim was a requirement) if he had not persuaded an amiable blonde youth to assume his gymnasium number and swim across the pool in his place.

So long as the cultural expectation for boys is dominated by the ideal of the muscular and aggressive male, the contribution of those less favorably endowed physically and more introverted psychologically will not be so completely utilized as it might be.

In an educational system designed to teach the art of living in a democratic and competitive society it is logical that sports and other leisure-time activities should play an important part. The social value of the common experiences shared by boys and girls in the schools of the nation in their pride and enthusiasm for the school team is a traditional phenomenon in American culture. Such sports are in most cases rigorously democratic and may provide an invaluable lesson. It is also a part of the American parent's conviction that it is a good thing for youth to have early training in the knowledge that in the life of a great democracy he is the better man who proves it.

When examined from the point of view of their function in the culture, intersectional games such as the Rose Bowl and the Cotton Bowl become instruments of national unity, and the provision of such instruments a duty of the colleges and universities. "It is a religious exercise of a kind a Greek would have understood, however remote it may be from the university as understood by Abelard or Saint Thomas Aquinas or John Harvard."[11]

Out of the experiment of democracy in American culture has come the belief that citizens are made not alone through the advancement of science and the spread of literacy but by an increased sharing in the responsibilities and privileges involved in the general welfare. Citizenship results from the profound realization that one's own destiny is inextricably bound to the destiny of the group.[12] Any educational means which tends to engender and strengthen this feeling of group solidarity, of shared responsibility and privilege, even if it be at a different level than the adult one of concern for the general welfare, amply justifies its existence as a fundamental part of American education.[13]

SPORT IN AMERICAN ART

The art of a nation is to a limited degree a mirror in which the culture is reflected. Sports have never achieved the place of prominence in American art which they have been accorded in certain other cultures, but the subject has not been entirely neglected. This fact was well illustrated by two special exhibitions of national importance, held within the last twenty years. The Metropolitan Museum of Art in New York City gave a special exhibition of "Sporting Prints and Paintings" in the spring of 1937, and late in 1944 an exhibition of "Sport in American Art" was held at the Museum of Fine Arts in Boston.

The exhibitions revealed that the popularity of a sport does not necessarily mean a corresponding emphasis in art. The universally popular sports of fishing and hunting, which lend themselves gracefully to artistic treatment, are well represented. Football and baseball, two of America's most popular sports, hardly appear at all. It may be that, since these sports do not compose on a canvas or a sheet of paper, artists have passed them by.

Some distinguished American artists, however, have clearly grasped the idea of using sport as a legitimate material for artistic expression rather than merely using their pens, pencils, and brushes to illustrate sport. Of these, perhaps the most important are Winslow Homer, Thomas Eakins, William James Glackens, and George Bellows. Nor should the many famous sporting scenes in the Currier and Ives lithographs be overlooked.

In the galleries and print rooms of American museums artistic interpretations of sport are rather meagerly represented. That it is quite otherwise with private collections was illustrated by the many things that came to light as a result of these two exhibitions.

SPORT AND THE CONDUCT OF GOVERNMENT AND
PUBLIC AFFAIRS

An English anthropologist, making a study of the national character of the American people, commented:

In conversation and in writing the metaphor most commonly used to describe the proper role of government is that of the umpire in some sporting event such as boxing or baseball; the umpire is not to make the rules which have already been laid down (in the Constitution) nor to take part in the contest which is the real object of the exercise; the umpire's duty is merely to prevent one of the contestants from taking an unfair advantage of the other.[14]

To anyone who sincerely attempts to understand the American character such an attitude is a natural concomitant, an almost inevitable outgrowth of the American way of life. Democracy itself is like a complex athletic game, and its existence depends, as much as upon anything else, upon the hearty willingness of citizens, *for the sake of the game*, to refrain from doing what they are physically perfectly free and able to do. As an example: a player in a game of tennis is physically free and at liberty to walk up to the net and drop the ball over instead of serving it, to put the ball in a gun and shoot it over, or to hire a small boy to carry it around the net. But the player is not mentally or morally free to do any of these things, because, if he did, he would be laughed off the court, put out of the game, and no one would play with him. Acceptable players and acceptable citizens respect the rules of the game, because they know that the rules make the game, and they believe in the game.[15] Democracy is impossible and freedom uncertain without this basic virtue of sportsmanship, since "freedom can live only in the minds of men who feel a moral compulsion to behave in political and in all other contests as a well trained athlete behaves in a game."[16]

The use of particular phrases, the evocative power of verbal symbols, has been widely and rather wisely exploited by all sorts of spokesmen on public affairs. Their use is credited as one of the chief means of uniting the United States and keeping it united.[17] Increasingly throughout the years of the twentieth century officials and other representatives of government have made a practice of translating the complexities of government into the easy idiom of sports.

President Wilson, at a Jackson Day Speech given in 1915, said: "If a man will not play on the team then he does not belong to the team. You see, I have spent a large part of my life in college, and I know what a team means when I see it; and I know what the captain of a team must have if he is going to win."[18]

Ellery Sedgwick, for so many years the distinguished editor of *Atlantic*, in discussing government control of muckraking journalism which flourished in the early nineteen-hundreds, commented: "The government shall not play the whole game itself, but shall see that the whole game is played fair and that the man who doesn't play fair is ruled off the field."[19]

In the distressing days of 1932 President Franklin Roosevelt referred to himself as the "quarterback," and Americans understood that he felt that he had the system and the plays to call a winning game. When his son later wrote a biography of his father, he described him as a man who got things done by "keeping his eye on the ball."

In explaining the reasons behind the use of the atomic bomb to end the Japanese War, a simile from the field of sports helped to clarify the point of view of the men concerned with that tremendous decision.

In war, as in a boxing match, it is seldom sound for the stronger combatant to moderate his blows whenever his opponent shows signs of weakening. To Stimson, at least, the only road to early victory was to exert maximum force with maximum speed. It was not the American responsibility to throw in the sponge for the Japanese; that was one thing they must do for themselves.[20]

In the early years of World War II a navy flyer, downed in the Battle of the Coral Sea, described the experience as being "like having a grandstand seat at the World Series," and all America knew exactly what he meant![21] And when the Japanese Peace Treaty was signed in San Francisco, a writer in *Harper's* explained to the public that the affair had been a team operation, in which "Secretary Acheson called the signals, Mr. Dulles carried the ball, and Mr. Rusk organized the interference."[22]

In reporting progress on the coal strike, *Newsweek*, December 2, 1946, commented that, although John L. Lewis had said nothing to urge his followers to work or not to work, they knew what was expected of them and that 140,000 of the 400,000 had "jumped the gun" ahead of the deadline.[23]

The Overseas Edition of *Time* dated March 3, 1946, reported that Russia's Andrei Gromyko found it necessary to "go to bat" for Albania.[24] And in New York the *Daily Worker*, July 10, 1946, explained to its readers that Australia's foreign minister, "who plays ball with the State Department," was trying to give the impression that the Security Council's functions would not be undermined.[25]

The use of sports terms and analogies reached an all-time high in the presidential campaign of 1952. Both of the major candidates, as well as newspapers writers and radio and television commentators, were naming political teams and prospective quarterbacks for such teams. The listener who had no acquaintance with the game of football, if one could be found, might have been extremely bewildered and would certainly have missed the nuances of meaning and innuendo which were so vividly clear to the listening sports fan.

SPORT AND THE PURSUIT OF WAR

The close relationship which has existed, both in reality and in the minds of men, between war and sport is not uniquely American. In fact, ever since words existed for fighting and playing, man has referred to war as a game.[26] Anthropologists have frequently reported that among primitive peoples athletics were practiced only secondarily for recreation and primarily for military training.[27]

A great deal of heroic and romantic fiction has been written about war as a noble game of honor and virtue. However consistently this ideal was belied in reality, it played an important part in developing civilization. It is from this ideal that chivalry sprang and hence, ultimately, international law. It was possible to consider war in the light of a game or contest so long as international law functioned, with its recognition of the ideal of a community of mankind with rights and claims for all, and specifically separating the state of war—by declaration—from peace, on the one hand, and criminal violence, on the other. It remained for the theory of "total war" to banish forever the idea or ideal of war as a game.

A strong rallying point of national feeling against Germany in World War I was provided by what was considered by Americans to be a total lack of chivalrous characteristics, of a sense of fair play, or a spirit of sportsmanship on the part of the enemy. Kleeberger, writing in 1919, gave expression to what was a widespread reaction:

The chief thing about this war which stirs us with righteous indignation, which causes us to loathe and hold in contempt an enemy who otherwise might have our wholesome respect, is this utter lack of chivalry among the German soldiery. We cannot understand it and we cannot forgive it.[28]

If twentieth-century total war had lost all resemblance to a game and degenerated into genocide and the flouting of international law, for the individual soldier it could still be best compared to a "rough and brutal team game."[29] In the words of a man who has been described as "the greatest living reporter of combat": "War's small picture is a series of end runs, off-tackle bucks and center rushes, and if the team does not hold together during each play, it loses yardage and the ball changes hands."[30]

When General Douglas MacArthur expressed the sentiment that it was the friendly strife of the sports field on which the seeds were sown "which in other years and on other fields will bear the fruits of victory," he was echoing a fundamental cultural belief. It is equally part of the nation's basic sportsmanship philosophy to believe that the real winning power comes from each man's love for his comrades rather than his hate for the other side.

TWENTIETH-CENTURY AMERICAN PRESIDENTS
AND THEIR SPORTS

In a sense the President of the United States is an exemplification of American culture as a whole, its spokesman and its symbol. Therefore, the sports tastes and practices of the man in the White House are a matter of interest to many Americans. It has also been demonstrated that presidential approval or disapproval, support and enthusiasm or lack of it, have more than once been influencing factors in the fortunes of sports and recreation for the nation as a whole. Outstanding examples are to be found in the presidential careers of the two Roosevelts. Their accomplishments in the field of conservation, and in federally aided means and opportunity for recreation, are a heritage the nation now enjoys.

The men who have occupied the White House represent the widest possible range of aptitude and ability for the job. There have been representatives from the log cabin and from the palatial estate; men with a college education and those with no formal schooling whatsoever. But it is doubtful if *any* man regardless of his ability could be elected President who publicly, in word or deed, displayed what a majority of Americans consider to be unsportsman-like behavior.

As an example, the presidential campaign of 1928 was not memorable for its display of sportsmanship, with its many undertones of religious intolerance. The two candidates, however, displayed a high quality of fair play and by most citizens were never held responsible for the mistaken zeal of their more partisan supporters. Early in the contest, Mr. Hoover expressed himself thus:

A great attribute of our political life has been the spirit of fair play with which our Presidential contests have been waged in former years and the sportsmanlike spirit in which we have accepted the result. We prove ourselves worthy of self-government and worthy of confidence as officials in proportion as we keep these contests free from abuse, free from mis-representation and free from words and acts which carry regret. Whatever the result we remain fellow countrymen.[31]

Governor Al Smith, the candidate opposing Mr. Hoover, paid tribute to the same principles of conduct:

No doubt the combination of a fine spirit of justice, fairness and good sportsmanship can lead to the development of the highest type of citizenship. It is, therefore, of great benefit to the State. Good sportsmanship is as important in politics as it is in business or any other field of human endeavor.[32]

American history reveals many instances in which this basic sense of what constitutes fair play, in the mind of the average citizen, has proved an effective deterrent to the overambitious or ruthless politician.

Twentieth-century American sportsmen were particularly fortunate in having such an advocate of sports and games, of the "strenuous life," as was embodied in the life and character of President Theodore Roosevelt. By the example of his own life, through consistent pressures applied in the various political offices which he held, and through his writing and speeches, Roosevelt won the respect and admiration of the ordinary citizen not only for himself but for active sports as an integral part of the American way of life.

Roosevelt's frequent use of such admonitions as "Don't squeal!" "Don't flinch!" and "Hit the line hard!" are reflections of his devotion to outdoor sports. Individuals may differ on the question as to whether the prize ring, the football field, and the fastnesses of big-game preserves are the ideal places in which to teach sturdy manhood to the young, but the phrases drawn from them and engrafted into the speech of our everyday life by Roosevelt will certainly survive with all their illustrative values even among those who take no delight in their sources.[33]

The chronicle of the sports tastes and accomplishments of this remarkable man who began life as a puny child, apparently doomed to a life of semi-invalidism, is amazing. He was a daring horseman, an enthusiastic rider to the hounds, an excellent shot, a good oarsman, a powerful swimmer, and a hiker of tremendous endurance. He boxed and wrestled and was reputed a master of the difficult art of jujitsu. He was a hard-hitting tennis player and an expert with the broadsword. He was equally at home in a canoe or on snowshoes or skis and knew more about camping than most professional guides.[34]

Aside from his official existence, Roosevelt found time to become an active leader in a number of important movements dedicated to the constructive side of outdoor life. He was founder of the Boone and Crockett Club, the foremost big-game hunting club of America, and one of the editors of its many publications. He was the leading spirit in the American Game Protective Association. He was also first honorary president of the Playground Association of America, a post which he held until the time of his death.

Although the sports proclivities of Theodore Roosevelt far overshadow any of his successors, with the single exception of Coolidge the twentieth-century Presidents have each had a special sport which they particularly enjoyed. Wilson, Taft, and Harding were golf enthusiasts, Hoover was a devotee of fishing, Roosevelt had an unfailing love of sailboating and deep-sea fishing, and Truman enjoyed swimming.

William Howard Taft was America's first enthusiastic golfing President. Speaking as guest of honor at the twenty-fifth anniversary dinner of St. Andrew's Golf Club, held at Delmonico's in November, 1913, he remarked:

> The game's virtues include, first of all self-restraint and call for mental discipline and ethical training. There should be no objections to playing it on the Sabbath day if one attends to his religious duties first. Church in the morning and golf in the afternoon on Sunday is an excellent compromise. It should be indulged in when opportunity arises, every man knows who has played the game that it rejuvenates and stretches the span of life.[35]

In May, 1917, President Wilson wrote a letter in which he advocated the retention of intercollegiate sports at institutions of higher learning. His purpose was not to afford diversion to the American people in the dark days to come, but because he believed such sports provided a contribution to America's defense through the correlation of physical development and mental quickness in action.[36]

President Harding served on the governing board of the United States Golf Association from 1921 until his death in 1923. He offered a trophy for intercity team contests in connection with public links championships. This was played the first time in Washington in 1923, being won by the Chicago team. There are golf courses in both San Francisco and Los Angeles named in memory of the most enthusiastic of all golfing Presidents.

President Hoover's devotion to the art and pleasure of fishing has been well delineated in his own words.[37] In pondering the question as to why Presidents fished, Mr. Hoover concluded that with the increased pressures of the office it became increasingly imperative for a President to be alone for a few hours once in a while. And, further, that there are only two occasions when Americans respect privacy—prayer and fishing. In addition, it seemed logical, since more people have gone in for fishing over more centuries than for any other human recreation.

In discussing the problems of modern leisure, Mr. Hoover admitted that he too went to movies and watched somebody else knock a ball over a fence or kick it over a goal post and enjoyed it. But he felt that, enjoyable as these "forms of organized joy" undoubtedly were, they were sadly lacking in the values which "surround the fish." Nor is it merely the fish itself but rather the "flow of stream, the stretch of mountain in their manifestation of the Maker, that soothes our troubles, shames our wickedness and inspires us to esteem our fellow men—especially other fishermen."[38]

Memorable in the minds and hearts of sports fans is the famous "green-light" action taken by President Roosevelt with regard to the continuance of professional baseball following Pearl Harbor. The following excerpts from the letter which the President wrote to Commissioner Landis reflect an understanding sympathy of the vital role of sports in the culture.

I honestly feel that it would be best for the country to keep baseball going. There will be fewer people unemployed and everybody will work longer hours and harder than ever before.

And that means that they ought to have a chance for recreation and for taking their minds off work even more than before.

Baseball provides a recreation which does not last over two

hours or two hours and a half, and which can be got for very little cost. And, incidentally, I hope that night baseball can be extended because it gives an opportunity to the day shift to see a game occasionally.

Here is another way of looking at it—if 300 teams use 5,000 or 6,000 players, these players are a definite recreational asset to at least 20,000,000 of their fellow citizens—and that in my judgment is thoroughly worthwhile.[39]

Indications are that Americans will have in Eisenhower the most sports-minded President to occupy the White House since the days of Theodore Roosevelt. Since high-school days when the young Eisenhower helped organize the first athletic association at Abilene High School, and became first president of the organization, he has been an enthusiastic participant and advocate of sports.[40] While at West Point Eisenhower won his "A" in football, but a fractured kneecap interrupted what might have been an outstanding record and put him out of the game. His continuing enthusiasm found an outlet, however, as cheer leader and as coach for the football squad at Cullum Hall.

One biographer reports that during the war the General played "everything from badminton to ping-pong at odd moments to relax from strain."[41] During his service at Supreme Headquarters, Allied Powers in Europe, just outside Paris, his staff knew of his fondness for golf and tried to get him out of the office in time for a game any day that time or weather permitted.

In letters to his only son, Eisenhower reveals his belief in sports as an important aspect of life by urging him to keep up with his tennis and to take an active part in all outdoor athletic sports.

16. Race Relations and the World of Sports: A Progress Report

ONE OF THE BEST INDICATIONS THAT SPORTS FANS ARE, IN ESSENCE, both democratic and tolerant Americans lies in the success of the headline athletes, both Negroes and Jews.[1] When a Jewish boxer wins a title, it is a better answer, for many, to the stereotype "Jews are physical cowards" than a lengthy scientific treatise. When Jackie Robinson is selected the most valuable player in the National League for 1949, it is a powerful antidote to another stereotype, that "Negroes are lazy, shiftless, and unreliable."

In America the word "champion" carries a magical connotation. The champion is the best, the man at the head of the class. When such a coveted title is carried by a member of any minority group, the boost to the morale of that group is incalculable and the blow to discrimination is strong and sure.

In a recent issue of one of the leading literary journals there is an article which contains heartening news for all Americans who are concerned with one of the nation's most difficult and distressing problems—discrimination and segregation of minority groups. The secretary of the National Association for the Advancement of Colored People is the author of "Time for a Progress Report," and he outlines in some detail the story of the real progress that has been made in at least fifteen different areas. Mr. White declares that the "most visible sign of change to most Americans is the cracking of the color line in professional sports, particularly professional baseball."[2]

The decade of the nineteen-forties will be long remembered

as marking the official entry of the Negro player into organized baseball. Commissioner Landis had for several years declared that there was no written or unwritten, formal or informal, understanding against the hiring of Negroes, that such action was entirely up to the club owners. Apparently the situation awaited the courage and imagination of a man like Branch Rickey, the owner of the Brooklyn baseball syndicate, "to throw Jim Crow out of the park to the oblivion where he belongs," as one sports writer put it.[3] Within a few years a dozen or more Negro players were playing such skilled ball that few persons thought of them any longer as Negroes but only as good ballplayers.[4]

This chapter will be devoted to a brief progress report on just a few aspects of the battle against discrimination in the field of sports in twentieth-century America. In these days when the enemies of America are doing such a thorough job of publicizing any sins of commission or omission, real or fancied, it may be that a recapitulation of the relative substantial gains that have been made is in order. Such an approach does not imply that the problems have been solved or that Americans may now be either smug or complacent about the situation. On the contrary much work remains to be done, and there are still wide gaps between the ideals of freedom from prejudice as publicly professed and what is done to implement such ideals.

Some distrust of the efficacy of sport as a bond between nations may be justified in the world's present state of nationalistic feeling. Sports may, as is sometimes charged, be only another cause of international misunderstanding.[5] Such doubts do not apply to the salutary effect of the elimination of *racial discrimination*, not only in sports but everywhere. Such discrimination anywhere and in any guise is a dilemma which transcends mere nationalism and is in fact a world-wide problem.

PROGRESS IN SCHOOLS AND COLLEGES

The statement would probably be affirmed by most educators that one of the widest channels through which intercultural relations progress in schools is in games and sports. It is commonplace in the northern sections of America for youngsters of all races, religions, and nationalities to play together on both intramural and interscholastic teams, building mutual respect for prowess, courage, and good sportsmanship.[6] Educators might further agree that children in school learn that the Negro people should be their equals in a democracy, yet, the moment they leave the playground, their attitudes too often come under the influence of adult prejudice.

Most educators are aware of the job to be done in intercultural relations and are alert to the possibilities within their scope of operation. It is too big a task, however, to be accomplished by the schools alone. Every victory that is won along this line in the adult world of either amateur or professional sports will help to reinforce the work of the schools.

There has been slow but steady progress in the elimination of racial discrimination in intercollegiate football since Walter Camp selected William H. Lewis of Harvard as center for his All-American teams of 1892 and 1893. By 1940 the team members of five mixed colleges had rendered the tribute of electing to team captaincy five different Negro players. In 1949 Levi Jackson, varsity football player at Yale University, was elected captain of the team. In 1951 players at the University of Pennsylvania chose as football captain for 1952 Bob Evans, six-foot-two tackle, a junior in premedicine. Evans and a teammate, Edward Bell, are the first Negroes to achieve prominence on the varsity team in the seventy-five-year history of football at that university.[7]

Even in Dixie progress could be noted. Chester Pierce of Harvard University stopped in the dormitories at the University of Virginia and played on Cavalier Field on the Charlottesville campus in October, 1947. And in the same year Wally Triplett and Dennis Hoggard of Penn State played against Southern Methodist University in the Cotton Bowl in Dallas, Texas, before thousands of cheering southerners.[8] For the first time in the history of Florida a college team with Negro players played against a white college team. This was when the University of Iowa played the University of Miami in the Miami Orange Bowl in 1950.[9] In 1951 the amount of discussion which was provoked, and the subsequent actions taken by various schools in the case of Johnny Bright and his broken jaw, indicates clearly that progress was being made in the matter of race relations in sport.[10]

It is interesting to note that the transformation of inter-collegiate football from a simple student-managed, student-coached game to a highly complex commercial operation, involving paid managers and high-salaried coaches, was the very thing that brought to an end a great deal of social and racial discrimination in the sport. In the judgment of some thoughtful students of the problem it was not until football became big business that college fraternities ceased to run the show from the sidelines. Prior to this time making the team (in some institutions) was sometimes as much a social as an athletic triumph. The advent of the professional coach, with his interest centered on athletic ability rather than social status, was the great leveling factor.[11]

And yet one of the most fundamental justifications or objectives of school and college athletics is vitiated when snobbery or racial prejudice prevents youth from developing a tolerance and admiration of all contestants regardless of race or creed or when unfettered opportunity is not provided for the participation of all students who have the desire or the ability to do so.[12]

CIVIL RIGHTS LEGISLATION, COURT ACTION, AND
INTERRACIAL SPORTS PARTICIPATION

Eighteen states have enacted civil rights laws to guarantee equality of access to public accommodation.[13] Only the state of Washington has a *general* civil rights statute, that is, one not enumerating specific places: "Every person who shall deny to any other person because of race, creed or color, the full enjoyment of any accommodations, advantages, facilities, or privileges of any place of public resort, accommodation, assemblage or amusement, shall be guilty of a misdemeanor."[14] The interpretation of the statutes and their enforcement in the various states have often involved sports facilities, sports participation, and attendance at sports events. For example, following a suit in New York in 1941 the statute was amended to include golf courses. In a recent New Jersey court decision a more liberal construction was given, and the court's decision was that the state's civil rights law applied to a refusal by an amusement park to admit Negroes to its swimming pool. The following comment was made at the time of the decision: "State civil rights acts have been widely honored in the breach, because persons discriminated against rarely have the time and the money to sue for damages or to obtain prosecution."[15] The riots which followed the use by Negroes of a newly opened swimming pool in one city, even though such use was not specifically forbidden by law, serve as a reminder of the work that remains to be done in this area of race relations.[16]

During June, 1951, in New Jersey, the State Division against Discrimination held public hearings for the first time since it began functioning six years before. The case involved a charge that Negro children had been turned away by the proprietor of a swimming pool when the children sought participation in a learn-to-swim program.[17] By July 31 the case was settled and the proprietor ordered to stop excluding Negroes. This was the first "cease and desist" order under the state's antidiscrimination law.[18] More than twenty years earlier a judge of the Superior Court in Los Angeles, California, had rendered a decision permanently enjoining the Department of Playgrounds and Recreation from making any segregation. At that time the Los Angeles City Council refused to carry the case to a higher court and since June, 1932, colored and white citizens have been permitted to use pools at the same hour.[19]

A United Press dispatch, datelined New Orleans, December 21, 1951, reported that the United States Fifth Circuit Court of Appeals had reversed a Texas federal court and held that Negroes might play on a Houston municipal golf course.[20] The city of Houston had contended that the course was "a facility and part of the park set apart under the segregation policy of the city . . . for use solely by white persons." It was claimed that other parks containing no golf courses had been reserved for Negroes.

Two additional actions taken in Florida during 1951–52 may be noted. First, there was the announcement of the first "mixed bout" ever to be held in the state, Kid Gavilan of Cuba defending his welterweight championship in Miami Stadium against Bobby Dykes of Miami. Second, the license of the first Negro jockey to ride at a Florida race track was approved.[21]

SOME RECENT ACTIONS OF RECREATION PARK BOARDS,
CITY COMMISSIONS, AND GOVERNING BODIES OF
SPORTS ORGANIZATIONS

In June, 1951, the Baltimore Park Board voted to end segregation at the four municipal golf courses and to allow interracial tennis matches on certain courts. The board also stated that it would allow mixed play on city athletic fields upon application and if such fields were available. There is an interesting clue to the force of publicity and public opinion which may underlie the action by the board in two stories picked up and reprinted in the *New York Times*. The first report (dated May 28, 1951) concerned the stopping by the Baltimore Park Police of a tennis match between Fort Meade and the Baltimore Tennis Club. This was immediately done when it was learned that the meet was to be interracial. The second report (dated June 13, 1951) told of how the park police in Baltimore had stopped a baseball game (after it had gone one inning) between members of the crew of a navy landing ship and a Negro team. The *U.S.S. Ashland* was in drydock for repairs, and the crew team, which had two Negro members, had scheduled a game with the Mohawks— without knowing or caring that it was a Negro team. In this instance the white members were in violation, since the park was restricted to Negro use.[22]

In December, 1951, the City Commission of Jacksonville, Florida, voted four to one in favor of opening the city's two municipal golf courses to Negroes. These courses are closed to white players on days they are to be used by Negroes.

Bowling has long been the number-one favorite in the list of activities sponsored by programs of industrial recreation. And yet, despite the growing numbers of Negroes in the labor force of the nation, they have until quite recently been barred from this sport in all but a few cities in the United States, where they were fortunate enough to have facilities for their exclusive use.

The American public was to become well acquainted during 1948–49 with the policy of discrimination and segregation practiced by the American Bowling Congress. The National Committee for Fair Play in Bowling, headed by Mayor Humphrey of Milwaukee, with Miss Betty Hicks, former United States women's tennis champion as co-chairman, was set up. Many prominent Americans, including former Senator James Mead and Philip Murray and Walter Reuther of the Congress of Industrial Organizations, were active in the fight.

Dr. Jay Nash, of New York University, was undoubtedly speaking for a majority of the members of his profession when he termed the committee the "torch bearer of a great ideal." By 1949 the aggressive crusade of the CIO had successfully ended the banning of Negro players from bowling.

The action of the United States Lawn Tennis Association in inviting the twenty-two-year-old Althea Gibson to play on the outdoor courts at Forest Hills shattered a long-standing policy of segregation and discrimination.[23] The subsequent invitation for Miss Gibson to participate in the British championship at Wimbledon was applauded by all sportsmen.[24]

CONTRIBUTIONS OF SOME PRIVATE AGENCIES TO INTERRACIAL PROGRAMS

The work done by the YMCA and the YWCA certainly belongs on the credit side of the ledger. Gifts of George Foster Peabody and John D. Rockerfeller made possible the first "Y" buildings for Negroes. But it was the offer made by Julius Rosenwald in 1911, an offer of $25,000 to every city in the United States that would provide an additional $75,000 for the construction of a YMCA building for the use of Negroes, that precipitated a real building program. In the two years following this challenging offer eight cities had constructed buildings, and eventually there were twenty-six buildings, including the large Harlem Branch, which was erected at a cost of over a million dollars. It is interesting to note that, of the $5,815,696 which these buildings cost, Negroes themselves gave $472,558.[25]

During World War I the Negro Associations sent 268 secretaries into home service and 49 into overseas army work. Today there are sixty-two Associations for colored men and boys in cities and industrial centers, and the Student Department reports 120 student Associations in colleges and secondary schools. One study reports that in recent years the official policy of the YWCA has been to operate on an interracial basis with regard to dormitories, committees, and in certain clubs and activities and that this same policy represents a "substantially greater common practice in the YMCA than is generally appreciated."[26]

Negro girls and women have participated in the Girl Scout movement since 1913, when the third American troop was organized in New Bedford, Massachusetts. In 1951 there were an estimated 1,507 integrated troops, mostly in the North and West, and 1,634 all-Negro troops, mostly in the South. There is ample evidence that racial barriers are breaking down. The weakening of the white newspaper taboo against publishing photographs of Negroes is one indication, and the fact that city-wide meetings of the scout organization have been held in some southern states on a completely nonsegregated basis, quietly and without fear, is another. Negro women hold many leadership posts in the Girl Scout movement in America.[27]

The American Red Cross has sponsored twenty-eight aquatic schools for Negroes in the South since 1939, and during that time more than fifteen hundred men and women have earned certificates as qualified water-safety instructors. Such schools as are conducted in the North are attended by both white and colored students, but the National Red Cross abides by southern custom and holds segregated schools in the South.[28]

The National Recreation Association has an impressive record of service and accomplishment in the struggle to obtain fuller recreational opportunities for Negroes. The fine attitude of this organization was demonstrated at the time of the Thirty-first Annual Congress held in New Orleans during 1949. If the conference had been scheduled in a hotel, it would have meant the exclusion of Negro recreation leaders. The meeting was therefore held in the civic auditorium to make possible the attendance of all leaders regardless of the color of their skin. This action by the National Recreation

Association may very well serve as a guide to other organizations.[29]

RACE DISCRIMINATION AND THE OLYMPIC GAMES

Up to 1936 there appears to be no semblance of a racial question in Olympic Games competition, but Hitler's vicious anti-Semitic campaign was well under way during the period of organization for the games in Berlin. Despite pledges by the Germans and a report by a member of the International Olympic Committee after a visit to Germany, the American Olympic Committee's decision to send a team to Berlin hinged on a very slim majority vote. There was very strong anti-Nazi feeling in this country, and unusual difficulties were encountered in raising the necessary funds to send the team. It was reliably reported that the Jewish population in the United States, because of the bitterness in the whole situation, raised more money to prevent the United States from sending a team to Berlin than was actually raised to finance the team. Also it was well known that there would be a number of Negro athletes on the United States track and field team, and it was also known that Hitler had declared the Negroes to be an inferior race.[30]

On the opening day Hitler personally congratulated the first three champions, two of whom were Germans. Then at last the high jump was completed, and a Negro boy from the United States had won. All eyes were upon Hitler's box to see what he would do, but he hastily departed, reportedly because it was late and looked like rain.

Word was sent to Hitler by the president of the International Olympic Committee that he was a patron of the games and hence a guest of honor but that, unless he was prepared to congratulate every winner, he should refrain from publicly congratulating any one of them. Hitler's explanation of his first day's activities was that it was the excitement of Germany's first Olympic victory, and he agreed to withhold further public greetings, which he did.

It is most interesting to note that the Negro athletes of the United States were referred to as "the Black Auxiliaries" by the Nazi newspapers, and there were many stories in American newspapers about how Hitler had snubbed the great American athlete Jesse Owens, four-gold-medal winner. Bill Henry termed the incident "an outstanding example of the type of myth fostered by excess emotionalism."[31] If anyone was slighted or snubbed, it was not Owens but Cornelius Johnson, who had won the high jump on the opening day. Hitler never had the opportunity of shaking hands with Owens.

Despite all the slighting remarks in the official Nazi newspaper, *Der Angriff*, Owens was "accepted by the Germans as an athletic marvel and they were really enthusiastic over his remarkable performances. . . . Owens was a hero on the streets of Berlin as well as a marvel on the dark red cinder-paths in the stadium."[32]

17. *America and International Sports*

SPORTS AS AN INSTRUMENT OF INTERNATIONAL POLICY

THERE IS NO PART OF AMERICAN LIFE IN THE TWENTIETH CEN-
tury that has been unaffected by the growing internationalism
which surrounds us at mid-century. Such obvious effects as
the millions of American soldiers who have served on foreign
soil in both world wars and the increased tax burden due
to commitments abroad are very much in the consciousness
of most citizens. A less serious and deadly aspect of internationalism is to be found in the sports life of the nation.

General Dwight D. Eisenhower, speaking in San Francisco
as a candidate for the presidency of the United States, referred to sports as one of the peaceful tools which should be
used in the waging of the international "cold-war" struggle
for the minds and wills of humanity.

Diplomacy, the spreading of ideas through every medium of
communication, mutual economic assistance, trade and barter,
friendly contacts through travel and correspondence and sports—
those represent. some of the political means to support essential
programs for mutual military assistance and collective security.[1]

. In December, 1951, the *Department of State Bulletin* devoted considerable space to a discussion of "The Soviet Athlete in International Competition." Reports from embassies
afforded positive proof that the Kremlin had launched a gigantic cultural offensive. This was designed to prove the Soviet
supremacy in the arts as well as on the athletic field. In the
Soviet philosophy, sports are apparently conceived primarily
as a tool of propaganda, an instrument of national policy, a
means of strengthening the party line of Soviet superiority
and further indoctrinating Communists. As to results, the

superiority of the Stalinist "socialist" athletics over "capitalist" athletics must be continually demonstrated.

If American sports are to be an effective instrument of international policy, a means of meeting the "big lie" with the "big truth," then they must continue to exemplify the highest standard of sportsmanship and fair play. The demand that American athletes win must yield to the demand that such athletes fight a good fight—*and may the best man win.* Nothing finer can be expected from American sportsmanship, for such sportsmanship is an exemplification of democracy at work.[2]

If the long record of international sports competition were to be compared with the similar record of international trade and diplomatic relations, and assessed against a comparable scale of measurement for the contribution each has made to promoting friendships and good will, American sportsmen would feel no need to be apologetic. With diligence and a spirit of dedication even more may be accomplished, for sportsmen have one of the finest tools for building the kind of understanding that may one day bring genuine peace. If a better world is to be built, it will surely be founded on fair play, the credo of the true sportsman.

THE INTERNATIONAL SPREAD OF SPORTS AS A PHASE OF CULTURE CHANGE

Culture change may be defined as the process by which the existing order of a given society—its social, spiritual, and material civilization—is transformed from one type to another. Culture change is a permanent factor of human civilization; it goes on everywhere and at all times.[3] In the twentieth century the process of culture change has assumed a magnitude and rapidity unprecedented in human history. Advances in communications and transportation and the world-wide developments of industrial and mercantile enterprises have tended to accelerate the rate of change beyond the capacity of social conditions, political institutions, and spiritual culture to adjust.

A great deal has been written about the spread of the ideas and the "gadgets" associated with Western civilization to all parts of the world. American movies, machinery, and Coca-Cola have encircled the globe. There is another aspect of the international spread of ideas and customs that has proceeded with less fanfare but which has for the past century been working subtle and profound changes nevertheless. The phenomenon has not gone entirely unnoticed. Both governments and missions have in general welcomed the spreading popularity of Western sports and games as an important factor of change and adaptation in the lives of people. The schools have been the main centers at which these sports are learned, although they also fan out from the urban centers at which native players have the advantage of being able to compete with non-native.[4]

THE INTERNATIONAL YMCA

There is one particular phase of the international spread of American sports and ideals of sportsmanship that deserves special attention—the work of the International Young Men's Christian Association. It would be difficult to estimate the extent of the contribution made by the YMCA in the field of physical education and amateur sport on every continent in the world. YMCA-trained men from Springfield and George Williams colleges have brought to many sections of the globe the initial experience which the people have had in modern competitive sports. While these colleges direct a program for the preparation of young men in all phases of YMCA work, it is in the field of physical recreation that their contribution has been most pronounced. The YMCA's are today functioning in some seventy-six countries, representing a more complete international roster than the United Nations!

The first foreign student entered the International YMCA

College in 1904, a young man from Australia, later to return to his native country to spread the gospel of Christianity and to work with people through the medium of games and sports. In 1908 another Springfield graduate, Dr. J. H. Gray, began his thirty years of service in India, China, and Burma, initiating programs of physical education and sports in which Indian people in huge numbers sought to take part.[5] For a number of years the Tokyo YMCA swimming pool was the only pool in Japan, and many Olympic swimmers practiced their strokes and secured their training in the splendid "Y" gymnasium.[6]

In 1910, Elwood S. Brown, later to become director-general of the Inter-Allied Games in France (1919), was sent to Manila as physical director of the American YMCA. One of the purposes of his mission, perhaps the main purpose, was to build up sports among the natives as well as the American civilian population in the Philippines. He was able to interest both groups in volleyball and softball, and, encouraged by Governor-General Forbes, participation in these activities became so widespread that one dealer in Manila before the advent of World War I sold eleven thousand volleyballs in one year.[7]

Competitive games were organized between the Americans and the Filipinos, then between the Japanese and the Filipinos, and finally the stage was set for establishing the Far Eastern Games, with China, Japan, and the Philippines participating. Aided by governmental support, great popular interest and enthusiasm were displayed in both China and Japan. Through Brown's efforts and the assistance of men and agencies working with him, modern athletics were developed in Siam and throughout the Malay Archipelago.

In 1928 Bangkok, Siam, was the largest city in the world without a YMCA. The International Committee raised a budget to pay for a secretary to be sent there, and in 1931 Walter Zimmerman formed a board of directors which eventually received formal government recognition in 1932. By 1937 the membership numbered more than four hundred men and boys of sixteen nationalities, and additional thousands benefited by the group activities sponsored by the organization.[8]

The fact that the American game of basketball today rivals soccer in popularity as an international sport is due primarily to the efforts of the International YMCA. Three years following the first introduction of the game in 1891, basketball had reached as far as Paris in one direction and Australia in the other. By 1900 China, Japan, and India had been introduced to the game. The Far Eastern Games (the Olympics of the Orient) have included basketball since 1924, and until World War II India, China, Japan, and the Philippine Islands competed for the championship.

In the Near East, basketball has long been a popular sport. In 1924 Roberts College in Constantinople, Turkey, became the first college in a country other than the United States to incorporate basketball in its curriculum. The complete rules have been translated into the Turkish, Greek, and Arabic languages.

South American countries have evidenced great enthusiasm for basketball, and the game has had a place on the program of the Latin-American Games since 1921. Ten years before the foundation of the International Federation of Amateur Basketball,[9] the South American Confederation was founded and thus became the first organization in the world to sponsor a championship contest between teams representing different countries.

For the first time in the history of the modern Olympic Games, basketball was included as part of the competition in 1936. Twenty-two teams were entered; the United States won first place, with Canada second and Mexico third.

Thus the strictly American game of basketball has had a wide and cosmopolitan career. Countries that may show a marked lack of enthusiasm for other segments of American culture, political and social, have adopted and enjoyed the game which is truly America's contribution to the world of sport.

ORGANIZATION, SUPERVISION, AND CONTROL OF INTERNATIONAL COMPETITION

International competition between track and field athletes and athletic teams representing the United States and those of other countries has a very long history, much of which lies buried in odd and fairly inaccessible sources. By comparison with the highly regulated and publicized events of today, such contests seem incredibly informal and rather sadly mismanaged. Prior to the 1890's almost no line separated the amateur from the professional in track and field athletics, and promoters were always to be found ready to shine up a trophy and take a chance on possible profits. If an element of the bizarre could be interjected, so much the better. For example, a Seneca Indian known as Deerfoot went to England in 1863, ran his many races in moccasins, and beat all of England's best men.[10] When a team of Irish athletes came to the United States in the autumn of 1888, their tour disintegrated so badly that some of the members had to work their passage home on cattle boats, and some took up permanent residence in this country. An unpaid $600 hotel bill in New York and outstanding debts at home amounting to $2,500 were just two of the unfortunate outcomes of this adventure. Two years later a team brought over from England by the Manhattan Athletic Club was rescued from the financial failures of appearances in Boston, Detroit, Buffalo, Chicago, and Philadelphia by a successful meet held in Madison Square Garden which netted $3,000.[11] Early intercollegiate contests in track and field represented a much better standard. The match arranged for Oxford and Cambridge against Yale and Harvard, held on the Queen's Club Grounds, West Kensington, London, July 22, 1899, was a very satisfactory experience for all concerned.

There are many complexities which surround international university competition, mostly growing out of a desire to preserve amateur status. This complicated matter has given rise to much controversy, some heated, some even bitter.[12] Prior to the Olympic Games of 1896 there were many international sports federations in existence. Associations or unions in gymnastics, swimming, rifle-shooting, and other sports attempted to deal individually with problems arising from amateur competition between countries. Following the Olympic Games of 1908 a movement was started to establish an organization which would really promote international solidarity and control. This led, following the 1912 Olympics, to the formation of the International Amateur Athletic Federation. The constitution of this federation provides that in each country a single organization shall exercise jurisdiction over both international and national aspects of competition. The American body upon which the control devolves, through sanctions and certification of eligibility, is the Amateur Athletic Union of the United States.

The choice of this organization was logical and inevitable at the time (1913). The Amateur Athletic Union was the only American organization of sufficiently cosmopolitan composition, long experience, and variety of contacts to be considered capable of performing the important duties of the American member in the International Federation. Thirty years before, the growth of athletic clubs and increasing competitions in track and field had brought about the necessity for a national association to control the sports competitions. The National Association of Amateur Athletes of America, organized in 1879 under the patronage of the New York Athletic Club, had attempted to govern the sport for a decade but eventually proved unable to enforce its decisions or to define an amateur. In 1888 the Amateur Athletic Union was organized and has been functioning continuously since that time. The Union is organized on a basis of district associations, or regional bodies covering the United States on a geographical basis, and has jurisdiction over the following sports: basketball, bobsledding, boxing, codeball, gymnastics, handball, horseshoe pitching, ice hockey, swimming, tobogganing, track and field, tug of war, volleyball, water polo (hard ball), water polo (soft ball), wrestling (catch-as-catch-can), and wrestling (Greco-Roman).

EXAMPLES OF INTERNATIONAL COMPETITION

International competitions in golf and tennis have elicited continued public interest over the last fifty years. While it is true that only a very small number of individuals are actually involved in contests such as the Davis Cup in tennis and the British Open in golf, the stimulus which has been given to these sports as a result of international competitions has been tremendous. Champions like Bobby Jones and Bill Tilden transcended the boundaries of national popularity and became known and admired by golf and tennis enthusiasts in all parts of the world where these sports are played.

The Davis Cup.—Over the years, since 1900, nations from every part of the world have played for the Davis Cup. Not only have most of the European countries been represented, but South American countries, Australia, Canada, and New Zealand as well. Players from Hawaii and the Philippine Islands have represented the Pacific area; Cuban and Mexican contestants as well as those from the United States have come from the Western Hemisphere; and from the opposite end of the globe, South Africans. The Far East has also been represented by players from China, India, and Japan.

The manner in which Davis Cup competition may become a matter of concern for diplomats is illustrated in a story from the 1928 contest. For the first time in the history of the cup, the challenge round was to be held in France, and in honor of the occasion a beautiful stadium had been built in the Bois at Auteuil. Newspapers were full of enthusiastic accounts of preparations. Then came word that the famous American player Tilden was in difficulties with the United States Lawn Tennis Association over alleged violations of the amateur rule and that he would not be allowed to play. The debarment of Tilden from the match was strongly resented by the French and was almost construed as a plot to ruin France's big moment of glory. To save the situation, the American ambassador to France intervened. He called the chairman of the Davis Cup Committee of the USLTA and asked that, for the sake of international good feeling, Tilden's suspension be withheld until after the challenge round had been played. This was done, and although Tilden won from Lacoste in the opening challenge round engagement, France took the other four and won the Davis Cup.[13]

The *"America's" Cup.*—Human beings have seldom failed to be aroused to great admiration and interest in contests involving demonstrations of speed resulting from the combination of human skill and expert craftsmanship. Such enthusiastic interest helped in the twentieth century to bring about the amazing developments in the automobile and the airplane. In the nineteenth century and early twentieth, there was a great concentration of such interest on ships and sailing, and most colorful of all, in the minds of many, were the famous international yacht races for the *America's* Cup.

The saga of the *America's* Cup began with some correspondence between an Englishman and some New York businessmen regarding an industrial exhibition to be held in London in 1851. The suggestion was made that a New York pilot boat be sent over to sail in the various regattas. The New York Yacht Club, which had been established in 1844, decided to build a yacht and send it over, and thus the *America* crossed the Atlantic in July, 1851, the first yacht to do so in either direction.[14] The *America* won what was then called the "Queen's Cup" in a match with British schooners sailing round the Isle of Wight.

Several years later, in 1857, the idea was conceived of making the cup an international trophy, to be held in custody by the New York Yacht Club "as a perpetual challenge cup open to competition by any yacht club." The first challenge did not materialize until 1870 when the British schooner *Cambria* raced the *Magie*. All business in New York was practically suspended to witness this first race, and a contemporary writer commented, years later, on "The Cup's Effects on American Maritime Affairs":

The *America's* Cup, as a British-offered prize, was but an unconsidered trifle in the affairs of a few yachtsmen. It was worth 100 ounces of silver—in those days less than $500. But in its effects on yachts and yachting, and on ships and shipping—more important still in effects on American men and maritime policy—who can calculate its results.[15]

Following 1899, when Sir Thomas Lipton sailed the first of his famous *Shamrock* series to try for the cup, the famous yachtsman gained warm supporters on both sides of the Atlantic. His gallantry and sportsmanship in the face of repeated defeats won the respect and admiration of all Americans. This Irishman who had come to America as plain Tom Lipton in 1865 and worked in New York City as a clerk, not returning to Glasgow until 1876, was as beloved in America as one of the country's own heroes.

INTERNATIONAL CO-OPERATION OF PROFESSIONAL
PERSONNEL

The years between 1900, with the first International Congress of Physical Education held in Paris, France, and 1952, with the World Seminars in Physical Education, Recreation, Health and Youth Work held at Helsinki, Finland, span more than a half-century of international co-operation and interchange of ideas among the professional leaders and scholars in many areas all over the world. The change in program emphasis from the study of gymnastics and methodology (in

1900) to constructive use of leisure and training for citizenship through the medium of sports and games (1952) is indicative of the changing role of physical education in the cultures of mankind.

The new century opened with the calling of an International Congress of Physical Education in Paris, France. Thomas Wood was the official American representative, and his report revealed the keen interest of the various participating countries in setting up an international basis for physical education, with national application to be adapted to local conditions.[16] Although the congress was more preoccupied with discussions of gymnastics than with games and sports, Professor Angelo Mosso, the famous Italian physiologist, had high praise for physical education in the United States. Mosso had recently been a visitor to America and was most favorably impressed. In contrasting conditions with those in France, he referred to the prominent position occupied by football and various other games. He also called attention to the fact that "all races except the Latin have gymnastics and athletics, and that a race, to develop, must have out-door sports."[17]

The first International Recreation Congress was held at Los Angeles, California, in 1932, under the auspices of the National Recreation Association. Thirty-three nations helped in the organization procedures, as members of the International Advisory Committee, and delegates from twenty-five countries met to "plan for the attainment of life and happiness by all their people." In the words of Joseph Lee:

The sources of human life and happiness that we are seeking are international, older and more deeply rooted than our differences. Every nation has its song, its games, its art, its drama, and its literature, its own approach to truth and understanding; each has its flag, the symbol of its personality; each brings its special contributions to the whole. But the Muses that have whispered to us are the same. It is because of this happy combination of unity and variety that we should meet and that we shall some day form a team.[18]

President Herbert Hoover, as honorary president of the congress, gave active assistance in launching the congress as an international project, and the co-operation of the State Department of the United States was secured in transmitting invitations to other governments.

At mid-century the State Department was continuing to evidence its confidence in the potential contribution of such endeavors to international understanding. During 1949–50 two hundred German community and youth leaders visited the United States as part of an exchange program. Following a two-week orientation period in New York City and Washington, leaders were assigned to various local recreation departments in a wide variety of geographic locations throughout the country for participation, observation, and training.

In the interest of promoting international co-operation and understanding in physical education throughout the Western Hemisphere, the Pan-American Congress of Physical Education has had three meetings: 1943, Rio de Janeiro; 1946, Mexico City; and 1950, Montevideo, Uruguay. One of the physical education leaders in the United States, Dr. C. H. McCloy of the State University of Iowa, is president of the Pan-American Institute of Physical Education.

Two of the leading American organizations for the promotion of physical education, the American Association for Health, Physical Education and Recreation and the American Academy of Physical Education, have active committees on international relations. These committees have functioned in promoting aid to programs abroad, in exploiting possibilities for the exchange of teaching personnel, in distributing publications to individuals in other countries, and in assisting in the entertainment of visitors to America.

THE OLYMPIC GAMES

As has been pointed out earlier in this chapter, international amateur competition, particularly between representatives of

England and America, has been in progress at various times for over a century in such sports as track, rowing, yachting, and tennis, but, until the Olympic Games were revived in 1896, no real start had been made on a truly international basis. Though Baron Pierre de Coubertin's dream of "one world in sports"[19] took on some significance at Athens, it was often a shaky and discouraging significance in later years, and a less courageous idealist than De Coubertin might have abandoned the whole idea. There were difficulties, bitterness, lack of co-operation in regard to the Olympic ideal, and bickering back and forth among nations. Tunis took a rather dim view of the whole Olympic situation when he said in 1928 that "the history of the modern Olympics records but few that did not leave a series of unfortunate incidents in their train," and he expressed grave doubt that the Olympic Games "are spreading peace and good will throughout the world, or that they bring together the various competitors in friendly social intercourse."[20]

He further believed that the American training system was not in keeping with the spirit of the games and the wishes of Baron de Coubertin and indicated the feeling of many that the intense training and the stressing of the will-to-win would tend to destroy the games.

Henry, twenty years later, did not take such a dim view.[21] While admitting the bickering among officials at London and other Olympic Games which followed, he believed that international relations had never been seriously affected. This view appears to be borne out by the testimony of America's Olympic competitors from 1932 on, which indicates that many fine international friendships have been made. While it is true that at times certain reporters have stirred up trouble between athletes and even between countries, such difficulties as have been started in this way have had little or no effect upon the games.

One interesting view of the 1952 competition in basketball

between Russia and the United States and of the fact that the United States was represented by players from industrial organizations, namely, Caterpillar Tractor Company and Phillips Oil Company, has been set forth by Castle. He indicates that the Russians took note of American industrial dominance in basketball and of American industrial teamwork operation. The idea of making sports an integral part of American industrial production was entirely new to the Russians, and, says Castle, "if the bortsch boys actually put into practice what they learned about American team work, maybe they'll become better world neighbors."[22]

Certain it is that the Olympic villages set up by the host cities, beginning with Los Angeles in 1932, did much to promote the friendly intercourse between athletes which is so important in any program of international relations.

It is also certain that the holding of the Olympic Games at Antwerp in 1920, almost immediately after a world conflict, gave definite indication of the growing feeling of internationalism and the desire to perpetuate the spirit of amateur sport on a world basis which had been dormant for eight years.

The games at Berlin in 1936 were held despite world events marking great international dissension, and this is further evidence of the desire on the part of Olympic officials to do everything possible to promote international good will through amateur sport. Baron de Coubertin's idea and ideal have been kept alive under the most severe handicaps, and the spirit shown at the games of 1948 and 1952 is the best indication of tremendous progress in international sports competition.

American internationalism reflected in the Olympic Games. —Some idea of the importance of the Olympic Games to the people of the United States can be gained from an examination of the quantity and quality of newspaper space and reporting devoted to them in the American press.[23]

The revival of the Olympics at Athens in 1896 received

scant attention beyond the fact that the United States team, if such it could be called, was merely a club group from the Boston Athletic Association augmented by two athletes, one from Princeton and one from Harvard who went "on their own."

The 1900 games at Paris received but minor comment on inside pages from the New York daily papers, "and nowhere were they referred to as Olympic Games."[24] The games at St. Louis in 1904 had to combat both a presidential campaign and the Russo-Japanese War and were lost in the shuffle, so to speak. On several days the *New York Times* carried no stories of what was happening in the international competition at St. Louis.

When the "off-year" Olympics were held at Athens again in 1906, some attention was paid to the fact that the United States was sending a team in a body on the *S.S. Barbarossa*, but here again other front-page events overshadowed the games, notably the San Francisco earthquake and fire.

Even stories about the 1908 games at London did not land on the front pages of American newspapers until the violent disputes arose between the United States and British officials, except, of course, the famous marathon race involving the winner Johnny Hayes (U.S.) and the disqualified Italian, Pietri Dorando, who collapsed and was practically carried across the finish line by British officials.

In so far as the United States is concerned, the Olympic Games did not become "front-page stuff" until they were held at Stockholm in 1912. There may have been a number of reasons for this, including the tremendous organization program of the Swedes, a better representation of nations, the publicity hang-over from the 1908 games in London, and the greater preparation of the American team. But, in all probability, one of the factors which had a great influence on public response to the games of 1912 and after was the gradual disintegration of America's isolation policy reflecting an international point of view and hence participation in international affairs including sports competition.

The American Olympic Committee applies the principle of associative activity.—It was not until after three Olympic competitions had been held that the United States had a truly representative Olympic team selected by the American Olympic Committee (whose honorary chairman was none other than President Theodore Roosevelt) and financed by a nation-wide subscription. Before 1906, our team was nothing more than a college and club affair financed without popular subscription and without special United States designations or uniforms. The unofficial games at Athens in 1906 were the first to achieve any particular semblance of organization. There were good reasons for prior lack of organization: (1) a political isolation policy on the part of the United States; (2) an internal dissension in the control of amateur sports; (3) the lack of a nation-wide college organization (such as the NCAA); and (4) two previous side shows which had been run in connection with the expositions at Paris and at St. Louis.

For the London games of 1908, the American Olympic Committee made preparations on a national scale with regional tryouts for track and field rather than selection by past performances. This practice was continued on a more elaborate scale for the games in Stockholm, and, when the 1916 games were canceled because of World War I, Olympic interest was kept alive to some extent by the selection of an All-American Track and Field Team.

When the 1920 games were announced for Antwerp, the American Olympic Committee was completely disorganized due to deaths and resignations, but a new committee, with the blessing of Honorary President Woodrow Wilson, immediately went to work inaugurating a more elaborate system of track and field tryouts in five different cities with the finals at Harvard. In addition, the committee was desirous of having America represented in all possible sports—tug of war, swimming (men and women), shooting, wrestling, boxing, rugby, football, rowing, fencing, modern pentathlon, cycling, equestrian, gymnastics, and winter sports. In addition to the tryouts for club and college athletes, army championships were held separately. This is further evidence of the changing attitude on the part of the armed services in regard to sports for their personnel.

The rather primitive organization of the International Olympic Committee coupled with the world-wide interest in sports generated by the Olympic Games brought into existence various international sports organizations to serve as governing bodies. For example, the International Amateur Athletic Federation, controlling track and field athletics, prescribes the program of events and the competitive conditions. Each sport included in the Olympic program has an international federation which provides for the rules and conduct of the international competition and which differs in some respects from those of national organizations in the various countries. These various federations and subsequent commissions (constituting a sort of executive committee) served to modernize Olympic Games competition in 1924 and thereafter.

In the beginning the American representatives at the International Amateur Athletic Federation meetings were AAU officials, and considerable controversy arose over the control of American participation in the Olympic Games. Only by the operation of the democratic *principle of associative activity* was the situation saved in 1921 when the American Olympic Association was formed by representatives of practically all of the national governing bodies of amateur sports.[25]

To head the American Olympic Committee for the 1928 games in Amsterdam, Major General Douglas MacArthur was selected, and, as would be expected, he organized the committee along military lines. One of the distinguishing characteristics of the preparations for the Ninth Olympic Games was the astonishing number of tryouts in which it was estimated twelve to fifteen thousand athletes participated.[26]

The American Olympic Committee organization has not changed materially since 1928, but the large number of track and field tryouts held in 1932 and 1936 was eliminated in 1948. In 1952 the armed services championship was added to the list of semifinals which included national championships of the Amateur Athletic Union and the National Collegiate Athletic Association.

One of the outstanding feats of Olympic organization of all time came with the establishment of the Olympic Village at the 1932 Games in Los Angeles. This move certainly illustrates the principle of associative activity, applied in an international way, and was responsible for the promotion of international good will and undoubtedly "did much to create the atmosphere of Olympic sportsmanship of which the founder of the games had dreamed."[27]

The amateur-professional controversy becomes an Olympic issue.—The problem of what constitutes a breach of amateur status has plagued authorities in American school and college sports since the beginning of the century. With all the various cultures involved in the Olympic Games, it is not surprising that there have been heated sessions of the International Olympic Committee devoted to the amateur-professional controversy.

To define an amateur was almost an impossibility because of the wide variety of viewpoints not only among nations but among the various international sport federations. The problem of "broken time" in football was one of the very sore points. "Broken time" refers to the payment received by a player for time lost from his job when in training for or actual competition in the Olympic Games.

Agitation for the "broken-time" rule caused the International Olympic Committee to give it consideration at the

Prague Congress of 1925, and, although the committee felt that abuses of this kind violated the spirit of amateurism, it "found difficulty in putting its opinion into definite language."[28] Sanctioned by the International Football Federation, largely because of the Continental attitude, but violently opposed by the English Football Association, the question of "broken time" was not settled until the Berlin Congress of May, 1930. This congress agreed that qualified athletes must not have received reimbursement or compensation for loss of salary. However, it left the question of defining "compensation for loss of salary" to its executive committee to settle with the Council of Delegates of the international federations.[29] The amateur status of a number of the leading French tennis players was questioned because of the "broken-time" rule, and in America grave doubts were cast upon the status of track athletes who could continually barnstorm just for the fun of making the trip.

Probably the two most publicized American cases involving amateur status are those of Jim Thorpe in 1912 and Charley Paddock in 1928. Paddock was cleared, but Thorpe was declared a professional and stripped of his laurels. Forty years afterward, when he was a sick and "down-and-out" old man, an unsuccessful movement was started to restore the sacred honors he had lost, clearly indicating the perennial American sympathy with "the underdog."

The fifty-year struggle to define an amateur for purposes of Olympic Games competition is probably not a closed issue. As the cultures of men and nations change, so will the conception of what constitutes amateur status change. At the moment in America the college athlete who receives what is commonly called an "athletic scholarship" is considered to be an amateur, but, according to a very strict interpretation of the Olympic regulation, he would not be so considered. There must be similar inconsistencies of interpretation among many of the nations currently competing in the Olympic

Games. It is a tribute to the patient effort of the International Olympic Committee that any common ground can be found on which to base international amateur sport competition.

Sunday scheduling of events at the Olympic Games.—In Chapter 7 the attitude of the American people in regard to holding sports events on Sunday, particularly in the early years of the century, was traced. The fact that some events at the Paris games in 1900 were scheduled on Sunday became something of an issue with United States authorities. The editor of *Outing* deplored the organization of the Paris games and indicated in no uncertain terms his general attitude on the matter, despite the claim of New York papers that Sunday games are more or less common in western United States.[30]

Following a vigorous protest by members of the United States delegation which reached the point of our refusal to send a team if events were scheduled on Sunday, the Paris Exposition authorities finally sent word that athletic events would not be held on Sunday. However, when the athletes from the United States arrived in Paris, they learned that the French officials had set the opening day for a Sunday.

After a long and bitter debate between the French authorities and the representatives of American college groups, the French agreed on a compromise. This they did not keep, largely because of pressure from other nations, and further complications arose when some American athletes decided to compete on Sunday. Altogether it was something of a mess, but the American athletes were good enough to win eight out of the ten Sunday finals.

Sunday scheduling was avoided at the St. Louis games in 1904 and at London in 1908, but no adverse comment was made about Sunday competitions at Stockholm in 1912. To indicate how viewpoints change in a very few years, the editor of *Outing* in 1908 made a strong plea for recreation on Sunday and urged that all playgrounds be opened.[31]

Women's participation in the Olympic Games.—According to one ancient Greek legend, the beginning of the Olympic Games in 776 B.C. involves a woman. According to another, the first woman spectator came as the result of a circumstance involving the mother of a contestant acting as his trainer after the death of his father.[32]

It is not strange, therefore, that when the modern Olympics were instituted at Athens in 1896, King George of Greece invited a large group of Danish girl gymnasts to give an exhibition on the opening day. The enthusiasm with which this exhibition was received augured well for women's participation in later years.

Throughout the early years of the twentieth century sports for women were stressed in the American press, and, after the inclusion of swimming competition for women in the Stockholm games of 1912, a concerted effort was made to send a team of American women swimmers to the next Olympiad. An eight-year interval between games together with the changed status of women caused by World War I undoubtedly had much to do with the decision to send a swimming team to Antwerp in 1920. There was, however, great objection from the professional women in physical education, and still is for that matter. In addition to swimming, women began competing at Antwerp in figure skating. Tennis singles and mixed doubles had been on the program since 1900, but women's doubles were not added until 1920 and were discontinued after 1924, when the American women's tennis team made a clean sweep with Helen Wills in singles and the team of Helen Wills and Mrs. George Wightman in doubles.

Track and field athletics for women were first put on the Olympic program at Amsterdam in 1928, and the light touches of femininity as well as the seriousness with which the girls took their work aroused comment.[33]

Fencing was added to women's Olympic competition at the Paris games of 1924, and gymnastics followed in 1928. Speed skating, skiing, and pair skating (men and women) have been added beginning with the Winter Games of 1936. Olympic competition for women at the Winter Games of 1936, 1948, and 1952 goes hand in hand with the increased interest of women in these activities and the part played by women in their development all over America. It is certainly realistic to believe that the phenomenal growth of winter sports in the United States dates from the Olympic Winter Games of 1932 held at Lake Placid, New York. Women have shared in this growth equally with men.

What of the future?—Baron de Coubertin's philosophy in relation to Olympic Games competition was centered on the welfare and glorification of the individual contestant, and throughout his long period of international service he fought against the introduction of team games. It was his contention that the larger and stronger nations would overwhelm the weaker and smaller nations by the sheer force of numbers in team games and thus detract from the importance of a single victory by a representative of a small nation.

In the team-game controversy he was overruled, but in his insistence on keeping the games free from any type of point score he was upheld. He recognized full well that point scores might immediately lead to a winner nation, then to a more intense nationalism, and, finally, to a wrecking of the spirit of the games and of the games themselves.

America demands a winner—it is one of the facets of our culture in all walks of life. It is true also that many nations have a passion for winning, but De Coubertin believed that stress on winning would overshadow international welfare. This in his mind was the important thing, and, as Henry remarks, "other world organizations, such as the United Nations, . . . have found themselves denied freedom of action for the international good by the selfishness of individual countries."[34]

The twentieth century has seen the birth of many organizations and devices designed to promote better international relations. Any estimate of the success or failure of the Olympic Games in contributing to the accomplishment of this goal should be made on a comparative basis. It seems reasonable to believe that any program which has "survived the life and death of nations, spanned devastating depressions, and lived through two world wars"[35] has amply demonstrated its potentialities for international good will.

18. *Spectator Sports—the Cement*
of Democracy

THE SPECTATOR ASPECT OF THE SPORTS LIFE OF AMERICA HAS probably received more widespread attention, at home and abroad, than any of the many facets of the picture as presented in this book. Few people will dispute the merits of personal participation in wholesome physical activities, but there is wide disagreement on the question of spectator sports. It is not too strange, therefore, that professional baseball should be selected by Soviet Russia as a subject for intensive anti-American propaganda.[1]

Spectator sports have undeniably played an ever expanding part in the social and economic life of America in the years of the twentieth century. Paid attendance figures are available for many major and minor sports, amateur and professional, and their total over a single year is a sizable sum even in these days of astronomical figures. If it were possible, however, to compile complete statistics on the actual number of individuals who read about such reports in the newspapers, books, and magazines, who listen to sports programs on the radio, and who remain firmly glued to a television set whenever a sports event is being shown, the totals would be astounding indeed.

Since spectator sports, in the widest sense of the word, would include also the contests played by youngsters on playgrounds and in special recreation areas, by workers in the thousands of industrially sponsored games, and by amateur groups in a variety of clubs and private organizations, a total spectator compilation would present almost unbelievable proportions.

Innumerable attempts have been made to analyze the factors which have given spectator sports the hold they have on Americans, and many attempts have been made to explain how they have woven themselves so deeply into our way of living. Increased leisure and a rising standard of living are a part of the answer, but not all. The American citizen with time on his hands and money to spend is also free to choose what he shall do with both. The answer as to why he has singled out sports for the attention he has may be an unconscious tribute to the part such activities play in the successful functioning of the culture. As one anthropologist states it: "Any cultural practice must be functional or it will disappear before long. . . . It must somehow contribute to the survival of the society or to the adjustment of the individual."[2] This chapter will attempt to give consideration to spectator sports as a cultural practice and to explore the manner in which they contribute to the survival of society and to the adjustment of the individual within the framework of twentieth-century American culture.

THE COMPETITOR

There are probably as many varieties of motives operating in the individual player of sports as there are individuals who play. One seemingly universal component is the desire to be watched. This is manifested at an extremely early age, as any mother or teacher of young children will testify. As soon as a particular skill is learned or attempted, the cry is "Watch me!" It may be assumed, therefore, that the desire for approval and for some form of mastery or superiority is fundamental in all individuals. Beginning with the accomplishments of childhood and extending up through the highest achievements of civilization, one of the strongest incentives to perfection, both individual and social, is the desire to be praised and honored for one's excellence.[3]

It is also evident that the culture within which the individual lives either operates to minimize or to reinforce this motivation, and thus there is another reason for the prevalence and popularity of spectator sports. In America, success must be recognized to be fully savored; it must be observed, recorded, envied, and applauded, and sometimes the amount of applause tends to be a measure of the achievement. It is because American democracy is a society of rising and not declining men that eminence is coveted, not disparaged, the provision being attached that such eminence be earned and not created by the social structure itself.[4]

There is great diversity of opinion within the culture as to the relative degree of harm and/or benefit which may accrue to the competitor in the so-called spectator sports, and especially when such competitors are in the school- and college-age group. Particularly among the older age groups, great concern is often expressed with regard to the harmful effects of excessive publicity and adulation on the character and future of the participants. In view of the case histories available representing both the harmful and the beneficial end results, perhaps the answer lies more in the personality and background of the individual competitor than in the circumstances which surround his competition or in the game itself.

Support for this point of view lies in the following excerpt from one of the nation's favorite writers of fiction in a discussion of the pros and cons of high-school athletics:

They help boys find a place in society, especially boys who might otherwise live on the fringes of the world. In games, such boys can be momentary heroes and win the wild approval of their community. Young fellows who wear ill-fitting clothes, whose fathers lie drunk in the town gutters, or whose mothers rouse whispers on street corners, boys whose entire future is nothingness can have their day of glory; and some of them like the taste of that glory and determine that the town gutters are not for them.[5]

AESTHETIC APPRECIATION

Trying to explain the fascination which sports have for the spectator to an individual who is relatively immune from such fascination is a little like trying to explain and communicate the beauty of a Beethoven symphony to the tone-deaf person. In common with any other aesthetic experience, the spectator-participant can get no more out of the experience than he brings to it in background, perception, or sensitivity. Yet the noblest qualities which can be perceived in things, rhythm and harmony, are there. The very words with which human beings try to explain the effects of beauty are the same as are used to denote the elements of play: tension, poise, balance, contrast, variation, solution, resolution.[6]

One of America's most esteemed authorities in matters of art, taste, and aesthetic experience makes the following comparison:

An example of the twentieth century dilettante *par excellence* is the baseball fan. If you compare his attitude toward his favorite pastime with that of a good art "lover," you find that they have a good deal in common. The fan (and the dilettante) is a highly skilled observer with a remarkable sense of the past and present status of his favorite pastime. He understands the nuances of technique and can distinguish between first-rate and not quite first-rate performance with the connoisseurship that comes from long exercise of judgment and constant refinement of perception. He may or may not be a practitioner himself. His is a spectator's skill and appreciation. He is confident in the expression of his judgment, but he doesn't hesitate to change his mind if continued performance doesn't bear him out. It is respect for his opinion (and consequently his patronage) that keeps his favorite after-hours occupation at the level of excellence it has achieved. It also keeps out the phonies. He isn't interested in reputations for their own sake; he is interested in quality of performance.[7]

It would be ridiculous to assume that all sports fans were sufficiently perceptive to be attuned to such an experience, and yet such appreciative spectators do constitute a substantial body among the total. Not all are equally capable of giving articulate expression to their reactions, as for instance in the following:

The sheer sensory satisfaction involved in watching players in a colorful and suspenseful contest is a deeply satisfying experience to many individuals. Add to this the emotional reaction of perceiving graceful bodily movement, nimbleness of foot, and power as expressed in play and you have glimpsed the art of sports.[8]

There are few indeed who would not admit that the aesthetic value of appreciating the art of the thing one sees or experiences is a desirable social goal and that life becomes an increasingly satisfying experience to those individuals capable of seeing all of life as an artistic expression.

For many, the appeal of spectator sports lies in the excitement of the crowd, the sensuous pleasure of the city dweller sitting in the shade of the grandstand, looking at the lush green of the playing field. It is a part of a healthy rebellion against the unrelieved realism of his daily life that seeks to make him walk sedately in a world where nothing but facts and common sense matter. Here he voluntarily enters into the play sphere and for the duration of the contest accepts its rules and values and puts himself under the spell of the world of sport. To the individual who is unable to make this transition the outcome of the contest has no meaning; he has put himself outside the play sphere. He is like the man who refused to attend the races because he knew very well that one horse could run faster than another.[9] And yet the best psychiatric thought of the day insists that the more complicated civilization becomes, and the more intense and elaborate the machinery of living is made, the more necessary it becomes to create the temporary retreat from reality which is called play.[10]

EMOTIONAL TENSION AND AGGRESSIVE BEHAVIOR

A growing body of evidence from the fields of psychology and psychiatry contributes to a better understanding of the role of sports and play activities with relation to the individual, both spectator and participant. On one point the evidence is practically unanimous, and that is the important value of play in the opportunities that it affords for the relief of repressed aggressions. This single function might in itself be sufficient to account for the invention and growth of games, with their enactment of the drama of struggle and danger. It might also explain why games and sports, though often frowned on and sometimes banned, have survived as a human institution and today are more firmly established than ever before over most of the world.[11]

The importance of vigorous physical activity in providing emotional release for the individual who participates is widely acknowledged and well understood. The existence of such benefits of release to the spectator is often denied, ignored, or misunderstood. And yet Menninger says:

> In defense of the spectator role it should be said that many people are almost entirely debarred from active competition of any sort because they feel weak or inferior, or fear retaliation. . . . Passive participation is the *only* outlet which such people can permit themselves and it is for that reason all the more necessary to them.[12]

The role of spectator sports in the relief of repressed aggressions and the release of emotional tensions is intimately related to the problem of spectator behavior. Vocal participation on the part of observers has always been an integral part of the game. In American culture, so long as such vocal participation is affirmative in character, taking the form of approval, applause, and approbation, it comes under the heading of acceptable behavior. When it takes the form of derision, booing, invective, and insult, it becomes a matter for grave concern and criticism. What is not generally understood is that both forms of behavior on the part of spectators have equally long histories and that in many cultures both have developed stylized and ritualized forms.

From the *Polynesian Researches* of missionary William Ellis, published in 1829, comes a vivid description of spectator behavior among Tahitians attending a *taupitis* (wrestling match):

The vanquished was scarcely stretched on the sand, when a shout of exultation burst from the victor's friends. Their drums struck up; the women rose, and danced in triumph over the fallen wrestler, and sung in defiance to the opposite party.[13]

While one party was drumming, dancing, and singing in pride of victory, all done with menacing defiance, the other party was equally vociferous in reciting the achievements of the vanquished and predicting the shortness of his rival's triumph.

Formal contests in invective and vituperation were widespread in pre-Islamic Arabia, abuse and derision of an adversary being one of the essentials of the competition.[14] Greek tradition has numerous traces of ceremonial slanging matches, and at the feasts of Demeter and Apollo men and women chanted songs of mutual derision. Of course, the Greeks used to stage contests in most anything that offered the possibility of a competitive struggle. Contests were held in singing, riddle-solving, keeping awake, and drinking. It is reported that Alexander celebrated the death of Kalanos by a gymnastic and musical contest with prizes for the heartiest drinkers, with the result that thirty-five competitors died on the spot, six at a later date, among them the prize winners.[15]

It would seem that an understanding of the behavior of spectators might more profitably be sought in the realm of custom, convention, and cultural pattern than in the realm of ethics and morality. Certainly such behavior is better understood if due recognition is given to the possibilities of emotional and aggressive release which are involved. In the words of one psychologist:

Booing is only applause turned inside out. A fellow cheers at a game to express his emotions—his emotions that follow approval. Why should he not boo to express his emotions that follow disapproval? They are just as genuine. They are just as inevitable. And they are quite as much in place. Few of us go to see games to study them. And disapproval is as much a part of enjoyment as approval is.[16]

SPECTATOR SPORTS AND MASS MEDIA OF COMMUNICATION

It is frequently asserted that all individuality in America is being destroyed as a result of mass education, mass amusement, mass production, ready-made clothes, and a popular press. The prevalence and popularity of spectator sports is usually included as a prime example in the picture of a people in the process of becoming more and more standardized. That this concept of the "mass mind" may be a delusion, as well as dangerous nonsense leading to a profound defeatism, is aptly expressed by a recent article in *Harper's:*

> The modern individual has an immense choice of occupation and amusement. So that the "mass" of sight-seers at any show place today is actually composed of individuals who have fully chosen to join that crowd and will join a different one tomorrow. What looks like a proof of the mob mind is really evidence of spreading interests among the people and a variety of occupations. And if some of these interests are "popular," aimed at a crowd which is not very critical or reflective, they are a good deal more so than interests which were the only recourse of their ancestors—dog-fighting, bear-baiting, the fit up melodrama or one-night stand, once a year, and booze.[17]

A great deal of the more sophisticated lamentation over this alleged regimentation comes from the "representatives of a class whose leisure and income has always enabled them to enjoy a relatively wide variety of pleasures."[18] To the average man the expanding opportunity to see and hear and to read about an increasing number of sports and games makes the cry of "regimentation" not only absurd but quite incomprehensible.

There is currently available a sizable body of research on the general subject of the effects of mass media, much of which has definite implications for the student of spectator sports and of their role in American culture.[19] Certain chapters of this book, which can be classified under the general title of "The Impact of Developments in Communication and Transportation," have related a part of the story of how much time and space has been devoted to giving Americans full opportunity to read about, listen to, and view sports through the media of newspaper and magazine, radio and television. The sheer volume of such material puts it in a category worthy of investigation along with music, daytime serials, mystery drama, comedy and variety, and quiz and audience-participation shows.

The most basic process thus far established by research on the effects of mass media is the phenomenon of self-selection. This is defined as the inevitable tendency of every product of mass media to determine its own audiences. In other words, whether a person voluntarily reads at all, what kind of material he reads, what kind he listens to, and what type of television program he chooses to see are apparently determined by his cultural status.

Every radio program, every book, every magazine thus tends to become known to and attract those persons who already like such material, and to remain unknown or at least unattended by persons who either dislike such material or, and perhaps more importantly, have had no experience with such material and no stimulus to develop the experience.[20]

It would be difficult to imagine the average American child growing up without any knowledge of or experience in sports and games. His earliest experiences are concerned with motor skills, with learning to run, to climb, to kick, to throw, and to ride on various types of play apparatus. He grows to adolescence in an atmosphere of playgrounds, physical education at school, and sports programs sponsored by the church and by youth organizations. He comes to maturity in a social environment that encourages such forms of sports expression. It seems fairly obvious then that herein lies a still further explanation of the popularity of spectator sports.[21]

Increasing recognition of the spectator role as an almost inescapable concomitant of America's complex twentieth-century development is shown in the treatment given the question by the Educational Policies Commission in their publication *Policies for Education in American Democracy*.[22] Under that section of the report devoted to the objectives of self-realization, the statement is made that the educated person is participant *and* spectator in many sports as well as other pastimes. The suggestion is made that, rather than quarrel about participation versus observation, it would seem more constructive to encourage both, since for the average person each activity supports and enriches the other.

There is included also an interesting commentary on the tendency to regard the role of spectator at certain recreational activities as being inferior to others. There are obviously many people who feel that a visit to the theater to watch professional actors perform is somehow more wholesome and praiseworthy than a visit to the baseball park to watch professional athletes. It would seem difficult to measure the relative intrinsic dramatic power in "watching the struggle on a darkening stage between Macbeth and his conscience" as against "watching under a warm sun a good nine-inning pitching duel."[23]

RITUAL AND CEREMONY

Every culture develops ritual forms in daily life which seem to be essential for the satisfaction of certain needs in the people who make up the culture. In the words of Herskovits, ritual is "a powerful agent in uniting a people. Whether they are active participants . . . themselves experiencing the emotional force of a rite, or whether they are spectators, the bonds that bind them to their fellows are strengthened by ceremonialism."[24] As a civilization develops in size, complexity, and becomes industrialized, old forms of dress and methods of doing things are replaced by standardized procedures and forms. Yet the need for ritual remains. In America this need has been met, in a measure, for millions through the medium of spectator sports. In furnishing socially approved forms of ritual and ceremony, spectator sports serve a definite cultural function.

The band, the drum majorettes, the drill team, the card stunts, the color guard, and the playing of the national anthem—all of these create an atmosphere of oneness and belonging which is too seldom achieved. They create a sharing of a common interest, an indispensable ingredient in a successfully functioning culture.

Sport is America's great outdoor theater, offering an exciting and colorful repertoire, with the big college-football game presenting the most spectacular appeal of all. It is not alone the pageantry, but the fact that the average football crowd brings to the stadium a passionate and partisan spirit, which is accelerated by the acrobatic cheerleaders and stirred by the marching bands, themselves as intensively trained as the athletes.

Hero-worship is not uniquely an American phenomenon or one of the present age alone. The fact that it reaches such extraordinary dimensions in the present day is due in part to the fact that the machinery exists in more complete form than ever before. In America each sport has its magic names and a whole corps of competent sports writers and sports announcers to chronicle the saga of their outstanding accomplishments. Thus is achieved the status of national hero. More than a hundred years ago Carlyle wrote, "Society is founded upon hero-worship," and it is quite apparent that the glamour and excitement still persist.

For there is joy in the coming of a hero. There is a fine thrill in a new champion suddenly revealed. There is solid satisfaction in standing beside him when the drums roll and the cameras click, lining the streets to bid him welcome, packing the banquet-halls to hear him praised, basking in the aura of his sudden fame, breaking the humdrum routine of an ordered living with a gala day, enjoying for a moment the thrill of self-identification with this fleeting bit of glory.[25]

SPORTS HERO IN THE CULTURE

The historian, Dixon Wecter, opens his book on *The Hero in America* with a paragraph extremely appropriate to an examination of the interrelationship of the phenomenon of hero-worship with athletics and athletes in American culture.

Hero-worship answers an urgent American need. The fan and the autograph hunter, now imitated elsewhere, are as native to the United States as the catbird and the Catawba grape. To fix our relation with greatness by means of a signature in an album, a lock of hair, a photograph, or a baseball that has scored a home run; to haunt stage doors and entries to locker-rooms; to pursue our favorites with candid cameras and sound recorders, invading their meditations and their honeymoons—this passion has made us the premier nation of hero-worshippers. Others, of course, have like impulses. The phlegmatic Cockney collects Famous Cricketers from the coupons in cigarette packets; the Spaniard helps to carry off a great matador on his shoulder. But only in the United States has the greeter become a profession and the ovation a fine art[26]

The game of baseball and the baseball player Babe Ruth are prime examples of the operation of the hero-worship motif as it functions in the culture. In addition to being widely acknowledged as the national sport, baseball is the one sport that has a formal shrine, built and maintained to perpetuate and immortalize the heroes and relics of the game. Opened in June, 1939, at Cooperstown, New York, baseball's Hall of Fame had more than a hundred thousand visitors in the first nine years of its existence. These visitors, whose names are signed to the register, came from all of the forty-eight states and from such other parts of the world as Spain, France, Germany, Great Britain, Japan, Mexico, Cuba, and Costa Rica.

The United States government lent prestige and support to the dedication of the shrine by authorizing a special issue of sixty-five million stamps to commemorate this hundredth anniversary of baseball. One million of these stamps were allotted to the Cooperstown Post Office, and 450,000 pieces of mail were dispatched from that post office on June 12, 1939.[27]

Three years previous to the opening, a most impressive list of individuals and organizations, representing a wide cross-section of the culture, had been enlisted to aid in the movement. There were generals and admirals from the army, navy, and marines; the United States Chamber of Commerce and the Commissioner of Education; the National Association of Broadcasters and the Baseball Writers Association of America; the National Collegiate Athletic Association, and the Boys' Clubs of America. Their efforts and support, coupled with the energy and promotional ability of the men within baseball, brought to completion this quarter-million-dollar project which had begun in 1917 as a dream—to build a memorial to Abner Doubleday.

It is most typically American that the decision should have been made that all candidates to the Hall of Fame be elected by vote. It also seems particularly fitting that the responsibility for their selection should be placed in the hands of the Baseball Writers Association of America.

Shrines must have their heroes, and this one has Babe Ruth, baseball's greatest and most colorful personality. Experts may disagree, but in a democracy a hero must be the people's choice, and by almost any standard of measurement the Bambino fulfils this first requirement. Nationally and internationally he was one of the most widely known of all Americans. Without minimizing the accomplishment of skilled publicity and friendly biography and oratory, he became the greatest crowd magnet in the history of the sport because the crowd admired and loved him. His heart and spirit very successfully relegated his feet of clay to the background shadows.

While a great deal of adult acclaim and appreciation was showered on Ruth, the essence of his popularity and of the hero-worship which surrounded him was the bond between the Babe and the kids of the nation. Though it is currently more fashionable to be cynical about such things, there is overwhelming evidence that his affection for children was completely sincere. Throughout his playing career and long afterward, even though such public appearances were an inconvenience and an annoyance, Babe never turned down a promise to go somewhere to visit kids.[28] During his long illness in the nineteen-forties the bulk of his mail came from youngsters. The climax to a lifetime of playing hero to the children of America came with the setting-up of the Babe Ruth Foundation, Inc., in May, 1947. The funds were to be "used to aid American youngsters to achieve good character from participation in sports and to offer scholarships and prizes to underprivileged boys, not necessarily connected with sports."[29]

Babe Ruth was accorded the supreme tribute of public prayer offered in his behalf. The commissioner of baseball had announced that Sunday, April 27, 1947, would be proclaimed "Babe Ruth Day" in every ball park in organized baseball, in order to give an opportunity to all fans to unite in a salute and join in prayer for the recovery of the champion. This was no collection scheme or fund-raising event but an expression of affection to one who had contributed so much to the national game. Sixty thousand people in Yankee Stadium listened to Francis Cardinal Spellman as he prayed:

> To Thee, we turn today and pray Thee: Be the spirit of our sports, the source of our spiritual inspiration and physical strength, for the upbuilding of our nation as, on this occasion, we honor a hero in the world of sport, a champion of fair play and a manly leader of youth in America.[30]

THE AMATEUR AND THE PROFESSIONAL

A discussion of spectator sports necessarily involves at least a brief examination of the amateur-professional controversy which flourished even before the twentieth century began and still remains an unresolved dilemma in the sports life of America.

Historically, the amateur rule comes from the cultural setting of the leisure classes of feudal Europe, carrying a distinction between the classes and the masses, with the disparaging implication that to work for pay is to be a hireling. Such a point of view was expressed by Plato in the *Dialogues* when he said, "For a teacher to receive pay for teaching is no better than prostitution." One of the unique features of the development of sports in America is the gradual transformation of the idea of sports for a privileged few, "gallant sportsmen to whom a dollar was just something for tradesmen to fret about,"[31] to sports for all those who have the desire or the ability to indulge.

It may be that the historical amateur tradition is one of the many traditions that, while forming an acknowledged part of the heritage of American sports, have undergone subtle changes and adaptations to the peculiarly American culture pattern. As an example, when Xenophon of Corinth, a month before he appeared at the stadium to take part in the Olympic Games of 464 B.C., solemnly swore as a part of his qualifying for participation that he was of pure Hellenic blood, he was perpetuating an idea that Americans have attempted to repudiate since the democracy began. Pindar's immortal ode may still thrill its readers, but this idea, antiquated and discredited before Hitler seized upon it, that the possession of a certain type of blood should qualify some individuals and disqualify others who lack it, is contradicted daily in democratic America.

A prominent social historian has made a very astute observation with regard to this controversy.

There was a technical distinction between amateur and professional athletics in the United States, insisted on with such pedantic precision that a player could be disqualified as an amateur for writing articles on his own sport or coaching a schoolboy for money in another game; but there was little psychological distinction. Both amateur and professional had the essentially professional attitude which takes training seriously, admires technical form and would make almost any sacrifice for victory.[32]

Arnold J. Toynbee's book, *A Study of History*, contains an acknowledgment of the importance of games and sports to the well-being of individuals living under the conditions imposed by a modern industrial culture. It also points out that there is more than an accidental relationship between the growth of organized games and sports and the rise of industrialism; and such sport is described as a "conscious attempt to counter-balance the soul-destroying specialization which the division of labor under industrialism entails." Toynbee does not let the matter rest there but goes on to deplore the growth of professional athletes, "more narrowly specialized and more extravagantly paid than any industrial technicians."[33]

This may be an oft-repeated error of mistaking the shadow for the substance. Repelled at the richness of the frosting, Toynbee has failed to remember the good solid layers of cake which support it. There would seem to be as much logic in viewing with alarm a magnificent opera performance at the Metropolitan or a symphony concert at Carnegie Hall, and ignoring the music-loving public which makes such performances possible.

The exercise of physical skill, mental acumen, and spiritual courage in the field of sports and games is as old and as integral a part of the cultures of mankind as the expression of these same human capacities in the fields of music and art. The rich and colorful heritage in this area of human experience is as much a part of the birthright of the children of earth as the songs that have been sung and the pictures that have been painted.

Why the supremely gifted in sports should be barred from that all-too-small company of artists whose talents bring fame and fortune, it is difficult to understand. It seems quite certain that a professional athlete in the course of his training never underwent a more rigorous regime than, say, Yehudi Menuhin. And if the steep ascent from obscurity to fame is always accomplished without chicanery or temptation, then all biographical and autobiographical evidence to the contrary must be disbelieved.

SPECTATOR SPORTS AS AN INTEGRATING FORCE
IN AMERICAN DEMOCRACY

Common interests, common loyalties, common enthusiasms —those are the great integrating factors in any culture. In America, sports have provided this common denominator in as great a degree as any other single factor. The team rosters of the great universities, athletic clubs, and professional teams have sometimes resembled the third-class passenger list of an ocean liner putting into the port of New York in the early years of the twentieth century. Throughout America the many groups with their various racial backgrounds and cultural heritages are often conscious of their differences from one another and eager to find a common meeting ground. When this group unites in an interest in or hero-worship of an athlete or a team, all at the same time, they feel a sense of homogeneity which they can acquire in no other way.[34]

The democratizing influence of spectator sports in American culture can scarcely be overestimated. In furnishing a common cultural interest, fostering understanding across class lines, and increasing the intimacy of association with different classes, spectator sports have contributed to those integrating forces which are vital and indispensable in the preservation of our democratic way of life. The lowliest individual in the economic or social scale may participate with equal benefit and pleasure in the spectator sports. The bleachers are equally cordial to coal-miners, politicians, and bank presidents.

Notes and Bibliography

NOTES AND BIBLIOGRAPHY TO CHAPTER 1

1. Cozens, Frederick W., and Stumpf, Florence. "Implications of Cultural Anthropology for Physical Education," *American Academy of Physical Education*, Professional Contributions No. 1, 1951, pp. 94.

2. Thomas, W. Beach. "Games on Paper, and Elsewhere," *Macmillan's Magazine*, 81 (December, 1899), 129–35.

3. Wecter, Dixon. *The Saga of American Society: A Record of Social Aspiration, 1607–1937*, p. 428. New York: Charles Scribner's Sons, 1937, pp. 504.

4. Jokl, Ernst. "The Future of Athletics," *Vigor*, 1 (December, 1947), 10–18. Published at Johannesburg by the National Advisory Council for Physical Education in collaboration with the Department of Health of the Union of South Africa.

5. Jones, R. W. "A Century of Sport," *World Communique*, 9 (June, 1950), 3. Published bimonthly at Geneva Headquarters of the World Alliance of Young Men's Christian Associations: 37 Quai Wilson, Geneva, Switzerland.

6. Information on foreign programs was taken from the quarterly bulletin *Physical Recreation*, for home and overseas circulation, the official journal of the Central Council of Physical Recreation, London, England. Headquarters office, 6 Bedford Square, London, W.C. 1.

7. Davidson, Marshall B. *Life in America*, Vol. 2. Boston: Houghton Mifflin Co., 1951, pp. 503.

8. Sherman, Stuart P. *Points of View*, p. 25. New York: Charles Scribner's Sons, 1924, pp. 363.

9. Dulles, Foster Rhea. *Twentieth Century America*. New York: Appleton-Century Co., 1940, pp. 441.

10. Commager, Henry Steele. *Living Ideas in America*. New York: Harper & Bros., 1951, pp. 776.

NOTES AND BIBLIOGRAPHY TO CHAPTER 2

1. Strunsky, Simeon. *The Living Tradition: Change and America*. New York: Doubleday, Doran & Co., 1939, pp. 454.
2. Stumpf, Florence, and Cozens, Frederick W. "Some Aspects of the Role of Games, Sports, and Recreational Activities in the Culture of Modern Primitive Peoples," *Research Quarterly*, 18 (October, 1947), 198–218; *ibid.*, 20 (March, 1949), 2–20.
3. Ortega y Gasset, José. *Toward a Philosophy of History*. New York: W. W. Norton & Co., 1941, pp. 273.
4. Linton, Ralph (ed.). *The Science of Man in the World Crisis*. New York: Columbia University Press, 1945, pp. 532.
5. Cozens, Frederick W., and Stumpf, Florence. "Sports and American Culture," *Idea and Experiment*, 2 (December, 1952), 12–15. (Printed by the University of California Press.)

NOTES AND BIBLIOGRAPHY TO CHAPTER 3

1. Menninger, Karl. *Love against Hate*. New York: Harcourt, Brace & Co., 1942, pp. 311.
2. Pier, Arthur Stanwood. "Work and Play," *Atlantic*, 94 (November, 1904), 669–75.
3. Elmer, M. C. *The Sociology of the Family*. Boston: Ginn & Co., 1945, pp. 520.
4. "Public Recreation Facilities," *Annals of the American Academy of Political and Social Science*, 35 (March, 1910), 380.
5. Barnes, Harry Elmer, and Ruedi, Oreen M. *The American Way of Life*. New York: Prentice-Hall, Inc., 1942, pp. 802.
6. Roosevelt, Theodore. *An Autobiography*, pp. 169–70. New York: Macmillan Co., 1913, pp. 597. (Permission to quote granted by present copyright holder, Charles Scribner's Sons, New York.)
7. Groves, Ernest R. *The American Woman*. New York: Greenberg, Publisher, Inc., 1937, pp. 438.
8. Beard, Mary Ritter. *Woman's Work in Municipalities*. New York: D. Appleton & Co., 1916, pp. 344.
9. Mead, Margaret. "What Women Want," *Fortune*, 34 (December, 1946), 6.
10. O'Hagan, Anne. "The Athletic Girl," *Munsey's*, 25 (August, 1901), 729–38.

11. Allen, Frances Anne. "Fig Leaves," *American Mercury*, 13 (January, 1928), 59–66.
12. Seldes, Gilbert. "Dress and Undress," *Mentor*, 17 (November, 1929), 15, 56, 60.
13. *Ibid.*
14. Bayles, James C. "Courage in Dress," *Independent*, 70 (May 11, 1911), 956–57.
15. Patten, Simon N. "The Standardization of Family Life," *Annals of the American Academy of Political and Social Science*, 48 (July, 1913), 81–90.
16. Dulles, Foster Rhea. *America Learns To Play*. New York: D. Appleton–Century Co., 1940, pp. 441.
17. Train, Arthur. *Puritan's Progress*. New York: Charles Scribner's Sons, 1931, pp. 477.
18. Carpenter, Niles. "Courtship Practices and Contemporary Social Change in America," *Annals of the American Academy of Political and Social Science*, 160 (March, 1932), 38–44.
19. Burgess, Ernest W., and Locke, Harvey J. *The Family: From Institution to Companionship*. New York: American Book Co., 1945, pp. 800.
20. Folsom, Joseph Kirk. *The Family and Democratic Society*. New York: John Wiley & Sons, Inc., 1943, pp. 755.
21. Mead, *op. cit.*, p. 6.
22. Rich, Margaret E. *Family Life Today*. Boston: Houghton Mifflin Co., 1928, pp. 244. Papers presented at a conference in celebration of the Fiftieth Anniversary of Family Social Work in America, held at Buffalo, October 2–5, 1927. Chapter IX, "New Tools of Leisure," by Karl de Schweinitz.
23. Faust, J. W. "Family Recreation the Most Fruitful Feature of Home Life," *School Life*, 14 (February, 1929), 101–3.
24. Folsom, Joseph K. "The Changing Role of the Family," *Annals of the American Academy of Political and Social Science*, 212 (1940), 64.
25. *Ibid.*
26. Mumford, Lewis. *Faith for Living*. New York: Harcourt, Brace & Co., 1940, pp. 333.
27. Mumford, Lewis. "The American Dwelling House," *American Mercury*, 19 (April, 1930), 474.
28. Hudnut, Joseph. *Architecture and the Spirit of Man*. Cambridge, Mass.: Harvard University Press, 1949, pp. 301.
29. Mumford, *op. cit.*, p. 474.

NOTES AND BIBLIOGRAPHY TO CHAPTER 4

1. Steiner, Jesse Frederick. *Americans at Play*. New York: Mc-Graw-Hill Book Co., Inc., 1933, pp. 199. Chapter VI, "Trends in Commercial Amusements."
2. Meyer, Harold D., and Brightbill, Charles K. *Community Recreation*. Boston: D. C. Heath & Co., 1948, pp. 704.
3. Perry, Clarence Arthur. "Is Commercial Recreation an Octopus?" *Playground*, 21 (February, 1928), 604–6.
4. Lewis, Oscar. "The Case of American Sport," *Independent*, 118 (June 18, 1927), 628–30.
5. Le Galliene, Richard. "Human Need of Coney Island," *Cosmopolitan*, 39 (July, 1905), 237–46.
6. Paine, Albert Bigelow. "The New Coney Island," *Century*, 68 (August, 1904), 529.
7. Gatlin, Dana. "Amusing America's Millions," *World's Work*, 26 (July, 1913), 325–40.
8. Willey, Day Allen. "The Trolley-Park," *Cosmopolitan*, 33 (July, 1902), 265–72.
9. Sullivan, James E. "Athletics and the Stadium," *Cosmopolitan*, 31 (September, 1901), 501–8.
10. "Physical Training at the St. Louis Fair," *Amer. Phys. Educ. Rev.*, 9 (March, 1904), 46–47.
11. Govett, L. A. *The King's Book of Sports*. London: Elliot Stock, 62, Paternoster Row, 1890, pp. 140.
12. Bailey, Gilbert. "20,000,000 Keglers," *New York Times Magazine*, April 3, 1949, pp. 48–49.
13. Meyer, Robert, Jr. *Festivals U.S.A.* New York: Ives Washburn, Inc., 1950, pp. 438.
14. Martin, H. B. *Fifty Years of American Golf*. New York: Dodd, Mead & Co., 1936, pp. 423.
15. Bartlett, Arthur. "They're Just Wild about Sports," *Saturday Evening Post*, 222 (December 24, 1949), 34–35, 41–42.
16. Martin, *op. cit.*, Chapter XXI, "American Inventive Genius."
17. Musser, H. Burton. *Turf Management*. New York: McGraw-Hill Book Co., 1950, pp. 354. Author and editor is professor of agronomy at Pennsylvania State College. Chapter 11, "Elements of Golf Course Design," is the work of two members of the American Society of Golf Course Architects.
18. Sparkes, Boyden. "Who Plays Golf and Where," *Saturday Evening Post*, 203 (September 6, 1930), 18–19.

19. "Our National Golf Bill," *Literary Digest*, 112 (March 5, 1932), 35.

20. Pirie, Alex. "The Business of the Golf Game," *Saturday Evening Post*, 203 (July 26, 1930), 36.

21. Wind, Herbert Warren. *The Story of American Golf*. New York: Farrar, Straus & Co., 1948, pp. 502.

22. Landman, Joan and David. *Where To Ski*. Boston: Houghton Mifflin Co., 1949, pp. 359.

23. "Where To Go," *Good Housekeeping*, 52 (June, 1911), 749–54.

24. This bureau was conducted under the auspices of the Playground and Recreation Association of America.

25. Benson, Reuel D., and Goldberg, Jacob A. *The Camp Counselor*. New York: McGraw-Hill Book Co., Inc., 1951, pp. 337. Chapter 1, "The Development of Organized Camping in the United States."

26. Mitchell, A. Viola, and Crawford, Ida B. *Camp Counseling*. Philadelphia: W. B. Saunders Co., 1950, pp. 388. Chapter 1, "The History and Growth of the Camping Movement."

27. Gulick, Luther Halsey. "The 'Why' of the Summer Camps for Boys and Girls," *Good Housekeeping*, 54 (June, 1912), 825–29.

28. Gardner, Edith M. "When Girls Go Camping," *Good Housekeeping*, 78 (June, 1924), 66.

29. Hopkins, Una Nixson. "The New Girls' Camp," *Ladies' Home Journal*, 31 (March, 1914), 11.

30. Gibson, H. W. *Camp Management*. New York: Greenberg, Publisher, Inc., 1939 (rev. ed.), pp. 304.

31. Gatlin, Dana. "Amusing America's Millions," *World's Work*, 26 (July, 1913), 340.

32. Tunis, John Roberts. *This Writing Game: Selections from Twenty Years of Freelancing*. New York: A. S. Barnes & Co., 1941, pp. 357. It has been said that no one writing about sport today approaches it with more intelligence, perception, and balance, as well as enthusiasm, than John Tunis.

33. Grombach, John V. *The Saga of Sock*. New York: A. S. Barnes & Co., 1949, pp. 381.

34. McGeehan, W. O. "Amalgamated Sports," *Saturday Evening Post*, 200 (June 9, 1928), 12–13.

35. Tunis, John. "A Nation of Onlookers," *Atlantic*, 160 (August, 1937), 141–50.

36. Meyer, *op. cit.*

37. Merz, Charles. *The Great American Band Wagon*. New York: Garden City Pub. Co., Inc., 1928, pp. 194.
38. Grombach, *op. cit.*
39. The International Boxing Club was referred to by the newspapers as "Octopus, Inc."
40. "Battle: Sports vs. Antitrust Bloodhounds," *Business Week*, October 20, 1951, pp. 20–21.
41. MacDougall, Curtis D. *Newsroom Problems and Policies*. New York: Macmillan Co., 1941, pp. 592. Quotation reprinted from an editorial in the *New Republic*, October 6, 1926, p. 122.
42. *Newsman's Holiday*. Cambridge, Mass.: Harvard University Press, 1942, pp. 203.
43. Spink, J. G. Taylor. *Judge Landis and Twenty-five Years of Baseball*. New York: Thomas Y. Crowell Co., 1947, pp. 306.
44. Mack, Connie. *My 66 Years in the Big Leagues*. Philadelphia: John C. Winston Co., 1950, pp. 246.
45. *Ibid.*, p. 190.
46. Daley, Arthur. "Why We Worship the Babe Ruths," *New York Times Magazine*, April 16, 1950, p. 19.

NOTES AND BIBLIOGRAPHY TO CHAPTER 5

1. Castle, Ames. "Teamwork Topics," *Industrial Sports Journal*, 12 (May 15, 1951), 6.
2. Diehl, Leonard J., and Eastwood, Floyd R. *Industrial Recreation: Its Development and Present Status*. Lafayette, Ind.: Purdue University, 1940, pp. 75.
3. Hapgood, Norman. *Industry and Progress*. New Haven: Yale University Press, 1911, pp. 123. Under Norman Hapgood as editor (1903–12), *Collier's* was a great force in public affairs.
4. Taylor, Frederick Winslow. *The Principles of Scientific Management*. New York: Harper & Bros., 1929, pp. 144.
5. Patterson, S. Howard. *Social Aspects of Industry*. New York: McGraw-Hill Book Co., Inc., 1943, pp. 536.
6. Tannebaum, Frank. *A Philosophy of Labor*. New York: Alfred A. Knopf, Inc., 1951, pp. 199.
7. Duggins, G. Herbert, and Eastwood, Floyd R. *Planning Industrial Recreation*. Lafayette, Ind.: Purdue University, 1941, pp. 82.
8. Patterson, Garnett. "Attitude of the National Labor Relations Board toward Industrial Recreation Programs." Chicago: Chi-

cago National Conference on Industrial Recreation, Lecture Reporting Service, 1939.

9. "Industrial Recreation," *Playground,* 14 (September, 1920), 356–67.

10. Tarbell, Ida M. "A Fine Place To Work," *American,* 80 (September, 1915), 38–41, 80.

11. "Women in Industry," *Outlook,* 125 (August 4, 1920), 598.

12. "Play or Grow Sour," *Collier's,* 65 (March 27, 1920), 19.

13. The CIO led the fight against the American Bowling Congress for the elimination of racial discrimination in that sport.

14. *The CIO News* (Detroit, Mich.), August 23, 1948, p. 10.

15. *Ibid.*

16. Olga Madar was a former schoolteacher who received her training in physical education and recreation at Michigan State Normal College. She became international recreational director in 1947.

17. Hearings, Special Subcommittee of the Committee on Education and Labor, House of Representatives (81st Cong.; H.R. 2026), *Community Recreation Services Act.* Washington, D.C.: United States Government Printing Office, 1949.

18. "Glamour Girls of Industry," *Industrial Sports Journal,* 12 (December 15, 1951), 9–10. Dubinsky has been called the Daniel Boone of industrial relations for his pioneer work from the labor-union angle.

19. "Mighty 66'ers Win Again!" *Industrial Sports Journal,* 12 (April 15, 1951), 16, 38.

20. 1. Dayton Air-Gems: This is a civic team representing five divisions of General Motors (Aeroproducts, Delco, Frigidaire, Inland, Moraine Products), plus National Cash Register Company and Wright Patterson Air Force Base.

2. Goodyear Tire and Rubber.

3. Allen-Bradley Corporation of Milwaukee.

4. Caterpillar Tractor Company, Peoria, Illinois.

5. Phillips Petroleum Company, Bartlesville, Oklahoma.

6. Denver Civic Basketball (formerly the Denver Chevrolet dealers).

7. Stewart Chevrolet Company of San Francisco.

8. Atlas-Pacific Engineering Company (Blue and Golds).

9. Rural Electrical Association of Artesia, New Mexico.

10. Santa Maria Dukes (civic team), Santa Maria, California.

11. Fibber McGee and Molly, National Broadcasting Company.

21. Morse, Wayne H. "U.S. Industrial Cagers To Play in Coming Olympics in Finland," *Industrial Sports Journal*, 13 (June 15, 1952), 22–23, 35.

22. "Industrial Hockey Squad To Represent U.S. in World Title Matches," *Industrial Sports Journal*, 12 (February 15, 1951), 7, 34.

23. Prezioso, Sal. "Cooperation of Industrial and Community Recreation," *Recreation*, 45 (November, 1951), 343–44.

24. "Industrial Recreation Meeting," *Recreation*, 45 (October, 1951), 301. This is the opinion of George Wilgus, personnel director of the Mutual Life Insurance Company.

25. Riedman, Sarah R. *Physiology of Work and Play*. New York: Dryden Press, 1950, pp. 584.

26. Creed, C. Edwin. "The Relationship of Recreational Participation to Industrial Efficiency," *Research Quarterly*, 17 (October, 1946), 193–203.

27. "Industry's Fact-finding Board Conducts Nationwide Employee-Recreation Survey," *Industrial Sports Journal*, 10 (March, 1950), 18, 36.

NOTES AND BIBLIOGRAPHY TO CHAPTER 6

1. Lundberg, George A.; Komarovsky, Mirra; and McInerny, Mary Alice. *Leisure: A Suburban Study*, Chapter 8. New York: Columbia University Press, 1934, pp. 396.

2. Barrows, Isabel C. (ed.). *Physical Training Conference of 1889*. Boston: Press of George H. Ellis, 1890, pp. 135.

3. Schlesinger, Arthur M. *Paths to the Present*, p. 9. New York: Macmillan Co., 1949, pp. 317. (Quotation used with the permission of the Macmillan Company.)

4. *Ibid.*

5. Whitton, Fred. "Higher Ideals in Secondary Education," *School Review*, 8 (April, 1900), 261–67.

6. Dewey, John. *The Educational Situation*, pp. 50–80. Chicago: University of Chicago Press, 1906 (Contributions to Education, No. III), pp. 104.

7. Elsson, Jay P. "What Really Is the Montessori Method?" *Ladies' Home Journal*, 29 (November, 1912), 30.
Nearing, Nellie, and Seeds, Scott. "Fitting the Public School to the Children," *Ladies' Home Journal*, 30 (March, 1913), 20.

Harrison, Elizabeth. "What the Kindergarten Has Done," *Ladies' Home Journal*, 28 (April, 1911), 23.

Irwin, Edward P. "Luther Burbank and Child Culture," *Overland Monthly*, 45 (July, 1905), 265–70.

Angell, Emmett D. "New Games in the School and Playground," *Ladies' Home Journal*, 21 (September, 1904), 9.

[Roosevelt, Theodore]. "The President's Objections to Modern School Methods," *Ladies' Home Journal*, 23 (January, 1907), 19.

8. Sargent, D. A. "The Place for Physical Training in the School and College Curriculum," *Amer. Phys. Educ. Rev.*, 5 (March, 1900), 9.

9. Johnson, George E. "Children's Games in the Andover Public Schools, as Means for Avoiding Over-Pressure," *Amer. Phys. Educ. Rev.*, 6 (June, 1901), 160–69.

10. McCurdy, J. H. "A Study of the Characteristics of Physical Training in the Public Schools of the United States," *Amer. Phys. Educ. Rev.*, 10 (September, 1905), 202–13.

11. Meylan, Geo. L. "Harvard University Oarsmen," *Amer. Phys. Educ. Rev.*, 9 (June, 1904), 124.

12. Lowman, G, S. "The Regulation and Control of Competitive Sport in Secondary Schools of the United States," *Amer. Phys. Educ. Rev.*, 12 (September, 1907), 241–55; *ibid.*, December, 1907, pp. 307–23.

Editorial. *Amer. Phys. Educ. Rev.*, 12 (December, 1907), 348.

13. Hetherington, Clark W. "The Demonstration Play School of 1913," *Amer. Phys. Educ. Rev.*, 20 (May, 1915), 282–94; *ibid.*, June, 1915, pp. 373–80; *ibid.*, October, 1915, pp. 429–45.

14. Sargent, Dudley A. "Are Athletics Making Girls Masculine?" *Ladies' Home Journal*, 29 (March, 1912), 11.

15. Ballintine, Harriet I. "The Value of Athletics to College Girls," *Amer. Phys. Educ. Rev.*, 6 (June, 1901), 153.

16. Hart, Lavinia. "A Girl's College Life," *Cosmopolitan*, 31 (June, 1901), 188–95.

17. The rise of intramural sports is particularly well developed in three books:

Mitchell, Elmer D. *Intramural Sports*. New York: A. S. Barnes & Co., 1939, pp. 324.

Brammell, P. Roy. *Intramural and Interscholastic Athletics*. (Office of Education, Bulletin No. 17, 1932, National Survey of Secondary Education, Monograph No. 27.) Washington, D.C.: Government Printing Office, 1933, pp. 143.

Means, Louis E. *The Organization and Administration of Intramural Sports.* St. Louis: C. V. Mosby Co., 1949, pp. 442.

18. Throughout the issues of the *American Physical Education Review* for 1916, 1917, and 1918 there are many evidences of the growing tendency to institute competition for all.

19. Particularly is this trend shown in the announced programs of the College Physical Education Association, the Athletic Research Society, and the American Physical Education Association. For a rather detailed report see Wilce, J. W. "Report of the Committee on Intramural Sports, Athletic Research Society, December 27, 1918," *Amer. Phys. Educ. Rev.*, 23 (April, 1918), 199–212; *ibid.*, May, 1918, pp. 279–86.

20. Curtis, Henry S. "The Relation of the Playgrounds to a System of Physical Training," *Amer. Phys. Educ. Rev.*, 13 (May, 1908), 248–49.

21. Articles and editorials in the issues of *Playground, American City,* and *American Physical Education Review* just prior to World War I offer ample evidence of the fact that many forces were advocating the wide use of the school plant for play purposes.

22. Hetherington, Clark W. *School Program in Physical Education.* Yonkers, N.Y.: World Book Co., 1922, pp. 132.

23. DeGroot, E. B. "President's Address," *Amer. Phys. Educ. Rev.*, 8 (March, 1903), 40–46.
    Meylan, Geo. L. "Athletics," *Amer. Phys. Educ. Rev.*, 10 (June, 1905), 157–63.

24. Dorgan, Ethel J. *Luther Halsey Gulick, 1865–1918.* New York: Bureau of Publications, Teachers College, Columbia University, 1934 (Contributions to Education, No. 635), pp. 180.

25. Wingate, George W. "The Public Schools Athletic League," *Outing*, 52 (May, 1908), 165–75.

26. Dorgan, *op. cit.*

27. Wingate, *op. cit.*

28. *Ibid.*

29. *Ibid.*

30. Reeve, Arthur B. "The World's Greatest Athletic Organization," *Outing*, 57 (October, 1910), 106–15. The list of cities which patterned their public school athletic leagues after the New York organization included New Orleans, Seattle, Balti-

more, Newark, Buffalo, Cleveland, Birmingham, Tacoma, Philadelphia, Chicago, Troy, San Francisco, Kansas City (Kan.), Oakland, and Helena.

31. McKenzie, R. Tait. *Exercise in Education and Medicine*. Philadelphia: W. B. Saunders Co., 1923 (3d ed.), pp. 601.

32. Reeve, *op. cit.*

33. Wagenhorst, Lewis H. *The Administration and Cost of High School Interscholastic Athletics*. New York: Teachers College, Columbia University, 1926 (Contributions to Education No. 205), pp. 134.

34. A news note in the *American Physical Education Review* for December, 1904, voiced the concern of the Massachusetts Teachers Association for the way in which athletic competition was developing and urged that organization to "do something about it."

35. Forsythe, Charles E. *The Administration of High School Athletics*. New York: Prentice-Hall, Inc., 1948, pp. 440.
See also "A Review of Athletics in the High Schools," *Athletic Journal*, 10 (June, 1930), 42–69.

36. *Ibid.*

37. Between 1905 and 1910 *Outlook* printed more than thirty articles on the control of college athletics in general and football in particular.

38. Ryan, W. Carson, Jr. *The Literature of American School and College Athletics*. New York: Carnegie Foundation for the Advancement of Teaching, 1929 (Bulletin No. 24), pp. 305.

39. Pierce, Palmer E. "The Intercollegiate Athletic Association of the United States," *Proceedings*, 1907, pp. 27–32.
Pierce, Palmer E. "The Intercollegiate Athletic Association of the United States," *Amer. Phys. Educ. Rev.*, 14 (February, 1909), 76–81.
Pierce, Palmer E. "The Intercollegiate Athletic Association of the United States," *ibid.*, 15 (February, 1910), 82–87.

40. Luehring, Frederick W. "Affiliated Organizations: XIV. The National Collegiate Athletic Association," *Jour. of Health & Phys. Educ.*, 18 (December, 1947), 707–9, 751–53. An excellent bibliography of twenty-six references is appended.
Scott, Harry A. *Competitive Sports in Schools and Colleges*. New York: Harper & Bros., 1951, pp. 604.

41. Scott, *op. cit.*

42. A partial list of the conferences in existence in 1929 is to be found in "A Review of Athletics in the College Conferences of 1929–1930," *Athletic Journal*, 10 (June, 1930), 25–42, 69. In this particular article only twenty-seven conference reports are listed.

43. These and other organizations have worked diligently for the proper organization and control of athletic competition and have made their influence felt in all sections of the country.

44. Scott, *op. cit.*
Babbitt, James A. "Present Condition of Gymnastics and Athletics in American Colleges," *Amer. Phys. Educ. Rev.*, 8 (December, 1903), 280–83.

45. "The Fifth Annual Meeting of the National Amateur Athletic Federation—Report of Colonel Henry Breckenridge, President," *Amer. Phys. Educ. Rev.*, 32 (January, 1927), 49.
Griffith, John L. "The Function of the National Amateur Athletic Federation," *Amer. Phys. Educ. Rev.*, 32 (May, 1927), 378.
Griffith, John L. "National Amateur Athletic Federation," *ibid.*, October, 1927, p. 632.

46. "A Merger: The Women's Division, NAAF, Becomes an Integral Part of the AAHPER," *Jour. of Health & Phys. Educ.*, 12 (January, 1941), 36–37.

47. Britt, Albert. "On the Sidelines," *Outing*, 80 (July, 1922), 161.
Griffith, John L. "The National Amateur Athletic Federation," *Athletic Journal*, 6 (August, 1925), 3–13, 46–47.

48. Proctor, Wm. M. (ed.). *The Junior College*. Stanford University: Stanford University Press, 1927, pp. 226. Merton E. Hill, who has an article in this volume on the rural junior college, should be credited with the quote.

49. Vande Bogart, G. H. "Physical Education and Athletics in Junior Colleges of the United States," *Athletic Journal*, 10 (April, 1930), 14–17, 54.

50. Eells, Walter C., and Davis, Harold M. "The Junior College Transfer in University Athletics," *School Review*, 37 (May, 1929), 371–76.

51. In connection with the publication of the *California State Manual of Physical Education*, a decathlon chart was prepared for teachers of physical education in California which popularized the testing of various sport skills.

52. Educational Policies Commission. *Research Memorandum on Education in the Depression.* New York: Social Science Research Council, 1937 (Bulletin No. 28), pp. 173.

53. Rogers, J. F. "What's Happening to Physical Education," *Jour. of Health & Phys. Educ.,* 4 (November, 1933), 17.
Scott, Harry A. "A Comparative Study of the Effects of the Financial Depression on Certain Vocational Aspects of College Physical Education," *Research Quarterly,* 5 (October, 1934), 97–106.
Steiner, Jesse F. *Research Memorandum on Recreation in the Depression.* New York: Social Science Research Council, 1937 (Bulletin No. 32), pp. 124.
Rogers, J. E. "How Has the Depression in Education Affected Physical Education?" *Jour. of Health & Phys. Educ.,* 5 (January, 1934), 12–13.

54. Larson, A. W. "Six Man Football," *Athletic Journal,* 18 (June, 1938), 40.

55. See *School and Society,* 46 (August, 1937), 177.

56. Mitchell, E. D. "Physical Education Utilizes CWA and FERA Help," *Jour. of Health & Phys. Educ.,* 5 (March, 1934), 20.

57. Mitchell, E. D. "Great Day for Women's Athletics," *Jour. of Health & Phys. Educ.,* 8 (April, 1937), 218.

58. Wrenn, C. Gilbert, and Harley, D. L. *Time on Their Hands.* Washington, D.C.: American Council on Education, 1941, pp. 266. A report on leisure, recreation, and young people, prepared for the American Youth Commission.
Reeves, Floyd W. "Youth—in the War Crisis and After," *Recreation,* 36 (November, 1942), 459.

59. "Recommendations of the American Youth Commission," *Jour. of Health & Phys. Educ.,* 11 (September, 1940), 339.

60. "A Plan for National Preparedness," *Jour. of Health & Phys. Educ.,* 11 (September, 1940), 397–99, 453–54. Gives the detail on the early consideration of the Schwert Bill.
"An Open Letter from Dr. Jones," *Jour. of Health & Phys. Educ.,* 11 (November, 1940), 523–27. The Schwert Bill details; the consideration of a new bill H.R. 1074, the text of which will be found in *Jour. of Health & Phys. Educ.,* 12 (February, 1941), 70–73.

61. "National Association News—Federal Bill Calls for Survey," *Jour. of Health & Phys. Educ.,* 12 (March, 1941), 157. H.R. 1798, introduced January 10, 1941.

62. "The High School Victory Corps" (editorial), *Jour. of Health & Phys. Educ.*, 13 (December, 1942), 590–91.

63. *Physical Fitness through Physical Education.* Washington, D.C.: Government Printing Office, 1942, pp. 102.
   Physical Fitness for Students in Colleges and Universities. Washington, D.C.: Government Printing Office, 1943, pp. 140. Both of these manuals were published by the Federal Security Agency, U.S. Office of Education.

64. *Physical Fitness Program for High Schools and Colleges.* Washington, D.C.: U.S. Navy, Training Division, Bureau of Aeronautics, 1942, pp. 57.

65. Schrader, Carl L. "Education of or through the Physical," *Jour. of Health & Phys. Educ.*, 14 (February, 1943), 87.
   McCloy, C. H. "A Common Denominator of Physical Condition," *Jour. of Health & Phys. Educ.*, 14 (February, 1943), 87.

66. Two editorials decry the gymnastic conditioning program and point out that our objectives cannot be achieved by such procedures:
   Oberteuffer, Delbert. "An Open Letter to Mr. McCloy and Mr. Schrader," *Jour. of Health & Phys. Educ.*, 14 (June, 1943), 310–11.
   Williams, Jesse F. "Who Are Our Friends," *Jour. of Health & Phys. Educ.*, 14 (June, 1943), 311.
   These two editorials are answered by McCloy, C. H. "A Reply to Our Critics," *Jour. of Health & Phys. Educ.*, 14 (December, 1943), 526–27.

67. Pieh, Robert. "The Little People," *Jour. of Health & Phys. Educ.*, 15 (May, 1944), 260. Pieh points out that if our leaders are squabbling over what to do, what course shall the little people take? Which way shall they go?

68. Brace, David K. "Physical Fitness in Schools and Colleges," *Jour. of Health & Phys. Educ.*, 15 (November, 1944), 490. Dr. Brace was at that time principal specialist in physical fitness, U.S. Office of Education.

69. Publications of the Athletic Institute (209 S. State St., Chicago 4, Ill.) resulting from national conferences include: *Planning Facilities for Athletics, Recreation, Physical and Health Education,* 1947; *Undergraduate Professional Preparation in Health Education, Physical Education and Recreation,* 1948; *Graduate Study in Health Education, Physical Education and Recreation,* 1950; *Physical Education for Chil-*

dren of Elementary School Age, 1951; *Recreation for Community Living (Guiding Principles)*, 1952.

70. Guthrie, Hunter. "No More Football for Us," *Saturday Evening Post*, 224 (October 13, 1951), 24–25, 115, 117–18.
    Cherry, Blair. "Why I Quit Coaching," *Saturday Evening Post*, 224 (October 20, 1951), 40–41, 145–47, 149.
71. Lardner, John. "My Case against Sport," *American*, 152 (October, 1951), 24–25, 111–13.
72. Bee, Clair. "I Know Why They Sold Out to the Gamblers," *Saturday Evening Post*, 224 (February 2, 1952), 26–27, 76–78, 80.

NOTES AND BIBLIOGRAPHY TO CHAPTER 7

1. Meland, Bernard Eugene. *America's Spiritual Culture*. New York: Harper & Bros., 1948, pp. 216.
2. Atkinson, Henry A. *The Church and the People's Play*. Boston: Pilgrim Press, 1915, pp. 259.
3. McConnell, Rev. S. D. "The Moral Side of Golf," *Outlook*, 65 (June 2, 1900), 299–301.
4. "A Methodist Bishop on Amusements," *Literary Digest*, 35 (August 24, 1907), 263–64.
5. "Sunday Laws and One-Day Morality," *Literary Digest*, 35 (August 17, 1907), 233.
6. Smith, Bertha Henry. "Everyday Church Work," *Munsey's*, 32 (January, 1905), 481–89.
7. Haweis, Rev. H. R. "The Church's Attitude towards Recreation," *Outlook*, 66 (September 22, 1900), 209–12.
8. Hoben, Allan. *The Minister and the Boy*. Chicago: University of Chicago Press, 1912, pp. 171.
9. *Ibid.* There are some sentences in the first chapter (p. 10) which set the tone of this very readable book: "Genius and success in life depend largely upon retaining the boyish quality of enthusiastic abandon to one's cause, the hearty release of one's entire energy in a given pursuit, and the conviction that the world is ever new and all things possible."
10. Richardson, Norman E. *The Religious Education of Adolescents*, p. 133. New York: Abingdon Press, 1913, pp. 191.
11. Gulick was at this time chairman of the Playground Extension Committee of the Russell Sage Foundation.
    Eliot, Charles W. *The Wise Direction of Church Activities*

toward Social Welfare. Bulletin No. 11, Department of Social and Public Service. Boston: American Unitarian Association, 1913, pp. 17.

Aronovici, Carol. *Knowing One's Own Community*. Bulletin No. 20, Department of Social and Public Service. Boston: American Unitarian Association, 1913, pp. 82.

12. Fisher, George J. "Athletics outside Educational Institutions," *Amer. Phys. Educ. Rev.*, 12 (June, 1907), 109–20.

13. Raycroft, Joseph E. "The Administration of Playground, Sunday School and Social Settlement Athletics in Chicago," *Amer. Phys. Educ. Rev.*, 15 (March, 1910), 185–86.

14. *America*, 1 (August, 1909), 273.

15. Brown, William Adams. *Church and State in Contemporary America*. New York: Charles Scribner's Sons, 1936, pp. 360. The International convention of the YMCA adopted the *Social Creed* in 1919, and the national convention of the YWCA adopted it in 1920.

16. Richardson, N. E., and Loomis, O. E. *The Boy Scout Movement Applied by the Church*. New York: Charles Scribner's Sons, 1915, pp. 445.

17. Nicholson, Edwin. *Education and the Boy Scout Movement in America*. New York: Teachers College, Columbia University, 1941, pp. 117.

18. Richardson and Loomis, *op. cit.*

19. Schlesinger, Arthur Meier. *Political and Social Growth of the American People, 1865–1940*. New York: Macmillan Co., 1941, pp. 783.

20. Brown, William Adams. *The Church in America*. New York: Macmillan Co., 1922, pp. 378.

21. Bell, Bernard Iddings. *Right and Wrong after the War*, pp. vii, viii. Boston: Houghton Mifflin Co., 1918, pp. 187.

22. Holt, Arthur Erastus. *Social Work in the Churches*. Boston: Pilgrim Press, 1922, pp. 131.

23. Brabham, Morizon William. *Planning Modern Church Buildings*. Nashville, Tenn.: Cokesbury Press, 1928, pp. 240.

24. "Church Takes Up Recreation Work," *Amer. Phys. Educ. Rev.*, 26 (November, 1921), 396.

25. McCann, Francis A. "Scouting and the Catholic Boy," *National Catholic Welfare Council Bulletin*, July, 1921. Washington, D.C.: National Catholic Welfare Council.

26. Douglass, H. Paul. *The Church in the Changing City*. New

York: George H. Doran Co., 1927, pp. 453. Conducted in 1925–26 under the Institute of Social and Religious Research. The distribution of the churches was among thirteen cities and included samples of the seven larger denominations.

27. Powell, Warren T. *Recreational Leadership for Church and Community*. New York: Methodist Book Concern, 1923, pp. 163.
    Wegener, A. B., *Church and Community Recreation*. New York: Macmillan Co., 1924.

28. LaPorte, William R. *Recreational Leadership for Boys*. New York: Methodist Book Concern, 1927, pp. 137.

29. Wegener, A. B. "How the YMCA Physical Directors May Work with the Churches," *Physical Training*, 20 (1922–23), 210–11.

30. Jones, Ashley. "Recreation and the Church," *Playground*, 19 (November, 1925), 435–38.
    Silver, Abba Hillel. "Leisure and the Church," *Physical Training*, 24 (March, 1927), 136–37.
    Manning, Rt. Rev. W. T. "The Churches and Wholesome Play," *Playground*, 20 (January, 1927), 537–38.

31. "Modern Sport Symbolized," *Sportsmanship*, 1 (January, 1929), 9. The unit known as a "bay" is a vertical section of the wall and outer aisle of the cathedral nave. There are fourteen bays, seven on each side of the nave. Cathedrals in European countries contain many scenes of sports life in their decoration. A hunting scene in a window in the Cathedral of León in Spain is believed to be the earliest representation of sport in the glass of a cathedral. Lifelike wrestlers are depicted in Bordeaux, Lens, Paris, Rouen, Chartres, Ely, and other European churches. At a church in Gloucester two football forwards pursue the ball, and at Exeter an athlete puts the weight.

32. "Saving Rural Church in Its Crisis," *Literary Digest*, 122 (December 5, 1936), p. 33.

33. "A Birthright Not for Sale" (editorial), *Christian Century*, 52 (October 2, 1935), 1230–31.

34. Cozens, Frederick W., and Stumpf, Florence. "Examining the Orientation Process," *Jour. of Health & Phys. Educ.*, 19 (September, 1948), 468–69, 502, 504.

35. Govett, L. A. *The King's Book of Sports*. London: Elliot Stock, 62, Paternoster Row, 1890, pp. 140.

36. Scollard, John. "Birth of the Blue Laws," *Mentor*, 18 (May, 1930), 46–49, 58–60.
37. White, William C. "Bye, Bye, Blue Laws," *Scribner's*, 94 (August, 1933), 107–9.
38. Huestis, Charles Herbert. "Sunday Manners," *Christian Century*, 49 (November 9, 1932), 1371–72.
39. "Baltimore over the Blues," *Literary Digest*, 113 (May 21, 1932), 19.
40. Martin, B. Joseph. "The History of the Attitudes of the Methodist Church in the United States of America toward Recreation." (Ph.D. thesis, University of Southern California, 1944.)
41. Skidmore, Rex A. *Mormon Recreation in Theory and Practice: A Study of Social Change.* Philadelphia: University of Pennsylvania, 1941, pp. 137.
42. Sizoo, Joseph R. "What Can the Churches Do for Abundant Living?" *Recreation*, 28 (January, 1935), 463–64, 501–2.

NOTES AND BIBLIOGRAPHY TO CHAPTER 8

1. "The Newspaper Fan," from The Contributor's Club, *Atlantic*, 101 (April, 1908), 573–74.
2. Chase, John S. (ed.). *Years of the Modern.* New York: Longmans, Green & Co., 1949, pp. 354. Erwin D. Canham, distinguished editor of the *Christian Science Monitor*, is a contributor to this volume. He inadvertently pays quite a tribute to the universality and power of sports language when he says that news must be made interesting and impelling, which means simplification and dramatization are imperative. He comments that the result is that the news is sometimes "suped-up," and the language of the sports page finds its way into events that are far too grave to be considered in such terms. However, the editor has the problem of *getting the news into people's minds—into the maximum number of people's minds—*and thus must compromise between sobriety and reader interest.
3. "The Press in the Contemporary Scene," *Annals of the American Academy of Political and Social Science*, 219 (January, 1942), 222.
4. Lee, Alfred M. *The Daily Newspaper in America.* New York: Macmillan Co., 1937, pp. 609.
5. Smith, Robert. *Baseball: A Historical Narrative of the Game,*

the Men Who Have Played, and Its Place in American Life.
New York: Simon & Schuster, 1947, pp. 362.

6. Nugent, William Henry. "The Sports Section," *American Mercury*, 16 (March, 1929), 328–38.

7. This statement is made by Nugent but is contradicted by Stanley Walker in his book *City Editor* (New York: Frederick A. Stokes Co., 1934, pp. 336). Walker claims that it was a hunch of James Gordon Bennett (and the younger Bennett) that led to the invention of news as news is known today—including sports news.

8. Irwin, Will. "The American Newspaper," *Collier's*, 46 (January 21, 1911), 15, 18.

9. MacNeil, Neil. *Without Fear or Favor*. New York: Harcourt, Brace & Co., 1940, pp. 414. A fine chapter on "Sports Editor" by a member of the staff of the *New York Times*.

10. Woodward, Stanley. *Sports Page*. New York: Simon & Schuster, 1949, pp. 230. The point is well illustrated by the legal story involved when the New York Yankees went to court seeking an order to restrain the Mexican League from stealing their players. The sports story becomes a police story when gamblers are caught "fixing" games. And sometimes it is predominantly a weather story, as on January 1, 1934, when the Los Angeles and Pasadena fire departments were called out to pump a lake off the surface of the Rose Bowl field.

11. Woodward defines "newspaper ethics" as "newspaper expediency" but says that the man who is consistently inaccurate is a bad newspaperman. Woodward's book, *Sports Page*, gives the results of a questionnaire survey conducted by the author. In answer to the first question asked, as to what percentage of editorial space is devoted to sports, 90 per cent reported that sports space took up between 12 and 15 per cent of the editorial space. The questionnaire gave conclusive evidence that, in the minds of circulation managers, the sports page sells the paper.

12. Gramling, Oliver. *AP: The Story of News*, p. 246. New York: Rinehart & Co., 1940, pp. 506.

13. *Editor and Publisher*, January 11, 1936, p. x.

14. Emery, Edwin. *History of the American Newspaper Publishers Association*. Minneapolis: University of Minnesota Press, 1950, pp. 263.

15. Gramling, *op. cit.*

16. Lee, *op. cit.*

17. Slosson, P. W. *The Great Crusade and After*. New York: Macmillan Co., 1930, pp. 486. Chapter X, "The Business of Sport," is very well done.

18. Strunsky, Simeon. *The Living Tradition: Change and America*. New York: Doubleday, Doran & Co., Inc., 1939, pp. 454. An astute observer and student of our national life writes of America's manners, morals, and mores.

19. Mack, Connie. *My 66 Years in the Big Leagues*. Philadelphia: John C. Winston Co., 1950, pp. 246.

20. *Newsmen's Holiday*. Nieman Essays—First Series. Cambridge, Mass.: Harvard University Press, 1942, pp. 203. Material in this section was taken largely from "Box Score," written by Victor O. Jones, sports editor of the *Boston Globe*, who was recipient of a Nieman Fellowship at Harvard University.

21. MacNeil, *op. cit.*

22. Brillhart, Donald. "The Sports Page and the Social Scene, 1929–1935." Unpublished manuscript, Univeristy of California, Berkeley, 1951.

23. Spink, J. G. Taylor. *Judge Landis and Twenty-five Years of Baseball*. New York: Thomas Y. Crowell Co., 1947, pp. 306. Written by the long-time publisher of one of baseball's most famous "sheets," *The Sporting News*.

24. Walker, Stanley. *City Editor*. New York: Frederick A. Stokes Co., 1934, pp. 336. A sentiment not shared by Mr. Walker, who feels it is fortunate some sports writers retain enough "of the old beer, beef and beans flavor to ward off anemia."

NOTES AND BIBLIOGRAPHY TO CHAPTER 9

1. Wood, James Playsted. *Magazines in the United States: Their Social and Economic Influence*. New York: Ronald Press Co., 1949, pp. 312.

2. Allen, Frederick Lewis. "American Magazines, 1741–1941," *Bulletin of the New York Public Library*, 45 (June, 1941), 439.

3. Swicegood, Gloria. "American Physical Recreation, 1900–1910: Cultural Reflections in Journalism." Unpublished manuscript, University of California, Berkeley, 1951.

4. Allen, Frederick Lewis. "One Hundred Years of Harper's," *Harper's*, 201 (October, 1950), 32.

5. Mott, Frank Luther. *History of American Magazines, 1865–*

1885. Cambridge, Mass.: Harvard University Press, 1938, pp. 649.

6. In the June, 1902, issue of the *Delineator* appears a pattern for a bathing suit, Butterick Pattern No. 6055, offered in nine sizes for ladies from thirty- to forty-six-inch bust measure; pattern No. 6056 was offered in six sizes from six to sixteen years of age. For a lady of medium size the bathing costume required six yards and one quarter of material forty-four inches wide. For a miss of twelve years, the costume required five yards and one quarter of material forty-four inches wide. The fashion notes recommended that black satin made an extremely stylish suit, especially with trimmings of black-and-white braid. White mohair, elaborated with scarlet braid, was suggested for children but not for adults (since it was considered too pronounced). For a less expensive costume ticking was mentioned as a serviceable fabric which would shed water readily.

7. Koues, Helen. "Fashions: Sports Clothes," *Good Housekeeping,* 84 (April, 1927), 18–19.

8. Walker, Emma E. "Good Health for Girls," *Ladies' Home Journal,* Vol. 19 (March, 1902); "Why Golf Is Good for Girls" (May, 1902); "Lawn Tennis as an Exercise for Girls" (June, 1902); "Why Rowing and Canoeing Are Good for Girls" (July, 1902); "Swimming as an Exercise for Girls" (August, 1902); "Side-Saddle versus Man's Saddle" (September, 1902).

9. It seems worth while to give a complete listing of the twelve articles, if only to illustrate the scope of interest in sports and athletics which was being encouraged at this early date in the century. The series "Athletics for Women" began in the *Delineator,* Vol. 59 (January, 1902): No. 1, "Physical Culture at Home," Anthony Barker; No. 2, "Gymnasium Work," Dr. Watson L. Savage; No. 3, "How To Fence–Instructions for Young Women," Regis Senac; No. 4, "Basket-Ball," Ellen Bernard Thompson; No. 5, "Swimming," Edwin Sandys; No. 6, "Bowling," Sophie Gundrum; No. 7, "Rowing," Lucille Eaton Hill; No. 8, "Golf," Frances C. Griscom, Jr.; No. 9, "Equestrianism." Belle Beach; No. 10, "Lawn Tennis," J. Parmly Paret; No. 11, "Track Athletics," Christine Terhune; No. 12, "Dancing," Melvin Ballou Gilbert.

10. *Good Housekeeping,* Vol. 31 (April, 1900).

11. Sangster, Margaret E. "Taking Risks," *Good Housekeeping,*

31 (July, 1900), 33–34. This was from a regular department of the magazine entitled "Talks with Fathers and Mothers."

12. Birney, Mrs. Theodore. "The Twentieth Century Girl," *Harper's Bazaar*, 33 (May 26, 1900), 224–27.

13. Ryan, W. Carson, Jr. *The Literature of American School and College Athletics.* New York: Carnegie Foundation for the Advancement of Teaching, 1929 (Bulletin No. 24), pp. 305.

14. Muir, John. "Three Adventures in Yosemite," *Century*, 83 (February, 1912), 657–61.
Muir, John. "The Forests of Yosemite Park," *Atlantic*, 85 (May, 1900), 493–507; "Hunting Big Redwoods," *ibid.*, 88 (September, 1901), 304–20.

15. Curtis, Henry S. "Vacation Schools and Playgrounds," *Harper's*, 105 (June, 1902), 22–29.

16. Riis, Jacob. "A Modern St. George," *Scribner's*, 50 (October, 1911), 384–402.

17. Hartt, Rollin Lynde. "The National Game," *Atlantic*, 102 (August, 1908), 220–31.

18. Pier, Arthur Stanwood. "Work and Play," *Atlantic*, 94 (November, 1904), 669–75.

19. Fallows, Alice K. "Temptations To Be Good," *Century*, 67 (December, 1903), 169–79.

20. Burlingame, Roger. "Mountains of Paper," *Harper's*, 201 (October, 1950), 229.

21. Wood, James Playsted. *Magazines in the United States: Their Social and Economic Influence.* New York: Ronald Press Co., 1949, pp. 312.

22. Calkins, Earnest Elmo. "Magazine into Marketplace," *Scribner's*, 51 (January, 1937), 19–24.

23. Hower, Ralph M. *The History of an Advertising Agency: N. W. Ayer and Son at Work, 1869–1939.* Cambridge, Mass.: Harvard University Press, 1939, pp. 652.

24. "Want To Be a Champion?" series, Wheaties Library of Sports, Department 55, Minneapolis 15, Minnesota: Carl L. Nordly, Director of Sports Library.

25. Green, Harold E. "Psychologists Help Radio Programs Become a National Institution," *Printer's Ink*, 221 (November, 8, 1947), 32–33, 67, 70, 72.

26. Martin L. Reynert, director of the Mooseheart Laboratory of Child Research.

NOTES AND BIBLIOGRAPHY TO CHAPTER 10

1. Willey, Malcolm M., and Rice, Stuart A. *Communication Agencies and Social Life*. New York: McGraw-Hill Book Co., Inc., 1933, pp. 229.
2. Bartlett, Kenneth G. "Social Impact of the Radio," *Annals of the American Academy of Political and Social Science*, 250 (March, 1947), 89–97.
3. Lee, Alfred M. *The Daily Newspaper in America*. New York: Macmillan Co., 1937, pp. 559. Lee reports that newspaper publishers gradually, but grudgingly, accepted play-by-play radio descriptions of sports events and tried to make the best of it.
4. Sherwood, R. E. "Beyond the Talkies–Television," *Scribner's*, 86 (July, 1929), 1–8.
5. Chase, Francis, Jr. *Sound and Fury*. New York: Harper & Bros., 1942, pp. 303.
6. Goldsmith, Alfred N., and Lescarboura, Austin C. *This Thing Called Broadcasting*. New York: Henry Holt & Co., 1930, pp. 362. Chapter XIV, "Radio and Sports."
7. West, Robert. *The Rape of Radio*. New York: Rodin Pub. Co., 1941, pp. 546. Chapter 11, "Radio Era of Sports."
8. *Ibid.*
9. Schechter, A. A., and Anthony, Edward. *I Live on Air*. New York: Frederick A. Stokes Co., 1941, pp. 582. Chapter VIII, "Kilocycle Kampus"; Chapter XVI, "Blow by Blow"; Chapter XXV, "Youth Has Its Fling." This volume includes a wonderful collection of sixty-four reproductions of photographs. The last of these is a picture of the empty Olympic Stadium at Helsinki, Finland, that was to house the world-wide sports events supposed to symbolize international good will.
10. *Ibid.*
11. *Variety Radio Directory: Second Annual Edition, 1938–1939*. New York: Variety, Inc., 1939, pp. 1436. These stations were: WHBQ, Memphis, Tennessee; WHLB, Virginia, Minnesota; KGHL, Billings, Montana; KRGV, Weslaco, Texas; WAZL, Hazelton, Pennsylvania.
12. *Ibid.*
13. "Giving Education the Air." Dr. William E. Bohn, Educational Director, Rand School, in the WEVD "University of the Air Series," Tuesday, June 21, 1938, as reported in Robert West's book, *The Rape of Radio* (see n. 7).

A melancholy note was sounded with regard to TV educational programs currently being sponsored by the Alfred P. Sloan Foundation, "American Inventory." Robert Lewis Shayon in the *Saturday Review of Literature* for September 22, 1951, commented that the program is "expository to a fault" and that, although the intent is high-minded, such programs are governed by the same laws of audience interest that rule entertainment generally. It is false to assume that because the producers are motivated, and because the subject is important, the interest of an audience can be captured.

14. Renegar, Horace. "The Role of Public Relations in Intercollegiate Athletics," *Athletic Journal*, 9 (May 1929), 32, 34.
15. Wight, Earl H. "Notes on Intercollegiate Atnletics." Unpublished manuscript, January 3, 1949. Professor Wight for many years was director of physical education at Fresno State College, California, and has had wide experience in intercollegiate athletics. He is presently assistant to the president of Fresno State College.

Wight also says that "the simple days when a college athlete played on his own time and at his own expense for the fun there was in the game are gone. The complex days when most college athletes expect financial subsidy and academic favors and play for what they get out of it are here."
16. Western Reserve University, Cleveland, Ohio (10,000 enrolment). As reported by *Variety Radio Directory, 1938-1939*.
17. Harvard and Princeton refused to sell radio rights, but Yale did not, as reported in Schechter and Anthony, *op. cit.*
18. West, *op. cit.* Jordan (see n. 19) in his study says that the first sports program was the University of Pennsylvania football game in 1940. However, comparative studies regarding the light available for the transmission of outdoor events such as baseball, football, etc., were presented in a report from the Institute of Radio Engineers at its New York Convention in 1937.
19. Jordan, Jerry N. *The Long-Range Effect of Television and Other Factors on Sports Attendance*. Washington, D.C.: Radio-Television Manufacturers Association, 1950, pp. 112.
20. Horton, Donald, and Barrett, Halsey V. "Commercials That Click on Television Sports Programs," *Printer's Ink*, 221 (October 24, 1947), 46–47.

NOTES AND BIBLIOGRAPHY TO CHAPTER 11

1. Morris, Lloyd. *Not So Long Ago.* New York: Random House, 1949, pp. 504.

2. Hart, Val. *The Story of American Roads.* New York: William Sloane Associates, Inc., 1950, pp. 243.

3. Kroeber, A. L. *Anthropology.* New York: Harcourt, Brace & Co., 1948, pp. 849. Particularly the section beginning on page 344, entitled "Invention and Play."

4. Anderson, Rudolph E. *The Story of the American Automobile.* Washington, D.C.: Public Affairs Press, 1950, pp. 301.

5. "The Road and the Automobile," *Outlook,* 71 (June 14, 1902), 445–46.

6. "The Automobile as a Rest Cure," from The Contributor's Club, *Atlantic,* 98 (September, 1906), 575–76.

7. Sward, Keith T. *The Legend of Henry Ford.* New York: Rinehart & Co., Inc., 1948, pp. 550.

8. Cohn, David L. *Combustion on Wheels.* Boston: Houghton Mifflin Co., 1944, pp. 272.

9. Albert, Allen D. "The Social Influence of the Automobile," *Scribner's,* 71 (June, 1922), 685–88.

10. Paine, Ralph D. "Discovering America by Motor," *Scribner's,* 53 (February, 1913), 137–48.

11. Lampton, William J. "The Fascination of Fast Motion," *Cosmopolitan,* 33 (June, 1902), 136.

12. Labatut, Jean, and Lane, Wheaton J. (eds.). *Highways in Our National Life.* Princeton, N.J.: Princeton University Press, 1950, pp. 506. A symposium, representing the combined knowledge of forty-eight contributors, undertaken by the Bureau of Urban Research of Princeton University.

13. Jay, John. *Skiing the Americas.* New York: Macmillan Co., 1947, pp. 257.

14. Cohn, David L. *The Good Old Days.* New York: Simon & Schuster, 1940, pp. 597.

15. Putnam, Harold (ed.). *The Dartmouth Book of Winter Sports.* New York: A. S. Barnes & Co., 1939, pp. 315.

16. The WPA built a million-dollar structure, Timberline Lodge, and installed a mile-long chair lift patterned after the one at Sun Valley, Idaho.

17. Landman, Joan and David. *Where To Ski.* Boston: Houghton Mifflin Co., 1949, pp. 359.

18. In the Foreword to the Landmans book (see n. 17), Lowell Thomas comments that the vast information presented is overwhelming evidence of the hold that skiing has taken on America in less than a generation. The book not only gives factual data and information that is complete and well organized but is full of sketches on historical backgrounds, colorful personalities, and special attributes of the various skiing areas in the United States and Canada.

19. Martin, H. B. *Fifty Years of American Golf*. New York: Dodd, Mead & Co., 1936, pp. 423.

20. The group called themselves the Mosholu Golf Club. They had searched for a suitable site and failed to find any, thus the petition for Van Cortlandt Park was a last resort.

21. Faulkner, Harold U. *The Quest for Social Justice, 1898-1914*. New York: Macmillan Co., 1931, pp. 390. Quoted from the section entitled, "The People at Play," p. 289.

22. Rice, Grantland. "Golf–the Billion Dollar Game," *Official Golf Guide*. New York: A. S. Barnes & Co., 1947, pp. 256.

23. Featherston, Dr. E. Glenn. "Transportation of Pupils: A Growing Problem," *School Life*, 31 (January, 1949), 4–6.

24. Gaumnitz, Walter H., and Tompkins, Ellsworth. "A Look at the Size of Our High Schools," *School Life*, 31 (June, 1949), 4–6.

25. Kolb, J. H., and Brunner, Edmund deS. *A Study of Rural Society*. Boston: Houghton Mifflin Co., 1935, pp. 642.

26. "Keep 'Em Rolling," *Athletic Journal*, 22 (April, 1942), 47.

27. Mitchell, A. Viola, and Crawford, Ida B. *Camp Counseling*. Philadelphia: W. B. Saunders Co., 1950, pp. 388.

28. Benson, Reuel A., and Goldberg, Jacob A. *The Camp Counselor*. New York: McGraw-Hill Book Co., Inc., 1951, pp. 337.

29. *Community School Camping*. Published by Lee M. Thurston, Superintendent of Public Instruction, Lansing, Michigan, 1951, pp. 39.

30. Clarke, James Mitchell. *Public School Camping*. Stanford University, Calif.: Stanford University Press, 1951, pp. 184.

31. Scott, Walter L. "Recreation Programs Encouraged through Federal Inter-Agency Committee," *School Life*, 29 (July, 1947), 7–9.

32. Trembly, Clifford. "What Is a National Park?" *Overland Monthly*, 66 (July, 1915), 14–22.

33. *Ibid.* This article is a very comprehensive summary of the vari-

ous federal agencies interested in recreation. In 1950 twelve million hunting licenses were issued in the United States. This was reported on Arthur Godfrey's television program, "Arthur Godfrey and His Friends," October 22, 1952.

34. *Newsweek,* 21 (June 7, 1943), 76.
35. Reported in *The Sporting News* and quoted by Jerry N. Jordan, *The Long-Range Effect of Television and Other Factors on Sports Attendance.* Washington, D.C.: Radio-Television Manufacturers Association, 1950, pp. 112.
36. Ogburn, William Fielding. *The Social Effects of Aviation.* Boston: Houghton Mifflin Co., 1946, pp. 755.

NOTES AND BIBLIOGRAPHY TO CHAPTER 12

1. The series of articles which John Muir wrote for the *Atlantic Monthly* in 1901, 1902, and 1903 includes such subjects as "The Forests of the Yosemite Park" (May, 1900), "The Wild Gardens of the Yosemite Park" (August, 1900), "Fountains and Streams of Yosemite National Park" (April, 1901), "Hunting Big Redwoods" (September, 1901), and "Sargent's Silva" (July, 1903).

   John Burroughs was also a frequent contributor to the *Atlantic Monthly* in the early years of the century: "The Literary Treatment of Nature" (July, 1904), "Camping with President Roosevelt" (May, 1906), "Nature and Animal Life" (August, 1907).

   In the pages of the *Ladies' Home Journal* for 1904 Stephen M. Dale writes of "Seeing Niagara Falls for the First Time" (June) and "Through the Yellowstone on a Coach" (August).

   Bradford Torrey writes particularly of the Southwest. In the *Atlantic Monthly* will be found "A Bunch of Texas and Arizona Birds" (July, 1903) and "A Bird-gazer at the Grand Cañon" (June, 1906). He, too, had been enticed into the Yosemite: "On Foot in the Yosemite" (August, 1910).

   Monroe, Harriet. "Arizona," *Atlantic Monthly,* 89 (June, 1902), 780–89.

   Thompson, Maurice. "An Archer on the Kankakee," *Atlantic Monthly,* 85 (June, 1900), 764–72.

2. "The Role of the Federal Government in the Field of Public Recreation." Washington, D.C.: Federal Inter-Agency Committee on Recreation, 1949, pp. 50. (Mimeographed pamphlet.)

3. "The Federal Government in Recreation," *Recreation*, 44 (June, 1950), 138–50. One of the early articles on the then sixteen national parks, which comprised 9,773 square miles, shows their location. See *Outing*, 74 (April, 1919), 34–35.

 Cahalane, Victor H. "Parks and People," *Recreation*, 43 (May, 1949), 73.

 The twenty-eight national parks comprise 11,347,269 acres, and the 146 national monuments make up the balance of the 21,000,000 acres. In 1948 a total of thirty million people visited these areas. As of 1948, 282 wildlife refuges were maintained by the Fish and Wildlife Service. In this year the number of licensed duck hunters was 1,722,677.

4. Meyer, Harold D., and Brightbill, Charles K. *Community Recreation: A Guide to Its Organization and Administration.* Boston: D. C. Heath & Co., 1948, pp. 704. Particularly valuable in this volume is Chapter 3, "The Federal Government and Recreation," pp. 59–71.

 Another excellent discussion of the federal government's activities in recreation will be found in Hutchinson, John L. *Principles of Recreation.* New York: A. S. Barnes & Co., 1949, pp. 310.

5. Wrenn, C. Gilbert, and Harley, D. L. *Time on Their Hands.* Washington, D.C.: American Council on Education, 1941, pp. 266. This volume is in the nature of a report to the American Youth Commission on Leisure, Recreation and Young People. Chapter VIII, on "Federal Recreation Functions and Agencies," pp. 202–46, is a particularly valuable reference for this chapter.

6. *Community Recreation Programs: A Study of WPA Recreation Projects*, p. 20. Washington, D.C.: Federal Works Agency, 1940, pp. 54.

 Williams, Aubrey. "The Contribution of Recreation to Recovery," *Recreation*, 28 (January, 1935), 480–81. Williams was at this time assistant director of the Federal Relief Administration.

 Lindeman, Eduard C. "Recreation and the Good Life," *Recreation*, 29 (December, 1935), 436. Dr. Lindeman was at this time the director of the Community Organization for Leisure, Works Progress Administration.

7. "The War Recreation Services of Several Federal and National Agencies," *Recreation*, 37 (June, 1943), 132–38, 185.

8. Wrenn and Harley, *op. cit.*

9. Meyer, Harold D., and Brightbill, Charles K. *State Recreation:*

Organization and Administration. New York: A. S. Barnes & Co., 1950, pp. 282.

10. "State Agencies and Recreation," *Recreation*, 40 (June, 1946), 115–37, 162.

11. One of the early, large state parks was the Palisades Interstate Park in New York and New Jersey with 29,000 acres. See Jessup, Elon H. "The Greatest Park in the World," *Outing*, 72 (August, 1918), 289–93, 342–44.

12. *Recreation in California* (compilation of laws relating to recreation). Sacramento: State of California, Recreation Commission, 1948, pp. 184.

13. *Sport's Golden Age: A Close-up of the Fabulous Twenties,* eds. Allison Danzig and Peter Brandwein. New York: Harper & Bros., 1948, pp. 296.
    Grombach, John V. *The Saga of Sock.* New York: A. S. Barnes & Co., 1949, pp. 381.

14. Spink, J. G. Taylor. *Judge Landis and Twenty-five Years of Baseball.* New York: Thomas Y. Crowell Co., 1947, pp. 306.

15. *Ibid.*

16. *Ibid.*

17. *Ibid.*

18. Stafford, Frank S. *State Administration of School Health, Physical Education and Recreation.* Washington, D.C.: Federal Security Agency, Office of Education, 1947 (Bulletin No. 13), pp. 33. .

19. "State Recreation Services," *Recreation*, 44 (June, 1950), 117–36. Fietz, Louise A. "The Role of the States in Recreation." Berkeley: University of California, Bureau of Public Administration, 1947, pp. 29. (Mimeographed.)

20. Faulkner, Harold U. *The Quest for Social Justice, 1898–1914.* New York: Macmillan Co., 1931, pp. 390.

21. Bendelow, Tom. "Municipal Golf," *American City*, 15 (July, 1916), 1–8.
    DeGroot, Edward B. "Recreation Facilities in Public Parks," *American City*, 10 (January, 1914), 9–15.

22. Nolen, John. "City Making," *American City* 1 (September, 1909), 15–19.
    Eliot, Chas. W. "The Indispensableness of City Planning," *American City*, 1 (September, 1909), 25–26.
    Olmsted, Frederick Law. "The Basic Principles of City Planning," *American City*, 3 (August, 1910), 67–72.

Ford, George B. "Digging Deeper into City Planning," *American City*, 6 (March, 1912), 557–58.

23. "Savannah and Its Renaissance," *American City*, 3 (August, 1910), 57–63.

"The Minneapolis Spirit," *American City*, 6 (January, 1912), 398–404.

Reported in *American City*, 4 (June, 1911), 269. Professor Henry V. Hubbard, an assistant professor of landscape architecture at Harvard, gave an address on "The Size and Distribution of Playgrounds and Similar Recreation Facilities" at the Toronto meeting of the National Conference on City Planning. A portion of the paper was discussed in *American City*, 11 (July, 1914), 24–26.

Lay, Charles Downing. "Parks and Playgrounds: A Program of Development," *American City*, 11 (November, 1914), 386.

24. Nolen, John. "Replanning Small Cities," *American City*, 4 (May, 1911), 238–39.

25. Nolen, John. "The Improvement of a Country Town," *American City*, 6 (May, 1912), 733–36.

26. *Ibid.*

27. Engle, William L. "Supervised Amusement Cuts Juvenile Crime by 96%," *American City*, 20 (December, 1919), 515–17.

28. Truxal, Andrew G. *Outdoor Recreation Legislation and Its Effectiveness*. New York: Columbia University Press, 1929, pp. 218. This volume contains a summary of American legislation for public outdoor recreation, 1915–27, and, in addition, a study of the association between recreation areas and juvenile delinquency in Manhattan, 1920.

29. Shanas, Ethel. *Recreation and Delinquency*. Chicago Recreation Commission, 1942, pp. 284.

30. Lee, Alfred McClung, and Lee, Elizabeth Bryant. *Social Problems in America: A Source Book*. New York: Henry Holt & Co., 1949, pp. 741. The quotation has been taken from a contribution by Edith Karlin Lesser, chief, information section, Mental Hygiene Division, U.S. Public Health Service, entitled "Neighborhood Factors in Delinquency," pp. 496–97.

31. The Playground Association of America later became the Playground and Recreation Association of America, and still later the National Recreation Association.

32. These and later figures cited throughout the chapter were ob-

tained from the *Year Books* of the National Recreation Association. These have been recently discontinued (since 1948).

33. "Public Recreation Facilities," *Annals of the American Academy of Political and Social Science*, 35 (March, 1910), 217–448. A short article by Bessie D. Stoddart on "Recreation Centers of Los Angeles, California." Henry S. Curtis in his article on "Provisions and Responsibility for Playgrounds" mentions a discussion in the House of Representatives involving the use of public funds for play purposes which is said to have consumed two days.

34. See n. 33.

35. Luehring, Frederick W. *Swimming Pool Standards*, p. 27. New York: A. S. Barnes & Co., 1939, pp. 273.

36. Potter, Florence Dangerfield. "How McKeesport Got Its Swimming Pool," *American City*, 7 (October, 1912), 318–23.

37. Gerhard, William Paul. "Public Bath Houses and Swimming Pools," *American City*, 11 (November, 1914), 357–67. Well illustrated are buildings at St. Paul and Newark, Sutro Baths (San Francisco), a power house converted to a public bath at Troy, N.Y., St. Louis Municipal Night-lighted Pool, the Mullanphy Swimming Pool at St. Louis, and the Patterson Park Open-Air Swimming Pool in Baltimore.
    Hinman, J. J., Jr. "The Swimming Pool and Its Operation," *American City*, 18 (April, 1918), 305–11.
    Mason, William P. "The Practical Design and Management of Swimming Pools," *American City*, 22 (March, 1920), 224–27. Mason was professor of chemistry at Rensselaer Polytechnic Institute, Troy, N.Y.

38. Millar, Louis de P. "The Municipal Plunge in Brookside Park, Pasadena," *American City*, 16 (June, 1917), 598–600.

39. A description of this rink will be found in *American City* for December, 1911. Size: 130 by 250 feet.

40. See n. 23.

41. "Skating the Best Winter Sport," *American City*, 18 (January, 1918), 47–48.

42. "Winter Recreation Provided and Protected," *American City*, 17 (December, 1917), 529–30.

43. Smith, F. A. Cushing. "Municipal Recreation on Inland Water-Fronts," *American City*, 12 (April, 1915), 291–98. The May, 1912, issue of *American City* contains an interesting account of "Fort Wayne's Civic Awakening" with special attention

given to the water front and to the beautification of the river-bank.

44. Angell, Herbert E. "A Farm That Became a Public Park," *American City*, 11 (August, 1914), 110–13. The beach and bath-house were featured.

45. Steiner, Jesse Frederick. *Americans at Play*. New York: McGraw-Hill Book Co., Inc., 1933, pp. 199.

46. *Ibid*.

47. Bendelow, *op. cit.*, pp. 1–8.

48. *The Playground*, Vol. 18 (April, 1924), yearbook number.

49. Figures taken from the *Year Books* of the National Recreation Association.

50. "The Growth of Winter Sports," *Recreation*, 34 (December, 1940), 520.

Among the pre–World War I articles depicting what *cities* had done in the way of providing for winter sports is one by Albert Britt, "St. Paul–the City That Discovered Winter," *Outing*, 69 (March, 1917), 661–76, which relates the story of a winter carnival–how it grew and what it did for the city. Britt followed this article by one in 1920 indicating that what St. Paul learned the rest of America is learning. Winter sports for all ages, young and old, are being enjoyed in the Northwest, Colorado, New Hampshire, and Lake Placid. See Britt, Albert. "A New Map of Winter," *Outing*, 78 (December, 1920), 107–10, 143–44.

Outing gave considerable attention to winter sports in the early twenties. In one issue (Vol. 79 [January, 1922]) appeared:

Foster, Thomas. "New England Plays All Winter," pp. 147–48.

Jessup, Elon. "Winter Climbing in New England," pp. 149–51, 186–88.

Harris, Fred H. "How I Learned To Ski," pp. 158–61, 188–89.

51. "Sports in America," *Recreation*, 40 (March, 1947), 641–43. This article does not refer specifically to recent trends in municipal recreation programs, but it serves as a guide to those operating community sports programs. The material in this article has since been published in a book by George D. Butler, *Community Sports and Athletics*, written for the National Recreation Association and published by A. S. Barnes & Co., New York, 1949.

52. "Sports in America," *op. cit.*

53. *Ibid*.

54. *Ibid.*
55. Dublin, Louis I. "Our Aging Population," *Recreation*, 43 (February, 1950), 538–39.
56. The May, 1949, issue of *Recreation* contains thirteen articles on recreation programs for oldsters.
57. "Recreation for Older People," *Recreation*, 34 (October, 1940), 432, 458.
58. "Softball for Oldsters," *Recreation*, 34 (March, 1941), 746–47.
59. "No Hits, No Runs, Plenty of Errors!" *Recreation*, 38 (October, 1944), 355, 381.
60. *Ibid.*
61. Brungardt, Theresa S. "Recreation for Older People in Rural Communities," *Recreation*, 40 (November, 1946), 416–18, 452, 453.

NOTES AND BIBLIOGRAPHY TO CHAPTER 13

1. "War-Time Lessons Applied to Peace." Extracts from an address by the Honorable Josephus Daniels, Secretary of the Navy, at the North Carolina Conference for Social Service, February 13, 1919, Raleigh, N.C. *Amer. Phys. Educ. Rev.*, 24 (March, 1919), 172–74.
2. Forman, Sidney. *West Point.* New York: Columbia University Press, 1950, pp. 255.
3. Slosson, Preston W. *The Great Crusade and After, 1914–1928.* New York: Macmillan Co., 1930, pp. 486.
4. Stimson, Henry L., and Bundy, McGeorge. *On Active Service in Peace and War.* New York: Harper & Bros., 1947, 1948, pp. 698.
5. Brown, Robert Bertrand. *War Camp Community Service Calls.* War Camp Community Service, 1918, pp. 49.
6. Crowder, Major General E. H. *The Spirit of Selective Service.* New York: Century Co., 1920, pp. 367.
7. Raycroft, Joseph E. "Training Camp Activities," *Amer. Phys. Educ. Rev.*, 23 (March, 1918), 143–50.
8. *Ibid.*
9. Mayo, Katherine. *"That Damn Y."* Boston: Houghton Mifflin Co., 1920, pp. 432.
10. *Summary of World War Work of the American Y.M.C.A.* Published by the International Committee, Y.M.C.A., 1920, pp. 239.

11. *The Inter-Allied Games.* Published by the Games Committee. Printed by Sté Ame de Publications Périodiques, Paris, 1919, pp. 496.
12. *Ibid.*
13. Wecter, Dixon. *When Johnny Comes Marching Home.* Boston: Houghton Mifflin Co., 1944, pp. 588.
14. *Ibid.*
15. Dulles, Foster Rhea. *The American Red Cross.* New York: Harper & Bros., 1950, pp. 554.
16. *Field Manual on Physical Training FM 21-20,* p. 9. U.S. War Department. Washington, D.C.: Government Printing Office, 1946, pp. 392.
17. Douglas, Lowell N. "Some Results of an AST Program in Physical Education," *Jour. of Health & Phys. Educ.,* 15 (May, 1944), 254, 290.
    Cozens, Frederick W. "The Program and Sport Choices of Navy V-12 Trainees," *Jour. of Health & Phys. Educ.,* 15 (December, 1944), 540–41, 581–82.
18. Sullivan, William H., Jr. "The Naval Aviation Physical Training Program," *Jour. of Health & Phys. Educ.,* 14 (January, 1943), 3–6, 53–56.
19. Niles, Donna I. "Physical Fitness and the W.A.A.C.," *Jour. of Health & Phys. Educ.,* 14 (October, 1943), 408–11, 448–50.
    Turnbull, Jenny E. "The Physical Training Program of the W.A.V.E.S.," *Jour. of Health & Phys. Educ.,* 14 (November, 1943), 470–72, 500.
20. "The War Recreation Services of Several Federal and National Agencies," *Recreation,* 37 (June, 1943), 132–38, 185.
21. *Free Time in the Armed Services.* Report of the President's Committee on Religion and Welfare in the Armed Forces. Washington, D.C.: Government Printing Office, 1951, pp. 79.
22. "News Notes," *Amer. Phys. Educ. Rev.,* 21 (October, 1916), 433.
23. "News Notes: A Special Message from the Greatest Recreation Congress Ever Attempted," *Amer. Phys. Educ. Rev.,* 21 (December, 1916), 553–56.
24. "270 Communities Organized for War Camp Community Service," *Playground,* 21 (October, 1918), 271–325.
25. "Patriotic Play Week," *Playground,* 12 (August, 1918), 175.
26. "Intensified Use of Recreation Grounds and Buildings," *American City,* 22 (June, 1920), 593–95.

27. Douglas, O. W. "Industrial Recreation," *American City*, 17 (October, 1917), 365–69.
28. Slosson, *op. cit.*
29. Flanagan, Lance. "A Study of the Sports Pages." Unpublished study, University of California, Berkeley, January, 1953, pp. 50.
30. *New York Times*, January 23, 1919, p. 10.
31. *Ibid.*, April 4, 1919, p. 10.
32. *Ibid.*, May 28, 1919, p. 13.
33. *San Francisco Chronicle*, November 14, 1919, p. 11.
34. *New York Times*, December 31, 1922, Sec. 2, p. 1.
35. "World at Play—New Course in Los Angeles," *Recreation*, 37 (May, 1943), 96–97.
   Friedman, Samuel L. "Recreation in Los Angeles 'Goes to War,'" *Recreation*, 36 (February, 1943), 614–17, 643.
36. Zaengle, Eleanore M. "Recreation after 1:00 A.M.," *Recreation*, 37 (April, 1943), 20–23, 50–51.
37. Beckwith, Eleanor. "'Y' Recreation on the Night Shift," *Recreation*, 37 (July, 1943), 199–200, 248.
38. In Volume 33 of *Recreation* (April, 1939, to March, 1940) there appeared twenty-nine articles on vigorous co-recreational activities (sports) together with four on social dancing and three on youth (boy-girl relationships).
39. Davis, Frank. "Proving Ground for Industrial Sports," *Aim*, 3 (November, 1944), 19–20, 63.
40. Wallace, Francis. "Pigskin Preview," *Saturday Evening Post*, 215 (September 19, 1942), 9–11.
   Newsweek, 20 (November 2, 1942), 74, in its section on "Sports" reported that football attendance had fallen off 25 per cent at the season's halfway mark; that ice hockey had suffered even more; and that the war and tottering finances had caused the entire American Hockey Association "to fold."
   Tunis, John. "Sports Return to 1900," *Harper's*, 186 (May, 1943), 633–38.
   Newsweek, 21 (June 7, 1943), 76, reports that the big leagues were not drawing as well as expected, that tracks in Florida and California were closed because of poor attendance, and that many college football schedules were either dropped completely or continued on a local basis.
41. *While You Were Gone: A Report on Wartime Life in the United States*, ed. Jack Goodman. New York: Simon & Schuster, 1946, pp. 625.

42. *Newsweek*, 21 (May 3, 1943), 82.
43. Tunis, John. "Sports Return to 1900," *op. cit.*, pp. 633–38; "Sports in Wartime," *New Republic*, 65 (April 3, 1944), 466–68.
44. "Fishing Gloom," *Business Week*, 668 (June 22, 1942), 34–35. *Newsweek*, 21 (January 4, 1943), 55–56, reported that the shortage of golf balls made it necessary to reprocess them, thus adding difficulty to the game.
    "Hunting–in Self-defense," *Business Week*, 715 (May 15, 1943), 28. The War Production Board ruled that ammunition would not be available for hunting only. Ranchers and farmers, in order to protect livestock, could obtain ammunition for the purpose of controlling predatory animals.
45. "Ball and Bat Crisis," *Business Week*, 822 (June 2, 1945), 41–42. Indicates that, though the major leagues would get almost their normal supply of balls (9,000 dozen) and bats (6,500), the sandlot and semi-pro teams would have to curtail their schedules and that military demands had left little for civilians. Tennis was booming because of a synthetic rubber ball which speeded up the game.
46. Some evidence of this can be gained from such reports as this: *Newsweek*, 21 (June 7, 1943), 76. Shows the tremendous increase in the sports activities in war plants, as, for example, the twenty-four hundred bowlers in a league at the Lockheed plant.

NOTES AND BIBLIOGRAPHY TO CHAPTER 14

1. Romney, G. Ott. *Off the Job Living*. New York: A. S. Barnes & Co., 1945, pp. 232.
2. Allen, Frederick Lewis. "The Big Change," *Harper's*, 201 (October, 1950), 145–60.
3. Inkersley, Arthur. "Golf in California," *Overland Monthly*, 35 (May, 1900), 209.
4. Merz, Charles. *The Great American Band Wagon*. New York: Garden City Pub. Co., Inc., 1928, pp. 263. (Permission to quote given by the copyright holder, Charles Merz, Editor, *New York Times*.)
5. Douglass, Albert A. "Alcoa's Golf Set-Up," *Industrial Sports Journal*, 12 (January, 1951), 12, 25.
6. "Golf at Heintz," *Industrial Sports Journal*, 12 (April 15, 1951), 14.

7. "Twilight Golf League," *Industrial Sports Journal*, 10 (June, 1950), 8, 32.
8. "Hole-in-One Golf at Tennessee Eastman," *Industrial Sports Journal*, 11 (September, 1950), 21.
9. "Sub-teen Golf," *Industrial Sports Journal*, 12 (July 15, 1951), 18.
10. "Midwest Industrial Golf Tourney," *Industrial Sports Journal*, 12 (June 15, 1951), 12.
11. Mulholland, Joe. "Industrial Golf League," *Industrial Sports Journal*, 10 (February, 1950), 12, 32.
12. Jordan, Jerry N. *The Long-Range Effect of Television and Other Factors on Sports Attendance*. Washington, D.C.: Radio-Television Manufacturers Association, 1950, pp. 112.
13. Hays, Arthur Garfield. *Democracy Works*. New York: Random House, 1939, pp. 334.
14. Allen, *op. cit.*
15. Bruce, Robert. "The Automobile," *Outing*, 36 (September, 1900), 703.
16. Strunsky, Simeon. *The Living Tradition*. New York: Doubleday, Doran & Co., Inc., 1939, pp. 454.
17. Cohn, David L. *The Good Old Days: A History of American Morals and Manners as Seen through the Sears, Roebuck Catalogs 1905 to the Present*. New York: Simon & Schuster, 1940, pp. 597.
18. Strunsky, *op. cit.*
19. Glueck, Eleanor Touroff. *The Community Use of Schools*. Baltimore: Williams & Wilkins Co., 1927, pp. 222.
20. Allen, *op. cit.*
21. Chambers, M. M. *Youth-serving Organizations*. Washington, D.C.: American Council on Education, 1941, pp. 237.
22. Daley, Arthur. "30,000 Little Leaguers," *American*, 151 (April, 1951), 42, 43, 134–36.
    "Kids World Series," *Life*, 29 (September 11, 1950), 11, 115–17.
    "A Place for Pee Wee," *Newsweek*, 38 (August 20, 1951), 8.
23. Archer, Jay. "Questions about Biddy Basketball," *Recreation*, 44 (October, 1950), 270.
24. *Ibid.*
25. Cloyd, Joseph. "Gangway for the Mighty Midgets," *American*, 154 (December, 1952), 28, 29, 83–85.
26. Hardwick, Mary. "Industry Takes Over Tennis Clinics," *Industrial Sports Journal*, 9 (September, 1949), 9, 17, 20.

27. Jarvis, William. "Junior Baseball Program," *Industrial Sports Journal*, 12 (April, 1951), 12, 31, 37.
28. Chambers, *op. cit.*

NOTES AND BIBLIOGRAPHY TO CHAPTER 15

1. Wing, Sherman W. "A Survey of Sports Vernacular as Found in Four Utah Newspapers during 1939–40." Unpublished Master's thesis, Brigham Young University, 1942, pp. 132.
2. Walker, Stanley. *City Editor.* New York: Frederick A. Stokes Co., 1934, pp. 336.
3. *Nation*, 97 (August 21, 1913), 161.
4. *Ibid.*, 111 (July 10, 1921), 43.
5. McCracken, Elizabeth. "American Children," *Outlook*, 101 (May 25, 1915), 209–18.
6. Brill, A. A. "The Why of the Fan," *North American Review*, 228 (October, 1929), 427–34.
7. Bryson, Lyman. *Science and Freedom.* New York: Columbia University Press, 1947, pp. 191.
8. Brogan, D. W. *The American Character*, pp. 135–36. New York: Alfred A. Knopf, Inc., 1944, pp. 169.
9. Stabley, Rhodes R. *Newspaper Editorials on American Education.* Ph.D. thesis, University of Pennsylvania, 1941, pp. 283.
10. Thurber, James. "University Days," from *My Life and Hard Times.* New York: Harper & Bros., 1933, pp. 153.
11. Brogan, *op. cit.*, p. 143. The historian Henry Steele Commager comments in the Bibliography of his book *The American Mind* (New Haven: Yale University Press, 1950) that Brogan is perhaps the best of the current commentators on the American character.
12. Hudnut, Joseph. *Architecture and the Spirit of Man.* Cambridge: Harvard University Press, 1949, pp. 301.
13. *Ibid.*
14. Gorer, Geoffrey. *The American People: A Study in National Character*, p. 36. New York: W. W. Norton & Co., Inc., 1948, pp. 246.
15. Sherman, Stuart P. *Points of View.* New York: Charles Scribner's Sons, 1924, pp. 363.
16. Bryson, *op. cit.*
17. Brogan, *op. cit.*, p. 143.

18. "President Wilson's Jackson Day Speech," *Nation*, 101 (January, 1915), 69–70.
19. Sedgwick, Ellery. "The Man with the Muck Rack," *American*, 62 (May, 1906), 111–12.
20. Stimson, Henry L., and Bundy, McGeorge. *On Active Service in Peace and War*. New York: Harper & Bros., 1947, 1948, pp. 698.
21. Wallace, Francis. *Dementia Pigskin*. New York: Rinehart & Co., Inc., 1951, pp. 252.
22. Beal, John R. "Bull's Eye for Dulles," *Harper's*, 203 (November, 1951), 88–94.
23. These illustrations were taken from Faden, I. B. *How America Speaks and Writes*. Stockholm: Almquist & Wiksells Skolbocker, 1949, pp. 362.
24. *Ibid.*
25. *Ibid.*
26. Huizinga, Johan. *Homo Ludens: A Study of the Play-Element in Culture*. London: Routledge & Kegan Paul Ltd., 1949, pp. 220.
27. Turney-High, Harry Holbert. *Primitive War, Its Practice and Concepts*. Columbia: University of South Carolina Press, 1949, pp. 277.
28. Kleeberger, Frank L. "American Athletics vs. German Militarism," *Amer. Phys. Educ. Rev.*, 24 (February, 1919), 83–89.
29. The expression was used by Field Marshall Sir Archibald Wavell.
30. Marshall, S. L. A. "Sports and War," *Recreation*, 46 (September, 1952), 192. Marshall is military critic of the *Detroit News*, and the designation of "greatest living reporter of combat" appeared in the *Combat Forces Journal* of the United States Army.
31. From a speech delivered at Elizabethton, Tennessee, by the then Secretary of Commerce, Herbert Hoover. This excerpt was reprinted in *Sportsmanship*, 1 (November, 1928), 3.
32. Reprinted in *Sportsmanship*, 1 (November, 1928), 4.
33. Leupp, Francis E. "A Review of President Roosevelt's Administration," *Outlook*, 91 (February 6, 1909), 298–307.
34. Willyoung, Arthur K. "Roosevelt the Greatest Outdoor Man," *Outing*, 74 (August, 1919), 273–77.
35. Reprinted in Martin, H. B. *Fifty Years of American Golf*, p. 263. New York: Dodd, Mead & Co., 1936, pp. 423.

36. "Baseball and the War," *Nation,* 107 (August, 1918), 137.

37. Hoover, Herbert. "Let's Go Fishin'," an article which first appeared in the April 22, 1944, issue of *Collier's* and was reprinted in *Recreation,* 38 (July, 1944), 171–73, 222.

38. *Ibid.*

39. Excerpts from a letter signed by Franklin D. Roosevelt, addressed to the Honorable Kenesaw M. Landis, dated at the White House, January 15, 1942. Reprinted in full on pages 278 and 279 of J. G. Taylor Spink's *Judge Landis and Twenty-five Years of Baseball.* New York: Thomas Y. Crowell Co., 1947, pp. 306.

40. Miller, Francis Trevelyan. *Eisenhower, Man and Soldier.* Philadelphia: John C. Winston Co., 1944, pp. 278.

41. Gunther, John. *Eisenhower, the Man and the Symbol.* New York: Harper & Bros., 1951, pp. 180.

NOTES AND BIBLIOGRAPHY TO CHAPTER 16

1. Ribalow, Harold U. *The Jew in American Sports.* New York: Block Pub. Co., 1949, pp. 288.

2. White, Walter. "Time for a Progress Report," *Saturday Review of Literature,* 34 (September 22, 1951), 9–10, 38–41.

3. Henderson, Edwin Bancroft. *The Negro in Sports.* Washington, D.C.: Associated Publishers, Inc., 1949 (rev. ed.), pp. 507.

4. *Ibid.*

5. Huxley, Aldous. *Ends and Means.* As reprinted in *Unseen Harvests.* New York: Macmillan Co., 1947, pp. 678.

6. Brameld, Theodore. *Ends and Means in Education.* New York: Harper & Bros., 1950, pp. 244.

7. *New York Times,* November 28, 1951.

8. Henderson, *op.cit.*

9. *New York Times,* October 18, 1951.

10. Johnny Bright received a broken jaw in a game between Oklahoma A. & M. and Drake. Drake spokesmen charged that movies of the game showed that Bright was hurt in an unprovoked incident. Relations were broken off between the two schools.

11. Frank, Stanley B. *The Jew in Sports.* New York: Miles Pub. Co., 1936, pp. 254.

12. Henderson, *op. cit.*

13. It is discouraging to note that only five states adopted such legislation in the twentieth century and that no state has been added to the list of eighteen since 1931.

14. Konitz, Milton R. "Legislation Guaranteeing Equality of Access to Places of Public Accommodation," *Annals of the American Academy of Political and Social Science*, 275 (May, 1951), 50.

15. *Ibid.*

16. *Time*, 54 (July 4, 1949), 15.

17. *New York Times*, June 8, 1951, p. 25.

18. *Ibid.*, July 31, 1951, p. 23.

19. "The Race Problem at Swimming Pools," *American City*, 47 (August, 1932), 76, 77.

20. *New York Times*, December 21, 1951, p. 16.

21. *Ibid.*, December 23, 1951, and November 28, 1951.

22. *Ibid.*, May 28, 1951, and June 13, 1951.

23. "Ladies and Gentlemen," *Time*, 56 (July 17, 1950), 74.

24. *New York Times*, May 31, 1951, p. 33.

25. Eddy, Sherwood. *A Century with Youth: A History of the YMCA from 1844 to 1944.* New York: Association Press, 1944, pp. 153.

26. Davis, Helen E. *The YMCA and Public Recreation, Informal Education, and Leisure-Time Programs.* New York: Association Press, 1946, pp. 196.

27. "Girl Scouts of America: Interracial Organization Celebrates Its 40th Anniversary," *Ebony*, March, 1952, pp. 46–47.

28. "Aquatic Schools," *Ebony*, August, 1952, p. 45.

29. Hutchinson, John L. *Principles of Recreation.* New York: A. S. Barnes & Co., 1949, pp. 310. Hutchinson acknowledges the implications of this choice in his chapter on "The Economic and Social Aspects of Recreation."

30. Kieran, John, and Daley, Arthur. *The Story of the Olympic Games 776 B.C.–1948 A.D.* Philadelphia: J. B. Lippincott Co., 1948, pp. 406.

31. Henry, Bill. *An Approved History of the Olympic Games.* New York: G. P. Putnam's Sons, 1948, pp. 371.

32. Kieran and Daley, *op.cit.*

NOTES AND BIBLIOGRAPHY TO CHAPTER 17

1. Reported in the *San Francisco Chronicle*, October 9, 1952, p. A.
2. Walsh, Richard B. "The Soviet Athlete in International Competition," *Department of State Bulletin*, 25 (December 24, 1951), 1007–10.
3. Malinowski, Bronislaw. *The Dynamics of Culture Change*, ed. Phyllis M. Kaberry. New Haven: Yale University Press, 1945, pp. 171.
4. Keesing, Felix M. *The South Seas in the Modern World*. New York: John Day Co., 1941, pp. 391.
5. Ten Brock, Edward. "Men Must Be Trained," *World Communique*, 9 (June, 1950), 20–21.
6. From an address by Soichi Saito. Printed in the *Proceedings, First International Recreation Congress, Los Angeles, California, July 23–29, 1932*, pp. 163–64.
7. *The Inter-Allied Games*. Published by the Games Committee. Engraved and printed by Sté Ame de Publications Périodiques, Paris, 1919, pp. 496.
   See also Jones, O. Garfield. "Athletics Helping the Filipino," *Outing*, 64 (August, 1914), 585–92.
8. Thompson, Virginia. *Thailand: The New Siam*, pp. 691–92. New York: Macmillan Co., 1941.
9. Ten countries met at Geneva in 1932 to discuss the variations in rules and playing codes. These were: Czechoslovakia, Portugal, Switzerland, Latvia, Italy, Argentina, Greece, Hungary, Bulgaria, and Romania. Rules as practiced in the United States were adopted.
10. Curtis, William B. "By-Gone International Athletic Contests," *Outing*, 36 (July, 1900), 350–57.
11. *Ibid.*
12. Savage, Howard J. *American College Athletics*. New York: Carnegie Foundation for the Advancement of Teaching, 1929 (Bulletin No. 23), pp. 383.
13. Danzig, Allison, and Brandwein, Peter (eds.). *Sport's Golden Age*. New York: Harper & Bros., 1948, pp. 296. Throughout the early years of the twentieth century *Outing* gave a considerable amount of space to Davis Cup play and stressed the development of young tennis players as the answer to keeping the cup in America. A succinct account of Dwight Davis, donor

of the cup, may be found in *Outing*, 68 (April, 1916), 32, under the title "Dwight Davis, Tennis Patron."

14. Lindsay, Nigel. *The America's Cup*. London: Heath Cranton Ltd., 1930, pp. 187.

15. Spears, John D. "The Cup's Effects on American Maritime Affairs," *Outing*, 38 (September, 1901), 679. Excellent historical material on the *America's* Cup races is to be found in *Outing* during the early years of the century.

16. Participating countries were France, Belgium, Austria, Spain, Sweden, England, United States, Italy, Hungary, Switzerland, Norway, Greece, Germany, Denmark, Japan, Romania, and Mexico.

17. From the report of Thomas D. Wood, datelined Geneva, Switzerland, September 16, 1900, and addressed to the editor of the *American Physical Education Review*. Printed in the *Amer. Phys. Educ. Rev.*, 5 (September, 1900), 269–74.

18. From the Preface to the *Proceedings of the First International Recreation Congress*, written by Joseph Lee, president of the National Recreation Association.

19. Henry, Bill. *An Approved History of the Olympic Games*. New York: G. P. Putnam's Sons, 1948, pp. 371. Quite early, *reporters* began to summarize the Olympic competition by attaching point scores to the various places. For example, at the Stockholm games in 1912, the first three places were given points 3, 2, 1, while at Antwerp, in 1920, six places were counted. See *Outing*, 60 (September, 1912), 767–68, and *ibid.*, 72 (January, 1921), 162–65.

20. Tunis, John R. *Sports, Heroics and Hysterics*. New York: John Day Co., 1928, pp. 293.

21. Henry, *op. cit.*

22. Castle, Ames. "Team Work," *Industrial Sports Journal*, 13 (September 15, 1952), 13.

23. Kieran, John, and Daley, Arthur. *The Story of the Olympic Games 776 B.C.–1948 A.D.* Philadelphia: J. B. Lippincott Co., 1948, pp. 406.

24. *Ibid.*

25. Weyand, Alexander M. *The Olympic Pageant*. New York: Macmillan Co., 1952, pp. 347.

26. *Ibid.*

27. Henry, *op. cit.*

28. *Ibid.*

29. *Ibid.*
30. *Outing,* 36 (June, 1900), 319.
31. *Ibid.,* 53 (December, 1908), 382–84.
32. Kieran and Daley, *op. cit.*
33. Weyand, *op. cit.*
34. Henry, *op. cit.*
35. *Ibid.*

NOTES AND BIBLIOGRAPHY TO CHAPTER 18

1. Stanky, Eddie. "All Out for 'Beizbol,'" *Saturday Review,* October 4, 1952, pp. 24–25. Eddie Stanky, manager of the St. Louis Cardinals, comments on an article in the Soviet publication *Smena.* Statements in the article include charges that the "Rodgers" (Dodgers) have a special training camp to school players in the bloodier side of "this beastly battle," that ballplayers often wind up "with ruined health" or "crippled," and that they are "in the situation of slaves, being bought and sold and thrown out of the door when they become unnecessary."
2. Kluckhohn, Clyde. *Mirror for Man,* p. 27. New York: Whittlesey House, copyright by McGraw-Hill Book Co., Inc., 1949, pp. 313.
3. Huizinga, Johan. *Homo Ludens: A Study of the Play Element in Culture.* London: Routledge & Kegan Paul Ltd., 1949, pp. 220.
4. Perry, Ralph Barton. *Characteristically American.* New York: Alfred A. Knopf, Inc., 1949, pp. 162.
5. Michener, James A. *The Fires of Spring,* p. 109. New York: Random House, 1949, pp. 495.
6. Huizinga, *op. cit.*
7. Lynes, Russell. "The Taste-makers," *Harper's,* 194 (June, 1947), 481–91.
8. Oktavek, Frank L. "Spectator Sports," *Recreation,* 27 (October, 1933), 320–22, 347.
9. Huizinga, *op. cit.*
10. Menninger, Karl. *Love against Hate,* p. 179. New York: Harcourt, Brace & Co., 1942, pp. 311.
11. Brill, A. A. "The Why of the Fan," *North American Review,* 228 (October, 1929), 427–34.
12. Menninger, *op. cit.*

13. Ellis, William. *Polynesian Researches*, p. 290. London: Fisher, Son, and Jackson, Newgate Street, 1829, Vol. 1, pp. 290.
14. Huizinga, *op. cit.*
15. *Ibid.*
16. *Athletic Journal*, 9 (January, 1929), 18.
17. Cary, Joyce. "The Mass Mind: Our Favorite Folly," *Harper's*, 122 (March, 1952), 25–27.
18. Dulles, Foster Rhea. *America Learns To Play*. New York: D. Appleton–Century Co., 1940, pp. 441.
19. Klapper, Joseph T. *The Effects of Mass Media*, p. 12. New York: Columbia University, Bureau of Applied Social Research, 1949, pp. 171.
20. *Ibid.*
21. Lawther, John D. *Psychology of Coaching*. New York: Prentice-Hall, Inc., 1951, pp. 333.
22. Educational Policies Commission. *Policies for Education in American Democracy*. Washington, D.C.: National Education Association and American Association of School Administrators, 1946, pp. 277.
23. *Ibid.*
24. Herskovits, Melville J. *Man and His Works*, p. 372. New York: Alfred A. Knopf, Inc., 1948, pp. 678.
25. Merz, Charles. *The Great American Band Wagon*, p. 229. New York: Garden City Pub. Co., Inc., 1928, pp. 263. (Permission to quote given by the copyright holder, Charles Merz, Editor, *New York Times*.)
26. Wecter, Dixon. *The Hero in America*, p. 1. New York: Charles Scribner's Sons, 1941, pp. 530.
27. Smith, Ken. *Baseball's Hall of Fame*. New York: A. S. Barnes & Co., 1947, pp. 244.
28. Meany, Tom. *Babe Ruth*. New York: A. S. Barnes & Co., 1947, pp. 180.
29. Ruth, Babe. *The Babe Ruth Story, as Told to Bob Considine*, p. 237. New York: E. P. Dutton Co., Inc., 1948, pp. 250. Copyright, 1948, George Herman Ruth.
30. *Ibid.*
31. Smith, Robert. *Baseball: A Historical Narrative of the Game, the Men Who Played, and Its Place in American Life*. New York: Simon & Schuster, 1947, pp. 362.

32. Slosson, P. W. *The Great Crusade and After*, pp. 271-72. New York: Macmillan Co., 1930, pp. 486. (Quotation used with the permission of the Macmillan Company.)

33. Toynbee, Arnold J. *A Study of History*. New York and London: Oxford University Press, 1947, pp. 617. (Abridgment of Vols. 1-6 by D. C. Somervell.)

34. Ringel, Fred J. (ed.). *America as Americans See It*. New York: Harcourt, Brace & Co., 1932, pp. 365. Bruce Bliven contributes an essay on "Worshipping the American Hero."

Index

347

extent of ownership, 143
use of sports themes by, 141
Radio alumni, 151
Radio Corporation of America, 220
Raycroft, Joseph E., 198
Recreation
  attitude toward, by church, 94
  camping program development, 165
  commercial, and urbanization, 13
  concern of government for, 16, 170
  co-recreation promoted in municipalities, 192
  expanding American philosophy of, 8
  home as a center of, 32
  industrial, 13
  and juvenile delinquency, 17
  and public welfare, 175
  in World War II, 210–14
  see also Facilities, recreational
Recreation, 212
Reeve, Arthur B., 73
Reno, 160
Reuther, Walter P., 57, 255
Rickard, Tex, 47, 120
Rickey, Branch, 250
Rifle competition, 72
Riis, Jacob, 24, 25, 227
Rio de Janeiro, 271
Ritual and ceremony in spectator sports, 292
Roberts College (Constantinople), 264
Robinson, Jackie, 249
Rochester Experiment, 226
Rockefeller, John D., 73, 256
Rogers, Will, 20
Roosevelt, Franklin D.
  and conservation measures, 173
  letter of, to Commissioner Landis, 247
  and sports language, 240
Roosevelt, Theodore
  as advocate of strenuous life, 245
  attitude of, toward golf, 219
  awards in rifle-shooting, 73

and conservation measures, 170, 173
  fights monopoly, 227
  football conference at White House, 75
  honorary chairman of the American Olympic Committee, 275
  honorary president of the National Recreation Association, 186
  and support of play in school curriculum, 65
  and support of playgrounds, 25
  as writer on outdoor recreation, 138
Roque, 193
Rosenwald, Julius, 256
Rowing, 69, 116, 136, 276
Rugby, 276
Russo-Japanese War, 274
Ruth, Babe, 119, 295

Sabbath laws
  early history of, 106
  repealed after World War I, 209
Sabbath Laws in the United States, 107
Sailing, 43, 175, 188, 246
St. Louis Arena, 49
St. Moritz skiing, 160
St. Nicholas Arena, 49
Saks-Fifth Avenue, 43
Salvation Army, 198
San Francisco, 274
San Francisco Chronicle, 122, 208
Santa Anita Handicap, 213
Saratoga, 39
Sargent, Dudley A., 66, 68
Saturday Evening Post, 90, 91, 129
Scandinavian nations, sports in, 2
Schmeling, Max, 146
Schneider, Hannes, 42
School
  attitude of, toward sports in curriculum, 14
  camps, 165
  effect on, of establishment of playgrounds, 71

School—*Continued*
effects of World War I on sports program of, 81, 82
growth of consolidated, 163
impact of American sports on, 7
and physical-fitness programs in war, 85
promotes race relations through sports, 251
as a recreation center, 226
sports in depression, 82
and sports life of America, 63
view of, at turn of century, 63
wider use of plant of, 71
Schwert Bill, 84
Scientific management and industrial recreation, 53
Scribner's, 129, 137, 138
Sears, Roebuck catalogue, 158, 224
Sedgwick, Ellery, 240
Selective Service Act
World War I, 80, 198
World War II, 201
Seton, Ernest Thompson, 138
Shaw, George Bernard, 120
Sheffield Scientific School, Yale University, 53
Shennescossett, 39
Sherman, Stuart, 8
Shooting, 72, 276
Shuffleboard, 193
Siam, 4, 263
Skating, 11, 29, 34, 47, 69, 72, 108, 166, 175, 188, 192, 211, 281
Skidmore, Rex A., 109
Skiing, 35, 116, 166, 172, 175, 189, 192, 205
development of commercial areas, 42
and Olympic Winter Games, 42, 159
resorts for, 159-60
see also Winter sports
Smith, Al, 244
Soccer, 56, 72, 86, 108, 148
Social Effects of Aviation, 168
Society of Secondary School Physical Directors, 71
Society of State Directors of

Health, Physical Education and Recreation, 77
Softball, 62, 81, 89, 148, 193, 212, 263
South Africa, 144
Southwest Conference, 150
Soviet athletes
in international competition, 260
and 1952 Olympics, 273
Soviet anti-American propaganda on professional baseball, 283
Spain, 3, 294
Spalding, A. G., Company, 40
Spectator behavior, 146, 156, 288
Spectator sports, 35, 129, 156, 158, 177, 208, 213
as cement of democracy, 283
effects of transportation on, 167-68
importance of, in twentieth century, 46
as integrating force in democracy, 299
and mass media of communication, 290
and the national economy, 6
role of, in the culture, 34
as "whipping boy" in athletic picture, 22
Spellman, Francis Cardinal, 296
Spirit of the Times, 113
Sporting goods equipment
and industrial recreation, 52
as part of national economy, 6
shortages during World War II, 214
Sports
advertising, and the periodical press, 138
aid to international understanding, 2, 3, 5
for all, rich and poor, 18
in American art, 238
church supports, 98
clothes, 132, 224; *see also* Dress
commercially sponsored, 6-7
and courtship practices, 29
in cultural heritage, 298
development of, for women, 68
and education, 235

AMERICA IN TWO CENTURIES:
An Inventory

An Arno Press Collection

American Association of Museums. **A Statistical Survey of Museums in the United States and Canada.** 1965

Andrews, Israel D. **On the Trade and Commerce of the British North American Colonies, and Upon the Trade of the Great Lakes and Rivers.** 1853

Audit Bureau of Circulations. **Scientific Space Selection.** 1921

Austin, E. L. and Odell Hauser. **The Sesqui-Centennial International Exposition.** 1929

Barnett, James H. **The American Christmas.** 1954

Barton, L| eslie | M. **A Study of 81 Principal American Markets.** 1925

Bennitt, Mark, comp. **History of the Louisiana Purchase Exposition.** 1905

Bowen, Eli. **The United States Post-Office Guide.** 1851

Bureau of Applied Social Research, Columbia University. **The People Look at Radio.** 1946

Burlingame, Roger. **Engines of Democracy:** Inventions and Society in Mature America. 1940

Burlingame, Roger. **March of the Iron Men:** A Social History of Union Through Invention. 1938

Burnham, W. Dean. **Presidential Ballots, 1836-1892.** 1955

Cochrane, Rexmond C. **Measures for Progress:** A History of the National Bureau of Standards. 1966

Cohn, David L. **The Good Old Days.** 1940

Cozens, Frederick W. and Florence Scovil Stumpf. **Sports in American Life.** 1953

Day, Edmund E. and Woodlief Thomas. **The Growth of Manufactures, 1899 to 1923.** 1928

Edwards, Richard Henry. **Popular Amusements.** 1915

Evans, Charles H., comp. **Exports, Domestic and Foreign, From the American Colonies to Great Britain, From 1697 to 1789, Inclusive;** Exports, Domestic, From the U.S. to All Countries, From 1789 to 1883, Inclusive. 1884

Federal Reserve System, Board of Governors. **All-Bank Statistics, United States, 1896-1955.** 1959

Flexner, Abraham. **Funds and Foundations:** Their Policies, Past and Present. 1952

Flint, Henry M. **The Railroads of the United States.** 1868

Folger, John K. and Charles B. Nam. **Education of the American Population.** 1967

Handel, Leo A. **Hollywood Looks At Its Audience:** A Report of Film Audience Research. 1950

Harlow, Alvin F. **Old Waybills:** The Romance of the Express Companies. 1934

Harrison, Shelby M. **Social Conditions in an American City:** A Summary of the Findings of the Springfield Survey. 1920

Homans, J. Smith, comp. **An Historical and Statistical Account of the Foreign Commerce of the United States.** 1857

Ingram, J. S. **The Centennial Exposition.** 1876

Institute of American Meat Packers and the School of Commerce and Administration of the University of Chicago. **The Packing Industry:** A Series of Lectures. 1924

Leech, D[aniel] D. T[ompkins]. **The Post Office Department of the United States of America.** 1879

Leggett, M. D., comp. **Subject-Matter Index of Patents for Inventions Issued by the United States Patent Office From 1790 to 1873, Inclusive.** 1874. Three vols.

Magazine Marketing Service. **M.M.S. County Buying Power Index.** 1942

Martin, Robert F. **National Income in the United States, 1799-1938.** 1939

McCullough, Edo. **World's Fair Midways.** 1966

Melish, John. **Surveys for Travellers, Emigrants and Others.** 1976

National Advertising Company. **America's Advertisers.** 1893

Peters, Harry T. **America On Stone:** The Other Printmakers to the American People. 1931

Peters, Harry T. **California On Stone.** 1935

Peters, Harry T. **Currier & Ives:** Printmakers to the American People. 1929/1931. Two vols.

Pownall, T[homas]. **A Topographical Description of the Dominions of the United States of America.** Edited by Lois Mulkearn. 1949

Reed, Alfred Zantzinger. **Present-Day Law Schools in the United States and Canada.** 1928

Reed, Alfred Zantzinger. **Training for the Public Profession of the Law.** 1921

Rogers, Meyric R. **American Interior Design.** 1947

Romaine, Lawrence B. **A Guide to American Trade Catalogs, 1744-1900.** 1960

Scammon, Richard M., comp. **America at the Polls:** A Handbook of American Presidential Election Statistics, 1920-1964. 1965

Smillie, Wilson G. **Public Health:** Its Promise for the Future. 1955

Thompson, Warren S. **Population: The Growth of Metropolitan Districts in the United States, 1900-1940.** 1947

Thorndike, E[dward] L. **Your City.** 1939

Truman, Ben[jamin] C. **History of the World's Fair.** 1893

U.S. Bureau of the Census, Department of Commerce. **Housing Construction Statistics: 1889 to 1964.** 1966

U.S. Census Office (12th Census). **Street and Electric Railways.** 1903

Urban Statistical Surveys. 1976

Wayland, Sloan and Edmund de S. Brunner. **The Educational Characteristics of the American People.** 1958

Woytinsky, W. S. **Employment and Wages in the United States.** 1953

U.S. Census Office (1st Census, 1790). **Return of the Whole Number of Persons Within the Several Districts of the United States.** 1802

U.S. Census Office (2nd Census, 1800). **Return of the Whole Number of Persons Within the Several Districts of the United States.** 1802

U.S. Census Office (3rd Census, 1810). **Aggregate Amount of Each Description of Persons Within the United States of America.** 1811

U.S. Census Office (4th Census, 1820). **Census for 1820.** 1821

U.S. Census Office (5th Census, 1830). **Abstract of the Returns of the Fifth Census.** 1832

U.S. Census Office (6th Census, 1840). **Compendium of the Enumeration of the Inhabitants and Statistics of the United States.** 1841

U.S. Census Office (7th Census, 1850). **The Seventh Census of the United States.** 1853

U.S. Census Office (8th Census, 1860). **Statistics of the United States in 1860.** 1866

U.S. Census Office (9th Census, 1870). **A Compendium of the Ninth Census.** 1872

U.S. Census Office (10th Census, 1880). **Compendium of the Tenth Census.** Parts I and II. 1883. Two vols.

U.S. Census Office (11th Census, 1890). **Abstract of the Eleventh Census.** 1894

U.S. Bureau of the Census (12th Census, 1900). **Abstract of the Twelfth Census of the United States.** 1904

U.S. Bureau of the Census (13th Census, 1910). **Thirteenth Census of the United States: Abstract of the Census.** 1913

U.S. Bureau of the Census (14th Census, 1920). **Abstract of the Fourteenth Census of the United States.** 1923

U.S. Bureau of the Census (15th Census, 1930). **Fifteenth Census of the United States: Abstract of the Census.** 1933

U.S. Bureau of the Census (16th Census, 1940). **Sixteenth Census of the United States: United States Summary.** 1943

U.S. Bureau of the Census (17th Census, 1950). **A Report of the Seventeenth Decennial Census of the United States: United States Summary.** 1953

U.S. Bureau of the Census (18th Census, 1960). **The Eighteenth Decennial Census of the United States: United States Summary.** 1964

U.S. Bureau of the Census (19th Census, 1970). **1970 Census of Population: United States Summary.** 1973. Two vols.